MW00987704

MODERN SLAVERY

SIDDHARTH KARA

MODERN SLAVERY

A GLOBAL PERSPECTIVE

Columbia University Press
New York

Columbia University Press
Publishers Since 1893
New York   Chichester, West Sussex
cup.columbia.edu

Library of Congress Cataloging-in-Publication Data
Names: Kara, Siddharth, author.
Title: Modern slavery : a global perspective / Siddharth Kara.
Description: New York : Columbia University Press, [2017] |
Includes bibliographical references and index.
Identifiers: LCCN 2017021711 (print) | LCCN 2017038682 (ebook) |
ISBN 9780231528023 (e-book) | ISBN 9780231158466 (cloth : alk. paper)
Subjects: LCSH: Human trafficking. | Prostitution. | Slavery. |
Globalization—Economic aspects.
Classification: LCC HQ281 (ebook) | LCC HQ281 .K367 2017 (print) |
DDC 306.3/62—dc23
LC record available at https://lccn.loc.gov/2017021711

Columbia University Press books are printed on permanent
and durable acid-free paper.

Printed in the United States of America

Cover design: Lisa Hamm
Cover image: © G.M.B. Akash / Panos Pictures

For my mother, Dinaz

CONTENTS

PREFACE

THIS BOOK REPRESENTS the culmination of sixteen years of research into modern slavery. During that time, I have investigated slavery in fifty-one countries and have comprehensively documented the cases of 5,439 slaves of all kinds. I traced human trafficking networks around the globe, witnessed the sale of human beings into slavery on six continents, and confronted some of the traffickers and organized crime networks that exploit people in bondage and servitude. My first book, *Sex Trafficking: Inside the Business of Modern Slavery*, outlined the most profitable form of slavery the world has ever seen. My second book, *Bonded Labor: Tackling the System of Slavery in South Asia*, outlined the form of slavery that ensnares more people than all other forms combined. This third book offers my overview of the most pervasive and salient manifestations of contemporary slavery I have documented. It represents the totality of what I know about slavery, the full evolution of my thinking on the topic, and my earnest efforts to contribute to the abolition of this savage institution. I focus on a handful of case studies that manifest many of the most important realities of slavery as they exist in the world today—from sex trafficking in Nigeria, to labor trafficking in the agricultural sector of California, to organ trafficking in South Asia and across the U.S.–Mexico border, to debt bondage in the construction sectors of Malaysia and Singapore, and finally to slavery in Thailand's seafood sector.

In my first two books, I placed a substantial focus on outlining the economic realities and key metrics of slavery as it exists in the world today. When I began my research in the summer of 2000, there was a gaping deficiency in slavery scholarship relating to data, metrics, and basic modeling of the offense. I believe my early work helped shift the mode of inquiry into contemporary forms of slavery by demonstrating the value of a business and economic understanding of the crime, as well as the importance of data and metrics relating to every facet of the offense—be it how many slaves there are by type, the profits generated by specific types of slavery from one country to another, the business models used to exploit slaves, or the expected economic value of a slave to the exploiter. This information was meant to provide baselines for measurement, to frame the scale and functioning of the phenomenon, and to inform antislavery policy and law.

In some sense, my journey into slavery has been the wrong way around. In recent years I have grown somewhat weary of metrics and data in the face of the immeasurable human suffering I have witnessed. The misery, degradation, and debasement of human life that I have seen in brothels, in factories, on ships, in agricultural fields, and in other venues of slave exploitation has taken an immense toll on my mind, heart, and health . . . as well as on my faith in humanity. My arguments on how to rid the world of slavery continue to be data-driven, but in this book I wanted to share with you the clearest possible picture of slavery, just as I have seen it—in all its depravity, greed, and disdain. At this stage in my journey, numbers no longer provide the comfort they once did, so I have returned to the beginning and tried to convey to you the torment of the slaves I have met, the forces that perpetuate their servitude, and the challenges I faced in trying to document their suffering. I do so solely in the hope that in some small measure these efforts will contribute to the eradication of this dehumanizing institution. Slavery has been an ignoble stain on the legitimacy of human civilization from the beginning. Although this truth only dawned on our collective consciousness a few centuries ago, the systems and forces that promote slavery remain as pervasive and entrenched in the global economic order as ever. Slavery debases human relations, invalidates the conduct of our lives, and indicts us all as participants in its ignominy. I hope this book will play some small role in moving you to action and will inspire new and more effective efforts to abolish slavery once and for all.

ACKNOWLEDGMENTS

THERE IS NO language to express my gratitude to each and every woman, child, and man who shared their stories with me. The dignity and fortitude of the enslaved and oppressed individuals I met across the years have both humbled and inspired me. They shall never be forgotten.

Hundreds of generous people around the world have contributed to my research during the past sixteen years. From local guides and drivers, to translators, to NGO personnel, to law enforcement, to colleagues and well-wishers in dozens of countries—I could not have completed my research without their assistance. I am especially grateful for all the goodwill I received from strangers, who had no reason to trust me, but without whose aid my research could not have been completed.

I am deeply grateful to my agent and friend Susan Cohen for her indefatigable support of my books, and of me as I struggle through them.

I remain profoundly indebted to my first editor, Peter Dimock, who saw something in me that to this day I do not see myself—the ability to write these stories. Without his faith and advocacy, my books would not exist.

Columbia University Press has given me a supportive home for my work since the first day they embarked on this campaign with me three books ago. It has been a pleasure being an author under their banner.

I could not have written a word, let alone embarked on so many soul-crushing journeys into the world of bondage and slavery, without the love and support of my family. I write especially in most affectionate memory of my second father, Vijay Shankardass, whose noble example of dignity, honor, and nobility I shall forever strive to achieve.

Above all there is my wife, my heart, my angel nonpareil, Aditi. When the world goes dark, you are my light. When all seems lost, you bring me home. I treasure your love beyond any capacity to express, so I shall say but this—with your hand in mine, life has meaning.

MODERN SLAVERY

CHAPTER 1

MODERN SLAVERY

An Overview

If slavery is not wrong, nothing is wrong.
—Abraham Lincoln

SITA'S LAST WISH

SHE STOOD LOW to the ground, hunched, eyes averted. Emaciated by misery and disease, she was next of kin to oblivion. Sita[1] was born to be a slave, at least for a portion of her life, and after that—an outcaste waiting to die. She is Bedia, a subjugated caste of former nomads in the state of Rajasthan, India. Unlike much of the nation, the Bedia prize their daughters, for they grow up to be prostitutes, and nothing else. It is the sole vocation they are allowed, by birth-curse, and it begins when they are children. They are told to be proud. They are told it is better than being a housewife. Bedia men only marry outside their community, and their wives have the lowest status of all. Sons born of these wives will one day peddle their sisters and hope to produce more Bedia daughters. The men live off the earnings of their child-raped girls. These children are the dismal face of slavery—an oppressed subclass of humanity fit only to be consumed, for profit.

I met Sita in a dusty village about forty kilometers outside the city of Bharatpur. Her mud-brick hut baked like an oven. Stray dogs with patches of missing fur skulked lazily between miserly pockets of shade. They growled, but meant no harm. Sita's breathing was labored; she knew she was not long for this world. Before the end, she wanted to tell her story. She knelt to touch my feet, but I waved her up and said that I should be touching hers instead. I reached out my hand and asked her to take it. She looked at me nervously; no one like her is allowed to touch the skin of someone like me, unless of course it is because she has been purchased. She folded her hands in a gesture of respectful decline. I understood. We sat on the dirt inside her hut, and I told her I would listen, as long as she wanted. She took a sudden, desperate breath, the kind meant to quell a gathering storm of pain. Then, she spoke.[2]

> My father died when I was nine. My mother took me and my brother to live with my uncle. I had my first period when I was thirteen. My uncle was happy. He sold my virginity to a businessman in Bharatpur for Rs 50,000 [~$960].[3] He slaughtered a goat and we did a ceremony called nathni utarna [literally "taking off the nose ring"]. This means I am ready to be a prostitute. My uncle bought me a new sari and took me to the businessman.
>
> That man kept me for two nights. What he did to me was so painful. I tried not to cry, but I could not stop. My tears did not make him stop either. After I returned home, my brother and my uncle arranged customers for me. They were men from Bharatpur and Agra and Jaipur. Tourists also. Some were Japanese from a car factory at Neemrana. There were European men also. I have seen so many colors of skin pressed against mine.
>
> I earned a good wage for my family doing prostitution. This made me feel proud. When I was fifteen, my uncle took me to Delhi. I did not want to leave my home. My mother protested, but what can she do? In my community a woman is only good to lie on her back. My uncle left me in a kotha [brothel] on GB Road. A gharwali [madam] named Manju paid him money. She told me I owed her Rs 20,000 [~$380] and after I repay this amount she will send money for my family. She told me my breasts must grow faster, so she gave me

injections. Manju was kind to me, but if I displeased her she beat me without mercy.

There were so many girls in that place. Some were younger than me, but most were older. One girl from Nepal named Kumari was like my sister. She took care of me and taught me how to make a man finish quickly so we can have more clients and make more money. My uncle came every three, four months to collect money from Manju. He brought me gifts from my mother, like this necklace. I did not see my mother for four years while I was in Delhi. Then I became sick. I knew what happened. It happens to all the girls at GB Road. It happened to Kumari one year earlier. She did not live very long.

Clients no longer had interest in me, so Manju sent me home. That was three months ago. I live here with my family. I am grateful that the Bedia men do not marry Bedia women. This means I can never have a Bedia daughter. My uncle is upset that I cannot work. He and his brother took two girls from another village and tell customers they are Bedia. They earn money from those girls now.

I tried to get an Aadhaar[4] card so I can find work, but the sarpanch[5] will not endorse my application. The upper classes discriminate against us, but they line up to sleep with our daughters. I am very weak, and I know I will not live very long from now. There is a school near this village for boys. I asked the teacher if he can teach me to write. He is kind and said he will help me. I want to write a book before I die. I want to tell my story so that people know how we are treated. I want to tell the girls in my community, there is no pride in being a slave for men. Do not let them make fools of you. This is not what God wants you to do.

Sita's eyes shivered as she spoke, but she shed no tears. She refused to pity herself, even though she recognized the bleakness of her predicament. There was no treatment available to her in the village for her HIV infection, and at barely nineteen she was forced to embrace the twilight of her life. Her tale of slavery and suffering was too bleak to bear. She was born an outcaste and a girl, two categories that sealed her wretched fate. She is the essence of slavery: a disadvantaged and oppressed individual valued only by virtue of her coerced service to those who matter more. She was never treated as equally human, equally dignified, or equally free as those who exploited her. That is the merciless formula that governs slavery in every corner of the world, from ancient times through to the modern age.

I spent several hours with Sita, as I wanted to learn as much as I could about her—as a woman, an Indian, a human. I saw glimpses of a little girl still sparkling within her battered heart. She had movie-star crushes and favorite foods, and she found solace in meditation. It was my honor to spend time with her, brief as it was.

Sita reiterated her wish to me several times—she wanted to write a book about her life, so that the Bedia girls who came after her might find the courage to reject their fates. I promised I would do my part to share her story with the world.

I knew I would never see Sita again. Before I left, I reached out my hands to her one last time. This time, she took them. I held her tight. I wanted to say so much, but only a few words emerged.

I am sorry. Please forgive us.

WHAT IS SLAVERY?

Sita was a slave, in every sense of the word. She was also a bonded laborer, a forced laborer, and a victim of child sex trafficking. To be clear, she was forced into prostitution as a child with no choice in the matter at any point in her life. Everyone but her profited from her degradation. She was exploited for the totality of her adolescence up to the point when there was nothing left to exploit. Although her case is unequivocal, the answer to the question "What is slavery?" can be quite elusive. There are many terms used in antislavery circles to describe various manifestations of the phenomenon, each of which has a codified definition in international law. However, the interpretation and application of these terms has been muddied by a lack of precision that renders it exceedingly difficult to address the offenses effectively. The terms are also used with varying agendas by the multitude of actors in the antislavery space, hence it is vital to understand more precisely just what these terms mean before one can properly address the crimes. Those terms are:

1. slavery (or modern slavery, or modern-day slavery)
2. forced labor
3. human trafficking
4. debt bondage/bonded labor

Slavery, aka Modern Slavery, aka Modern-Day Slavery

The system of slavery dates back to prehistoric hunting societies.[6] The millennia that have passed since that time have provided, one might assume, ample opportunity for scholars to reach consensus as to what the word *slavery* means. However, the term has been applied to different modes of human subjugation in different cultural contexts across the centuries, giving it broad and sometimes contradictory meanings. The most common use of the word refers to the practice of treating people like property, or chattel, hence the term *chattel slavery*. For much of human history, slaves were ontologically inferior individuals who were owned by ontologically superior people. The lines between slave owner and slave were always immutable and strictly enforced by law, culture, and religion. Slaves did not have the right to exit the relationship unless it was granted to them by their owners, and their labor was exerted almost entirely for the benefit of these owners. Slaves were most often acquired through military conquest, as in the ancient Greek, Roman, Egyptian, Mughal, Aztec, and Ottoman empires. The system of treating and exploiting people as property has continued from antiquity through to the Western colonial period, the Atlantic slave trade, and into the twenty-first century.

There are, however, other systems of slavery across human history that were not as binary as traditional chattel slavery. As I describe in *Bonded Labor*,[7] some Eastern conceptions of the institution of slavery during ancient times were more nuanced than the binary free/unfree, owner/owned system of chattel slavery. To be sure, even medieval systems of peonage and serfdom were not traditional systems of human ownership, but they still amounted to slavery and are often referred to as such. In South Asia, the concept of slavery begins with the Sanskrit word *dasas*, which is typically translated as "slave." The word in fact refers to a range of subservient conditions and classes of individuals who were analogous to

Western slaves. These individuals might have been owned outright, placed in a lifetime of bondage in exchange for food and shelter, sold into slavery to discharge a debt, or enslaved after military conquest. As with Western slaves, they had few, if any, rights under the law, and pathways to freedom were virtually nonexistent aside from being granted freedom by their owners. Similar systems of nuanced, caste-based or conquest-based slavery were common throughout the ancient Muslim world, the South American empires, and in Chinese and Japanese cultures. Despite these variegated manifestations of slavery, the system has always been based on expressions of power and violence, in addition to minimization of labor costs, economic exploitation, racism, sexism, alienation, and the superiority of one class of persons over another.

The first internationally accepted definition of slavery was established roughly 90 years after slavery was first abolished in the British Empire. This definition was provided in the League of Nations Slavery Convention in 1926: "Slavery is the status or condition of a person over whom any or all of the powers attaching to the right of ownership are exercised."[8] Per this definition, slavery is described as the condition of a person who is treated like property. Power is exerted over the person based on a legal and accepted right of human ownership. This definition would be applicable to most every instance of slavery in the pre-Abolitionist era, especially in the West. However, it has become more complicated to apply this term today because there are no longer any legal rights of ownership over human beings anywhere in the world. Indeed, the institution of owning and trading people like property has been rejected in various ways dating back to at least the third century BCE, when Emperor Ashoka outlawed the slave trade in the Mauryan Empire. Several empires and countries subsequently abolished slavery (or parts of the practice), but in most cases the system remained socially accepted and in fact almost always became legally reinstituted after it had been outlawed.

The sustained abolition of slavery as we know it began in earnest in 1807 with the Slave Trade Abolition Act in England, followed in 1833 with the Slavery Abolition Act. The post-Enlightenment era abolitionist movement spread across colonial powers, arrived in the United States in 1865 with the Thirteenth Amendment abolition of slavery, and continued around the world well past the League of Nations Slavery Convention with countries such as Saudi Arabia and Yemen abolishing slavery in 1962 and Mauritania as late as 2007. The crucial question in the modern context is, "If there are no legal rights of ownership of another person that convey power to the owner that can be exercised over said person, is there any slavery left in the world?"

Scholars and activists have come to use the terms *modern slavery, modern-day slavery, slavery-like practices,* or *contemporary forms of slavery* to describe the condition of a person who is treated in much the same way that slaves who were legally owned in the past were treated. Just because a condition has been made illegal on paper does not mean it does not exist in practice. Ascertaining just how these forms of modern slavery relate to the long-standing practice of traditional slavery remains unclear. In answer to this question, two camps have emerged.

The first camp asserts that *modern slavery* is a catch-all phrase that encapsulates all practices and conditions similar to old-world slavery, such as forced labor, human trafficking, debt bondage, and certain vestiges of old-world slavery that persist in countries like Niger, Mauritania, India, and Nepal.

The second camp asserts that the use of the term *slavery* should be restricted to the historic institution of chattel slavery and those few modern instances that equally manifest the extreme levels of control, abuse, and economic exploitation that were inherent in the system of chattel slavery and legal human ownership. Harvard scholar Orlando Patterson provides perhaps the most eloquent definition of slavery in this context as "the permanent, violent domination of natally alienated and generally dishonored persons."[9] Patterson argues that slavery requires severe degrees of violent domination of people stripped from their homeland and cultural contexts in a way that dishonors them as human beings. In this way, only the most extreme cases of what people describe today as modern slavery would be included, such as sex trafficking or servitude in the Thai fishing sector. Everything else would be just what it is—forced labor, bonded labor, forced marriage, severe labor exploitation, and so forth.

I have vacillated across the years on how best to use the word *slavery* in the modern context. The scholar in me veers toward Professor Patterson— slavery is a very specific, dehumanizing, violent form of domination and exploitation whose severity should be respected by not diluting the word to mean forms of severe labor exploitation found in the world today. On the other hand, slavery (or words that mean something like it) across cultures and time has occupied a spectrum of conditions, and perhaps it is prudent not to be too restrictive in the application of the term. To be sure, in the contemporary era one is attempting to assess a range of deeply exploitative and oftentimes dehumanizing and alienating power relationships that can be as onerous as slavery from centuries ago. The activist in me feels, therefore, that terms like *modern slavery* or *contemporary slavery* can be responsibly used as umbrella terms that capture the range of practices predicated on achieving dominance and exploitation similar to those that occurred within the old-world system of chattel slavery.

For the purposes of this book, and for general application in my antislavery work, I have for the time being sided with camp one. That is, I use the terms *slavery* or *modern slavery* as umbrella terms that describe the various faces of contemporary bondage and servitude that occur in the world today, in the hope that doing so will provide a more efficient framework for discussing the spectrum of servile labor exploitation practices. For the avoidance of doubt, I have no intention of using these terms with a view toward evoking emotional responses for the sake of sensationalism.

In my first two books, I provide definitions of slavery in a way that would allow the term to be operationalized from legal and research standpoints. This means that the definitions seek to provide clarity on the specific criteria that could be applied in criminal law or data-gathering contexts to determine whether a case is slavery. These definitions focus on the determining elements of the offense; however, I have come to feel that perhaps it would be more useful to reframe my definition in terms that are intended to capture the deeper essence of slavery in the contemporary context. I offer, therefore, a more essential definition, which can be operationalized through a determination of the conditions or indicators that would satisfy the concept:

> *Slavery* is a system of dishonoring and degrading people through the violent coercion of their labor activity in conditions that dehumanize them.

Every person I documented in my research and determined to be a slave fulfilled this definition. These are people caught in systems of servile labor exploitation that severely dishonor and degrade them. The coercion of their labor activity (any labor that generates economic value) must contain an element of violence to descend to the level of slavery. Violence does not mean physical harm alone; rather, it indicates any manner of threat against any person who matters to the slave, as well as verbal and psychological abuses, and also the deprivation of security or sustenance as penalties for lack of submission. Finally, coercion of labor must take place in conditions that dehumanize the individual. This can mean physical conditions of filth, putridity, or other conditions that amount to a subhuman working environment. It also can mean that the individual's freedoms are restricted— especially freedom of movement, which is a core freedom that makes us human. When the totality of these debasing conditions results in the systematic degradation of a person through the violent coercion of his or her labor activity in conditions that strip the person of his or her dignity and humanity, that, to me, is a slave.

Forced Labor

Four years after the first international legal definition of slavery, the International Labour Organisation (ILO) provided the first international legal definition of forced labor in the ILO Forced Labour Convention (No. 29): "All work or service which is exacted from any person under the menace of any penalty and for which the said person has not offered himself voluntarily."[10] The immediate context for this definition in 1930 was the recognition that chattel slavery was an institution that had been abolished from most of the planet, so a new term was needed to describe conditions akin to slavery that were not predicated on rights of ownership. The term also was defined in relation to the exploitative labor practices being perpetrated by colonial powers, in which millions of people were subjugated in slavelike conditions despite the abolition on paper of the practice.

The key elements to the ILO definition of forced labor are (1) coercion and (2) involuntariness of the labor. These terms are not defined in the convention; hence, scholars and legal experts have endeavored to determine what these terms mean and what levels of coercion and lack of consent are required to make a determination of forced labor. Scholars have established various indicators of these qualities to create an analytical basis of determination. There remains no definitive list of indicators nor a singular method through which these indicators are deemed to establish the conditions. There is, however, general consensus that some of the essential indicators to coercion include verbal, physical, sexual abuse or threats to the victim, family members, or other workers; confiscation of identity or work documents; the denial of sufficient food and water; living and working in the same place; excessive surveillance; manipulation of debts; the threat of deportation; and other measures along these lines.[11] Some of the indicators of involuntariness include the inability to leave the workplace or to pursue other work options without permission; being cut off from communications with friends and family; working excessive hours without overtime payment; having to ask permission for restroom breaks; having to work despite illness or injury; not being allowed sufficient time off for rest or holidays; lack of adequate safety equipment, toilet, and sanitation; and other measures along these lines.[12]

There are varying approaches to the question of whether each of these indicators is to be treated equally, or whether some might be construed as "strong" and others as "less strong." I have adopted the approach of having strong and less strong indicators in my assessments. For example, under coercion, I consider physical or sexual abuse to be strong indicators of coercion and excessive surveillance to be less strong. Under involuntariness, I consider restrictions on freedoms of movement and employment (especially when workers are locked inside the workplace) to be strong indicators, and not being allowed sufficient time off for rest or holidays to be less strong. See appendix C for an example of an intake questionnaire I used to document various forms of slavery, including the list of indicators for coercion and involuntariness I used to establish forced labor under ILO Convention No. 29.

Once one determines what indicators will be assessed and whether some are to be strong or less strong, one must then ascertain how many of the indicators are required to establish each of the conditions of coercion and involuntariness. A scoring technique of one point per indicator, or perhaps two or three points for strong indicators, can be used. The approach I have taken is that all strong indicators and at least half of the remaining less strong indicators must be present to determine each condition of coercion and involuntariness, and, of course, both conditions are required to make a determination of forced labor. This is a conservative approach that eliminates many cases that might reasonably be construed as forced labor. Having said this, if all the strong indicators are present, it is invariably the case that a majority of the remaining indicators are also present. Hence, the only alternate approach I could take would be to revert to a scoring technique that might allow for only one or two strong indicators and a handful of the other indicators to be sufficient. This would result in my having documented many more cases of forced labor across the years.

There is vigorous debate in policy circles as to whether slavery and forced labor are the same phenomenon, and if not, what the differences would be. The general consensus appears to be that slavery (when used as an umbrella term) is almost, but not quite, synonymous with forced labor. There are a few categories of slavery that are not captured by forced labor, primarily because they occur outside the context of employment, such as forced marriage,[13] child marriage,[14] and children in armed conflict.[15] Beyond these categories, slavery and forced labor generally describe the same array of severely exploitative and degrading labor practices.

Human Trafficking

Exactly seven decades after the ILO Forced Labour Convention (No. 29), a new term entered antislavery common parlance: human trafficking. The United Nations Protocol to Prevent, Suppress and Punish Trafficking in Persons Especially Women and Children, supplementing the United Nations Convention Against Transnational Organized Crime (2000), also known as the "Palermo Protocol," established the first international definition of the crime of human trafficking:

> "Trafficking in persons" shall mean the recruitment, transportation, transfer, harbouring or receipt of persons, by means of the threat or use of force or other forms of coercion, of abduction, of fraud, of deception, of the abuse of power or of a position of vulnerability or of the giving or receiving of payments or benefits to achieve the consent of a person having control over another person, for the purpose of exploitation. Exploitation shall include, at a minimum, the exploitation of the prostitution of others or other forms of sexual exploitation, forced labour or services, slavery or practices similar to slavery, servitude or the removal of organs.[16]

Most countries that subsequently established laws prohibiting human trafficking adopted definitions similar to the Palermo Protocol, usually with minor adjustments. For example, the definition of human trafficking in the United States Trafficking Victims Protection Act of 2000 does not include the removal of organs as one of the purposes for which a person can be deemed a victim of human trafficking. Nonetheless, almost every domestic legal instrument on human trafficking includes three elements to the offense as set forth by the Palermo Protocol:

A *process or action*: the recruitment, transportation, transfer, harboring, or receipt of a person
Through a particular means: force, fraud, or coercion
For a particular purpose: forced labor, sexual exploitation, debt bondage, slavery, practices similar to slavery

All three elements must be present to make a determination of human trafficking, except for children, in which case the "particular means" element is not required.[17] When the trafficking takes place for the purpose of sexual exploitation, it is called sex trafficking; when it takes place for the purpose of labor exploitation, it is called labor trafficking; and when it takes place for the purpose of the removal of organs, it is called organ trafficking.

No sooner had the definition of human trafficking been codified in the Palermo Protocol than did several confusions arise. These confusions continue to complicate antitrafficking and antislavery efforts to this day.

The first confusion relates to the term itself: human trafficking. The term connotes that people are being moved and that this is an essential element to the offense. The crimes of drug trafficking or arms trafficking, for example, involve the illicit transport or sale of drugs or weapons; hence, without even reviewing the definition of human trafficking one would infer that it involves the illicit movement or sale of people. This connotation led many scholars, activists, policy makers, and jurists to conclude that human trafficking must involve the illicit "traffic" of people across national borders for the purposes identified in the Palermo definition. However, it is entirely possible for a person to be "trafficked" within his or her home country (from a rural area to a city, for example). It is also entirely possible that the other processes of "obtaining" or "harboring" might not involve movement of people at all and in fact usually identify the actions of the recipient or a middle man in the victim's journey. Hence, from the outset, the term confused the nature of the crime as being fundamentally about the movement of people, and this confusion persists no matter how many efforts have been made to clarify it.

The inherent terminological confusion relating to movement of people was reinforced by the second issue with the definition—that it is included in a supplement to a transnational organized crime convention. This contextual factor suggests that the offense is concerned with the illicit transnational movement of people, or at least it focuses on this aspect of the offense as opposed to the purpose of this movement, which is the exploitation. The primary reason the connotations of movement and illicit crossing of borders are problematic is that most of the activists and policy makers who use the term *human trafficking* proffer it as a synonym to the term *slavery*. This usage suggests that slavery involves a transnational traffic in persons for exploitative purposes, as opposed to the exploitative purposes themselves. Policy makers have worked assiduously since the Palermo Protocol to clarify that human trafficking is not about movement but rather is about slavery. They have also worked to clarify that the crime does not require movement of any kind, and that only third-party involvement in the recruitment or delivery of a person into slavelike conditions is required, or that this person is involved in the exploitation themselves. One might then ask, "Why not just call it slavery?" This question evokes the preceding question as to whether slavery is a term that should refer to the narrow array of conditions that are similar to old-world chattel slavery, or whether slavery should be used as an umbrella term that refers to all modes of servile labor exploitation found in the world today. Those who would like to use human trafficking as a synonym for the word *slavery* would perforce use the word as an umbrella term, but this may or may not be useful or accurate, and doing so has already led to considerable confusion as to what the term actually means. Human trafficking simply does not sound like slavery, and no matter how many times people try to use the terms as synonyms, they likely never will be comfortably or intuitively accepted as such.

The third issue created by the term *human trafficking* has been confusion with the crime of human smuggling.[18] Human smuggling involves third parties who facilitate irregular migration across national borders, such as *coyotes* who help migrants without documentation cross from Mexico into the United States, or *trolleys* who help migrants without documentation travel from Africa to Europe. Because the phenomenon involves third parties who facilitate the illicit crossing of sovereign borders, human smuggling and human trafficking are often confused. Indeed, countless victims of human trafficking are incorrectly identified as smuggled migrants simply because they are in a country without proper documentation. As such, they are typically deported without a second look at the conditions (i.e., forced labor or forced prostitution) they might have been suffering in the destination country. For this reason, I have argued that any irregular migrant identified in a destination country should first be screened for forced labor exploitation prior to considerations of their violation of local laws, especially migration or prostitution. Human trafficking should thus be construed as human smuggling that takes place with force, fraud, or coercion prior to the movement, and forced labor or slavery after.

There are other confusions relating to the specific elements of the offense of human trafficking, namely, what actions are included under the requirements of force, fraud, or coercion, and what exactly is sexual exploitation? Is all commercial sex activity inherently exploitative, or only some? If slavery is one of the purposes of human trafficking, can human trafficking then also be used as a synonym for slavery? The overlap between the processes involved in force or coercion and many of the stated purposes of the offense—primarily being forced or coerced labor—creates additional confusion in establishing cases of human trafficking. Clearly, there is scope to tighten the definition, if not to adopt a new term that sounds more like that which it is trying to describe—that is, slavery, not irregular transnational movement.

The final and perhaps most fundamental question that has arisen since the term "human trafficking" was codified is whether it should be construed as slavery, or the *process* of entering a person into slavery. The answer to this question has considerable ramifications for antislavery activism, policy, and law. *My recommendation is that the term "human trafficking" should be used to describe the process of entering a person into slavery, not slavery itself.* This usage tightens the term to the phenomenon it is trying to describe (the traffic in people for the purpose of enslaving them) and also avoids much of the confusion that arises from the use of the term as a synonym for all forms of slavery. Using terms that more accurately describe the phenomena to which they refer is the first step in achieving the terminological and definitional clarity that can guide more effective efforts to tackle slavery in the world today.

Debt Bondage/Bonded Labor

Debt bondage or bonded labor is the most pervasive form of slavery in the world today. More people are ensnared in slavery through debt bondage than all other forms of slavery combined. Debt bondage exists in every corner of the world, but it is most heavily concentrated in South Asia. I outline the reasons for the persistence and concentration of bonded labor in South Asia in my second book, *Bonded Labor*.[19] Some of the primary reasons include, inter alia, immense poverty, the caste system,[20] corruption, a lack of access to formal credit markets, the inability of rural poor to access markets and infrastructure, and social apathy to the plight of low-caste and outcaste communities.

Debt bondage was born in feudal economies and was once the predominant mode of labor relations in agricultural settings around the world, from medieval Europe, to Mughal India, to Tokugawa Japan, to the peonage system of the American South after the Civil War.[21] The phenomenon was first defined under international law in the United Nations Supplementary Convention on the Abolition of Slavery, the Slave Trade, and Institutions and Practices Similar to Slavery (1956) as: "The status or condition arising from a pledge by a debtor of his personal services or those of a person under his control as security for a debt, if the value of those services as reasonably assessed is not applied towards the liquidation of the debt or the length and nature of those services are not respectively limited or defined."[22]

In 1976, India passed its Bonded Labour System (Abolition) Act, which includes an extensive definition of bonded labor as a system of forced or partly forced labor in which an individual takes an advance in exchange for his or any dependant's pledged labor or service, and is confined to a specific geographic area, cannot work for someone else, or is not allowed to sell his labor or goods at market value.[23] India's bonded labor definition covers more of the nuanced scenarios in which debt bondage exploitation can take place beyond an unreasonable asymmetry between the value of credit and labor found in the 1956 UN definition; however, the basic mechanisms and ultimate mode of the exploitation are similar.

In *Bonded Labor*, I include my own definition of bonded labor as:

> The condition of any person whose liberty is unlawfully restricted while the person is coerced through any means to render labor or services, regardless of compensation, including those who enter the condition because of the absence of a reasonable alternative, where that person or a relation initially agreed to pledge his labor or service as repayment for an advance of any kind.[24]

Whichever definition one applies, debt bondage involves the exploitative interlinking of labor and credit agreements between parties. On one side of the agreement, a party who possesses a surplus of assets and capital provides credit to the other party, who, because he or she lacks almost any assets or capital, pledges his labor to work off the loan. Given the sharp power imbalances between the parties, the laborer is often severely exploited. Bonded labor occurs when that exploitation becomes so severe that it manifests as slavery. In these cases, once the capital is borrowed, numerous tactics are used by the lender to extract slave labor. The borrower is often coerced to work for meager wages to repay the debt. Exorbitant interest rates of 10 to 20 percent per month are charged, and additional money lent for medicine, clothes, or basic subsistence is added to the debt. In most cases of bonded labor, up to one-half or more of the debtor's wages are deducted for debt repayment, and further deductions are often made as penalties for breaking rules, poor work performance, or at the whims of the exploiter. Sometimes the debts last a few years, and sometimes the debt may be passed on to future generations if the original borrower perishes without having repaid the debt (according to the lender). Most often, the terms of debt bondage agreements last a few years or can be on a seasonal basis in certain industries, such as agriculture.

The existence of debt bondage outside of South Asia is most often initiated through up-front fees that a debtor is forced to pay to a recruiter to secure identity documents, training, work permits, and travel for a work opportunity in a foreign country, usually in construction, domestic work, seafood, agriculture, or commercial sex. *Bonded Labor* covers the phenomenon's existence in South Asia, and I outline the practice of debt bondage beyond South Asia in chapter 6 of this book.

Scholars, economists, and policy makers have asked whether debt bondage should be considered slavery.[25] The question usually centers on the issue of whether the debtor willingly enters into the agreement, in which case this voluntary entry would vitiate the element of coercion typically required to establish slavery. Where slavery is used as an umbrella term, debt bondage is undoubtedly included. Where slavery is used more restrictively, most cases of debt bondage I have documented would still be considered slavery, but many cases of seasonal bonded labor or less severe cases of debt bondage in which the debtor may have alternatives or not be as aggressively coerced, manipulated, and exploited may not apply. I have focused on these more severe cases of debt bondage in my research, of which there are millions around the world, and I have no problem categorizing them as slavery.

Overlapping Categories

It is vital to note that there is substantial overlap between the aforementioned categories of servile labor exploitation. Any one person could easily belong to two, three, or even all four categories, which in some sense argues for the use of slavery as an umbrella term that captures these similar and highly overlapping practices. For example, many victims of labor trafficking in California's agricultural sector (see chapter 3) are also victims of debt bondage. Debt bondage victims in domestic work or construction (see chapter 6) are also very often victims of labor trafficking. The exploited individuals in Thailand's seafood industry (see chapter 7) are almost all victims of labor trafficking and debt bondage. Most of these victims also would be considered forced laborers, and all of them must be considered slaves. Nonetheless, when it comes to categorization by type of slavery, there are invariably certain indications as to the dominant mode or nature of the exploitation. Identifying these dominant modes is crucial when it comes to considerations of how to address the abuses. Appendix A describes my approach to categorization in more detail and acknowledges the substantial overlaps between these categories.

KEY METRICS OF SLAVERY

One of the most crippling deficiencies of the contemporary antislavery movement has been a lack of reliable data. This data deficiency has hampered efforts to persuade governments and charitable foundations to invest sufficient funds and attention to the issue, to persuade corporations that their supply chains might be tainted by various forms of slavery, and to establish legitimacy and credibility in the eyes of the world. Rather than focus on research, the movement has historically focused on sensationalism and emotional rhetoric. The atmosphere began to change around the turn of the last decade when the antislavery movement finally began to devote more attention to data and measurement. Since that time, there has been a marked increase in the number of data-driven research projects on various aspects of slavery. There are still substantial gaps, but I am confident these will be filled in due course. Two of the most important questions about slavery finally receiving meaningful attention are "How many slaves are there?" and "How much profit is generated from their exploitation?"

The Number of Slaves in the World

My estimate of the number of slaves in the world at the end of the year 2016 is **31.2 million**. This number is broken down into three categories:

Debt bondage: 19.1 million
Human trafficking: 4.8 million
Other forced labor:[26] 7.3 million

Although my model on the number of slaves in the world by type requires extrapolation, I have strived to be as conservative as possible in all calculations. Refer to appendix A for further details and discussion on the derivation of the numbers.

Table 1.1 provides a breakdown of each type of slavery by region. Roughly six out of ten slaves in the world are in South Asia. This is primarily a function of the fact the approximately 80 percent of the world's debt bondage slaves are in the region. It is also a function of the fact that the region possesses roughly 70 percent of the people in the world living in poverty. South

TABLE 1.1 Number of Slaves by Region, 2016[1]

	DEBT BONDAGE/ BONDED LABOR	HUMAN TRAFFICKING	OTHER FORCED LABOR	TOTAL SLAVES	PERCENT OF TOTAL (%)
South Asia	15.5	1.3	2.3	19.1	61.2
East Asia and Pacific	1.5	1.2	2.4	5.1	16.3
Western Europe	0.2	0.4	0.3	0.9	2.9
Central and Eastern Europe	0.2	0.4	0.3	0.9	2.9
Latin America	0.4	0.4	0.4	1.2	3.8
Africa	0.5	0.5	0.8	1.8	5.8
Middle East	0.7	0.5	0.7	1.9	6.1
North America	0.1	0.1	0.1	0.3	1.0
Total	**19.1**	**4.8**	**7.3**	**31.2**	**100.0**

[1] Values in millions.

Asia is unquestionably ground zero for slavery, but Africa and the Middle East also contain relatively high per capita levels of slavery.

There are two other credible estimates of the number of slaves and forced laborers in the world: one from the International Labour Organisation (ILO), and one from the Walk Free Foundation. The ILO has published two estimates on the number of forced laborers in the world (not exactly the same as slaves). In 2005, they estimated there were 12.3 million people in forced labor,[27] and in 2012 they estimated there were 20.9 million people in forced labor.[28] The increase from 2005 to 2012 is not based on actual increases in forced labor but rather on an improvement in sample size and methodology and extrapolation assumptions. I was engaged by the ILO as one of a handful of experts to advise on the 2012 estimate and can confirm that the process was both rigorous and conservative. The estimate is based on a capture-recapture (CR)[29] sampling methodology of reports of forced labor by NGOs and the media, which are then entered into an extrapolation model to generate forced labor estimates by region. The ILO continues to refine its estimate every few years, and I believe it produces the most reliable estimate of forced labor in the world.

The other estimate comes from the Walk Free Foundation, which produces a "Global Slavery Index" (GSI). This index provides estimates of the number of slaves in the world based on household surveys conducted by the Gallup organization. The most recent estimate in 2016 is that there are 45.8 million slaves in the world.[30] The GSI provides estimates by country as well, with the top countries being India (18.3 million), China (3.4 million), Pakistan (2.1 million), Uzbekistan (1.2 million), and North Korea (1.1 million).[31] On a percent of total population enslaved basis, the countries with the highest levels of slavery are North Korea (4.4 percent), Uzbekistan (4.0 percent), Cambodia (1.6 percent), Qatar (1.4 percent), and India (1.4 percent).[32]

These three estimates provide a range of roughly 21 to 46 million people in forced labor or slavery in the world. I suspect the truth is somewhere in between these numbers. One cannot compare them fully, as they use different methodologies, rely on different sources of data, make different assumptions that are used for extrapolation, and apply different definitions. Still, they constitute more rigorous estimates than were being produced a decade earlier and provide a reasonable sense of the scale of slavery in the world today.

The Profits of Slavery

Only two estimates of the profits generated by slavery and forced labor are available: one produced by the ILO and one produced by me. In 2005, the ILO estimated that the 12.3 million forced laborers in the world generated profits for their exploiters of $32 billion.[33] In 2012, the ILO estimated that the 20.9 million forced laborers in the world generated profits for their exploiters of $150 billion.[34] The sharp increase in profits is not strictly linked to the increase in the number of forced laborers in the estimates; rather, it is the result of a more refined economic model of forced labor, including the fact that forced prostitution is responsible for $100 billion, or two-thirds, of this estimate. The ILO's updated estimate of forced prostitution profits was partially drawn from my estimates in Sex Trafficking.[35] The ILO's most current data suggest the average annual profits per forced laborer is approximately $7,175. In Sex Trafficking, I estimated there were 28.4 million slaves in the world generating $92 billion in profits for their exploiters, with sex slaves

TABLE 1.2 Summary of Slavery Estimates and Metrics

	ILO (2012)	WALK FREE (2016)	KARA (2016)
Total Slaves/Forced Laborers	20.9 million	45.8 million	31.2 million
Total Annual Profits	$150 billion	—	$124 billion
Annual Profits per Slave[1]	$7,175	—	$3,978
Average Cost of a Slave[1]	—	—	$550
Annualized ROI of a Slave[1]	—	—	383%

[1] "Kara" values are global weighted averages.

Sources: ILO Data from "ILO Global Estimate on Forced Labor" Geneva, 2012; Walk Free Data from www.walkfree.org.

being responsible for almost 40 percent of these profits. My current estimates are that the 31.2 million slaves in the world generate $124.1 billion in profits for their exploiters, with sex slaves being responsible for $62.3 billion, or 50.2 percent of the profits, even though they represent only 5.8 percent of the total slaves in the world (see appendix A for details). These data suggest global weighted average annual profits per slave of $3,978, with a high of $36,064 in annual profits per sex trafficking victim, and a low of $1,056 per debt bondage slave. Table 1.2 summarizes the key data on total slaves/forced laborers and profits.

In addition to data on total slaves and the profits generated by slavery, I have calculated that the global weighted average cost of a slave is $550. The global weighted average annualized return on investment (ROI) of all forms of slavery is 383 percent (see appendix A for details).

Comparative Analysis of Slavery

From the early days of my research, it was clear to me that slavery is motivated by greed. Slavers are not cruel and exploitative simply for the sake of it. They are cruel and exploitative in pursuit of what they really want—profit. This focus on the profit motive of slavery guided much of my data gathering as I sought to understand just how profitable modern slavery is. As it turns out, slavery today is more profitable than I could have imagined. Profits on a per slave basis can range from a few thousand dollars to a few hundred thousand dollars per year, with total annual slavery profits estimated to be as high at $150 billion (ILO). These astounding numbers made me wonder how the profitability of slavery today compares to slavery centuries ago. As I investigated this comparison further, several contrasts between old-world slavery and modern-day slavery emerged, and these contrasts made it abundantly clear exactly why slavery persists and permeates almost every corner of the global economy.

Table 1.3 highlights some of the most important comparisons of slavery two centuries ago versus today. The first difference is that slave trading/ human trafficking two centuries ago involved lengthy, expensive journeys as compared to quick, inexpensive journeys today. Centuries ago, it could take months or more to transport a slave from the point of origin in Africa or the Middle East to the point of exploitation in the Americas or Asia. For example, in the Atlantic slave trade, the slave was first acquired somewhere in the interior of the African continent and transported to the West African coast. Around 20 to 25 percent of slaves perished during this portion of

TABLE 1.3 Comparative Analysis of Old World Slavery to Slavery Today

OLD WORLD (1810)	TODAY (2016)
Lengthy, expensive journeys to transport slaves	Short, inexpensive journeys to transport slaves
Limited avenues for exploitation (agriculture, domestic work, construction)	Numerous avenues for exploitation (dozens of industries)
Weighted average cost of a slave: ~$4,900–$5,500 (2016 USD)	Weighted average cost of a slave: ~$550
Weighted average annual ROI: 10–20%	Weighted average annual ROI: ~170–1,000%
Typically enslaved up to a lifetime	Typically enslaved a few years or less
Legal rights of ownership over other human beings	No legal rights of ownership over other human beings

the journey.[36] Once at the coast, the slaves were purchased and transported across the Atlantic to the Americas. Another 10 to 15 percent of slaves perished during this stage, known as the "Middle Passage."[37] The very time-consuming and expensive nature of the transport, as well as the high mortality rate during the journey, meant that when a slave finally arrived in the Americas and was auctioned for sale, the price was not cheap. Prices were also pushed upward because it could very well be quite some time before a new slave would be available to purchase should something happen to the former one. By contest, slaves today can be transported from one end of the planet to the other relatively quickly and for a small cost compared to the profits enjoyed through their exploitation. I am not aware of any mortality rate studies on modern slavery transport, but results from my own research indicate a fairly low percentage. All in all, the entire proposition of transporting slaves is significantly cheaper, quicker, and involves much less attrition than at any point in human history.

The second comparison is that in old-world slavery the industries in which slaves could be exploited were limited primarily to agriculture, domestic work, construction, and certain skilled trades, such as blacksmith. Other slaves were forced into military service, and, of course, slaves were sexually exploited by their owners. Of all these sectors, only agriculture generated meaningful and large-scale profits, which were nevertheless limited to one or two harvests per year depending on the crop. Slaves were forced into brothels as well, but commercial sex and sex tourism were not nearly the bourgeoning businesses they are today thanks to the speed and inexpensiveness of travel. Unlike the past, slaves today are exploited in dozens of industries linked to the global economy, including agriculture, mining, construction, apparel, manufacturing, seafood, beauty products, and commercial sex. In short, slaves are exploited in more industries than ever before, almost all of which generate significant profits.

The third comparison was the most challenging for me to assess: the average cost of a slave. To make the comparison, I gathered data on the prices of slaves during the early 1800s and compared these data to acquisition prices I gathered for slaves today. Data on slave prices from centuries ago is patchy and inconsistent. Slave prices tend to be more available for slaves sold in the American South and in the territories of the East India Trading Company than for sales in Africa, South America, and the Middle East.

Nonetheless, I can safely say that two centuries ago there was a wide variance in the acquisition costs of a slave, anywhere from $0 for a person born into slavery to upward of $30,000 in 2016 U.S. dollars[38] for a young, healthy African male slave sold in the American South. Premiums were also paid for certain skills, such as blacksmith or carpenter, and discounts for other qualities, such as older age or physical impairment.[39] I was not able to determine a precise global weighted average price of a slave two centuries ago; however, I feel confident saying that the number is somewhere between $4,900 and $5,500 in 2016 U.S. dollars. My data for slaves in the modern age is more comprehensive. As with the old world, the range is wide, anywhere from $0 for a person born into slavery to upward of $10,000 for a trafficked virgin sex slave sold in Western Europe or North America. However, the global weighted average is much lower, approximately $550. The weighted average is pulled down significantly by the high number of debt bondage slaves in South Asia, most of whom are in lower-profit sectors such as agriculture, apparel, or stone breaking and have correspondingly lower acquisition costs of anywhere from $50 to $500. Although slaves can be relatively expensive even today, there has been a sharp downward trend in the acquisition cost of a slave across the last two centuries of more than 90 percent. This downward trend in slave prices is primarily driven by (1) a sharp increase in the total number of people living in poverty and other highly vulnerable conditions, (2) a sharp drop in transportation costs, and (3) a sharp increase in transportation speed. These three factors create a nearly limitless supply of potential slaves who can be readily acquired and quickly and inexpensively moved from a point of origin to a point of exploitation, driving down the cost of slaves in general. A fourth element relates to mass migration events, almost always catalyzed by military conflict or environmental catastrophe, which also helps make slaves much cheaper than before; in essence they are transporting themselves from the point of origin to a point of exploitation and need only be recruited by a trafficker/slave exploiter at some point along the way.

The fourth comparison relates to the profitability of slavery, as measured by annual return on investment (ROI).[40] In the old world, I calculate the ROI of slavery to be around 10 to 20 percent per year. The ROI was primarily generated through agricultural work and semiskilled trade work. Slavery in domestic work and construction is economically beneficial through the avoidance of costs, which also can be construed as profit because the expense savings can be used for other capital investments. The much higher average up-front costs of a slave in the old world places significant downward pressure on the annual ROI. The annual ROI with slavery in the modern era, however, can be anywhere from 170 percent for debt bondage slaves to over 1,000 percent for sex trafficking. This astounding upward shift in the profitability of slavery is primarily a function of the sharp drop in the up-front price of a slave and a significant increase in the number and variation of sectors in which slave labor can be profitably exploited. The ROI metric alone explains the prevalence and persistence of modern slavery—it is far and away more profitable now than at any point in human history.

The preceding comparisons give rise to a fifth comparison: in the old world slaves tended to be exploited for their lifetimes, whereas today individuals are exploited for much shorter periods of time. Due to the significant up-front costs of a slave centuries ago, and the relatively modest rate of capital recoupment, the slave owner tended to exploit his slave for a longer period of time. That is not to say that slaves were not killed, brutalized, or bartered between slave owners, but in any scenario they were by and large slaves for most, if not all, of their lives. There are certainly slaves today who are exploited for decades or longer, especially in certain forms of generational debt bondage or hereditary slavery that persist in Asia and Africa. However, most slaves, especially trafficked slaves, may be exploited for just a few months or at most a few years. These individuals may endure repeated spells of slavery throughout their lives, but in totality the aggregate duration of slavery today is much shorter than in the past. This shift is primarily due to the fact that the capital investment for acquiring a slave is much less today and can be recouped within just a few months. After that point, the slave owner is generating massive profits. There is a ready supply of countless new potential slaves who can be acquired quickly and inexpensively, so the slave exploiter can also chew up his slave, spit him out, and acquire a new one with relative ease. Because slavery is no longer legal, this increased turnover also allows the slave exploiter to minimize risks associated with keeping a single slave for too long, given the chances that she or he may form ties with someone who could help with escape, or the slave may try to escape him- or herself, which could potentially lead to an investigation by law enforcement, even if rarely. In a way, human life has become more expendable than ever before. Slaves can be acquired, exploited, and discarded (or worse) in relatively short time periods and still provide immense profits for their exploiters.

The sixth and final comparison relates to the legal status of slavery. In the old world, slavery was legal, accepted, and normal. One could buy and sell people under the law and exert power over them as if they were any other form of property. Today one cannot legally own another human being; however, power can still be exerted over them as if they were property. The illegality of slavery and its rejection by humanity would suggest that there is meaningful risk associated with attempting to re-create the practice. For various reasons outlined later in this chapter, there is still an appallingly small level of risk associated with most of the slave exploitation that takes place in the world today. This deficiency in the global response to slavery has allowed the practice to persist in various forms across the global economy—often in the shadows but in broad daylight as well. Until slavery is perceived as a high-cost and high-risk form of labor exploitation, this reality will not change.

The aforementioned six comparisons give rise to a crucial thesis on modern slavery:

The immensity and pervasiveness of slavery in the modern era is driven by the ability of exploiters to generate substantial profits at almost no real risk through the callous exploitation of a global subclass of humanity whose degradation is tacitly accepted by every participant in the economic system that consumes their suffering.

The four elements to this thesis that must be addressed are (1) immense profits, (2) lack of real risk, (3) vulnerable subclass of humanity, and (4) tacit acceptance of the suffering of slaves. First, the profitability of slavery must be eliminated. Second, efforts to do so must be tied to the creation of significant risk associated with slave exploitation so that the perception of any rational economic actor is that the crime does not pay. Third, efforts must be made to protect and empower the global subclass of humanity upon which traffickers and slave exploiters most often prey, especially women, children, and minority ethnic communities. Finally, a radical shift in global consciousness is required; namely, a permanent rejection of the apathetic and deplorable acceptance that it is reasonable to inflict servitude on the downtrodden so long as their suffering is transformed into the cheap and delightful goods we purchase every day.

Throughout this book I endeavor to describe the array of efforts that I feel can achieve these goals by inverting the core thesis that drives modern slavery.

SUMMARY OF CASES DOCUMENTED FOR THIS BOOK

The data and trends described in this book and the appendixes that form the foundation of my arguments of how to eradicate slavery are drawn from a total of 5,439 cases of slavery that I have documented since the beginning of my research in the year 2000. One of the questionnaires I used to document these cases can be found in appendix C. Table 1.4 provides a summary of some of the key metrics from the data I collected.

I did not keep track of all of the incomplete cases I attempted to document, but I have a good sense that this number is at least five times the total number of cases I was able to document in full. I may not have been able to complete an interview with a potential slave for a number of reasons: he or she may not have wanted to finish the conversation out of fear or discomfort; he or she may not have been able to provide enough information for me to include the case in my findings; or there may have been interruptions or other problems with the interview.

Throughout my research, I upheld two principles: (1) do no harm and (2) the least important aspect of my research is my research. I always erred on the side of extreme caution in putting informants or their families in a situation that might cause any discomfort or risk. I never prioritized trying to document a case over adhering to this principle. I followed Institutional Review Board principles on human subject research at all times,[41] including the practice of explaining my intentions and the purpose of the questions before asking for consent to speak, never asking questions without consent, and never documenting or publishing identifying information on the informant that could put the person at risk. With minors, I asked for consent from a responsible adult where one was available (usually parents or the person running the shelter), or assent from a child when there was not a responsible or trustworthy adult present (usually in places of exploitation). It is impossible to conduct firsthand research into slavery without putting oneself at risk, and it is impossible to avoid all possible risk factors for the informant, but I made every effort to minimize these risks, and when in doubt, I refrained from pushing forward.

TABLE 1.4 Summary Metrics of Slavery Cases Documented

	TOTAL CASES	AVERAGE DURATION OF SLAVERY (YEARS)[1]	FEMALE/ MALE RATIO (%)	AVERAGE AGE SLAVERY BEGAN (YEARS)	LIVING IN POVERTY (%)	MINORITY ETHNIC GROUP (%)	FOREIGN MIGRANT (%)
Bonded Labor/Debt Bondage	2,292	5.1	45/55	21.1	97	94	28
Labor Trafficking	1,356	3.1	39/61	21.7	94	90	74
Sex Trafficking	920	3.8	94/6	15.4	90	82	55
Other Forced Labor	871	3.5	48/52	18.2	92	87	29
Total/Weighted Average	**5,439**	**4.4**	**58/42**	**19.8**	**94**	**90**	**44**

[1] Includes assumptions by type of slavery as well as considerations as to whether the individual was documented during or after a spell of slavery so that between one-fifth and one-half of the total duration of servitude remains after the point the individual was documented.

KEY FEATURES SHARED BY SLAVES

The slaves I have documented share a handful of key features, and under-standing these features is necessary to guide more effective antislavery efforts. Not every slave possesses every one of these features, and some fea-tures are more prevalent than others, but the following elements consistently appear in the cases I documented.

Poverty

Roughly 94 percent of the slaves I have documented lived in chronic poverty or had fallen into poverty not long before their exploitation began. Poverty is the most common feature shared by slaves today, and it is perhaps the most powerful indicator of vulnerability to potential enslavement. When one considers that approximately 40 percent of the planet, or 3.1 billion peo-ple, live on incomes of less than $3.10 per day, it is reasonable to posit that there is a near limitless supply of potential slaves around the world. Extreme poverty drives risky migration and acceptance of an offer from a recruiter/trafficker even if the individual knows it may lead to a negative outcome. For these and other reasons, poverty is unquestionably one of the most merci-less forms of violence and injustice in the world, and it invariably leads to a plethora of human rights catastrophes. That we live in a world in which the top 100 wealthy individuals have more combined wealth than the bottom 3.5 billion people combined represents a complete failure of the contemporary economic order. Global capitalism must take responsibility for promoting these indecent income disparities and for perpetuating an economic system that is both unjust and unsustainable.

Minority Ethnicity or Caste

Approximately 90 percent of the slaves I documented belonged to minority ethnic groups or low-caste/outcaste communities. These communities tend to be the poorest and most disenfranchised people in mainstream societies. They lack access to education, economic opportunity, basic rights, and social safety nets, all of which render them ever-at-the-edge of catastrophe and almost-always-ready to accept offers that lead to servitude. Caste is a particularly powerful force of social oppression whose persistence can be found primarily in South Asia and Africa. Bonded labor in South Asia is the form of slavery in which I found the highest proportion of outcaste communities, with more than 99 percent of cases. Whether it is the Roma in Europe, hill tribes in the Mekong subregion, *dalits* in South Asia, indigenous peoples in South America, or tribal people in Africa, the lower classes of the world are deemed less equal as human beings by those in the upper classes/castes; hence, their exploitation is oftentimes (and perversely) seen as a beneficial outcome for them, as well as a condition natural to them. These anachronistic attitudes permeate the consciousness of mainstream societies in most parts of the world, distorting social relations, prejudicing economic and judicial systems, and perpetuating the oppression of the lower classes with impunity.

Foreign Migration

Approximately 44 percent of the slaves I documented were foreign migrants. This figure does not include domestic migrants who had traveled from a rural area to an urban center in the same country in search of work. The highest levels of foreign migration were perforce in the cases of human trafficking for forced labor and forced prostitution. The movement abroad may have resulted from lack of a reasonable options for income and survival in their home country or from en masse distress migration due to military conflict, social collapse, or environmental catastrophe. Refugee camps are a common source of recruitment by traffickers. Being a foreign migrant renders individuals inherently more vulnerable and divorced from basic rights and protections. It also promotes high levels of isolation that directly facilitate slavery. Of all the slaves I documented who were foreign migrants, 61 percent of them migrated on an irregular basis. Internal migration also can lead to isolation and lack of access to rights, such as seasonal brick-making migrants who move from one state to another in India, or urban slum dwellers in Brazil who migrate to the Amazon interior for forced labor in logging or iron smelting. Of equal interest are those cases that do not involve migration. These cases tend to involve debt bondage in South Asia in sectors such as agriculture, beedi rolling, or stone breaking, as well as people who live in urban slums who end up in forced labor and vulnerable teens who end up in forced prostitution in their home cities. Although migration is not necessary for slavery, mass migration events are particularly sourced by opportunistic human traffickers to recruit new victims.

Other Features Shared by Slaves

Several other features are common to the slaves I documented. A majority of them were isolated—both before being enslaved and even more so during their enslavement. Isolation from social protections, infrastructure, markets, health care, and education are strong predictors of various forms of exploitation, including slavery. A lack of education and literacy are also common factors. Unstable family units, lack of access to formal credit markets (especially in debt bondage cases), and statelessness are common features in many of the cases of slavery I have documented.

The final feature shared by almost every slave that I met across the years is in some ways the most crucial—the lack of a reasonable alternative. To be sure, the aforementioned features all contribute to creating a situation in which an individual does not have any reasonable alternative to entering him- or herself or a family member into a condition of servitude. When faced with conditions of extreme poverty, violence, displacement, low-caste status, or other vulnerabilities, no amount of awareness of the possibility of being exploited can deter an individual from accepting an offer whose outcome is likely to be slavery.[42] Sadly, slavery might end up providing levels of food and shelter that are a relative improvement over the individual's alternative. This improvement is often cited by slave exploiters as justification that the individual is not being exploited but in fact is being done a favor. On the contrary, the fact that slavery can in some cases be a welfare-enhancing condition for an individual is no justification for the validity of slavery. It is a biting indictment of our collective failure to provide a decent existence for all people on this planet.

FORCES THAT PROMOTE SLAVERY

To design an effective response to slavery, it is vital to understand the forces that promote slavery around the world. I believe the most helpful way to frame these forces is in terms of supply and demand.

Supply-Side Forces

The supply-side forces of slavery are informed by the features that slaves share. Forces such as poverty, minority ethnicity, migration, gender violence, lack of access to formal credit markets, lack of education, and population displacement are some of the chief forces that promote the supply of potential slaves. In addition, the supply of slaves is promoted by systemic forces such as corruption, lawlessness, military conflict, and societal apathy for the plight of slaves. These and other forces have facilitated the supply of potential slaves for centuries. All of these supply-side factors must be addressed, though even the most optimistic activist would concede that substantial reductions in poverty, gender violence, minority bias, and corruption will take time. Accordingly, I have focused more on analyzing the demand-side forces of slavery, which I believe are more vulnerable to near-term intervention.

Demand-Side Forces

The specific forces of demand for any particular sector that exploits slaves varies. For example, male demand to purchase women and children for sex is an essential component to the demand side of the sex trafficking industry but is not present in slavery in the seafood sector. However, for any industry that exploits slaves, there are always two economic forces of demand: (1) exploiter demand for maximum profit and (2) consumer demand for lower retail prices. A closer look at these two forces reveals both the optimal points of intervention in the business of slavery and the underlying logic of the system as it exists today.

For almost any business, labor is typically the highest cost component to operating expenses, representing anywhere from 25 percent to 50 percent of costs depending on the industry. Throughout history, producers have tried to find ways to minimize labor costs. Slavery is the extreme of this effort because slaves afford a virtually nil cost of labor. With drastically reduced labor costs, total operating costs of the business are substantially reduced, allowing the company to maximize profit. However, significantly lower labor costs also allow producers to pursue another imperative—to become more competitive by lowering retail prices. The need to lower retail prices is driven in large part by consumer demand to pay less for goods and services. In a globalized economy where products are available to us in nearby shops from all over the world, the need to be competitive on price is greater than ever. This *globalization of competition* is one of the key differences between the economic logic of old-world slavery and slavery in the context of the global economy. Producers are not just competing with the company down the road but with companies from all over the world. As a result, slavery and other forms of severe labor exploitation have evolved from the old world into the globalized world as a means through which unscrupulous producers compete to advance profits as well as to maximize price competitiveness. Underregulated labor markets are targeted by producers to minimize labor costs, be it the seafood sector of Thailand, mobile phone manufacturing in China, or garment production in Bangladesh. I contend that there is a tacit understanding between Western multinationals (and their governments) and the governments of developing economies to look the other way regarding labor conditions so profits and price can be optimized. This relationship is a driving force of global capitalism, and it has resulted in vast increases in suffering among the poorest and most disenfranchised people of the world.

Consumers understandably prefer goods and services that are less expensive. However, if consumers were to find out that their food, mobile phones, and clothes are produced through slavery or child labor, they might opt to pay a little more for goods that they could be sure were untainted by severe labor exploitation. Just how much more a consumer would be willing to pay for an untainted good would depend on the good itself, as well as the reliability of the assurance that it is untainted. Many consumers may nevertheless not have sufficient disposable income to pay more for untainted goods, so one might reasonably ask whether they have a right to access cheap goods even if the price point can only be achieved through labor exploitation. I believe this is a false question because there will almost always be some profit margin that the seller could forgo to provide goods at prices that even relatively poor consumers could still afford. These hypotheses must be tested through research, but I contend that most people do not wish to wear clothes or eat food produced through slavery. As consumers become aware of the tainted nature of many global supply chains, I believe they will express a demand to be sold untainted goods. The next stage in antislavery activity must therefore involve cooperation by industry, governments, and nonprofits to formulate a reliable and economically viable system of supply-chain certification to meet the demand by consumers that the goods they purchase are free of slavery and child labor. Consumer demand is one of the most powerful forces that can help achieve a near-term change in the system of slavery around the world; however, one sector is left out of this consumer-based argument, and that is commercial sex.

In my experience, consumers of commercial sex are less sensitive to the possibility that the service they are purchasing is provided through slavery. They are, however, sensitive to price and risk. In *Sex Trafficking*, I presented a hypothesis that male demand to purchase commercial sex is highly elastic. This thesis suggests that consumer demand fluctuates significantly relating to shifts in price. I corroborated this hypothesis with a small sample size of four male consumers in a brothel in India, whose demand curve demonstrated an elasticity of demand of 1.9 (highly elastic).[43] I have since completed a more extensive survey of sixty male consumers of commercial sex in India, Denmark, Mexico, and the United States. Although there is variation between countries, the aggregate demand curve of all sixty male consumers is 1.82. This indicates that when the retail price of a commercial sex act doubles, demand among these sixty consumers drops by 76 percent. This result reinforces the hypothesis in *Sex Trafficking* and affirms that demand-side interventions have the most potential to reduce sex trafficking in the near term.

The results of this research also led me to think about a new set of demand-side tactics to attack sex trafficking. Although the demand curve establishes an economic elasticity, implied in this result is the fact that male demand to purchase cheap sex could very well be sensitive to deterrence-focused interventions in addition to those predicated on creating upward shocks in retail prices. Put another way, if demand fluctuates significantly based on price, it can very well fluctuate significantly based on risk, achieved via efforts to deter the purchase more directly. Interventions focused on deterring the purchase of commercial sex can best be tested in jurisdictions where the purchase is criminalized. One can then measure policies such as prison time, naming and shaming, or placement on a sex offender list, among others. Policies like these are being tested in small pockets around the world, with some of the most interesting and persuasive work being done by Demand Abolition, based in Boston. I believe that demand-side efforts to elevate cost and risk to the consumer (and trafficker) provide the best chance of having a major impact on the business of sex trafficking. And make no mistake, sex trafficking, like all forms of slavery, is a business.

THE BUSINESS OF SLAVERY

Slavery is a business, and the business of slavery is thriving. Despite substantial increases in awareness of slavery in recent years, a plethora of new laws on the issue, and a newfound focus on research, the global climate remains relatively friendly to the business of slavery. As a result, systems of human servitude persist around the world. Put another way, the drive to capitalize on the underregulated labor markets that feed the business of modern slavery remains more powerful than efforts to rid the world of slavery. As a result, slavery and other forms of severe labor exploitation have become embedded in much of the global economy.

Slavery remains good business primarily because that business generates substantial profits. In an effort to understand just how profitable the business of slavery is, I introduced the concept of the "exploitation value" (EV) of a slave in *Sex Trafficking*.[44] This crude economic term is not intended to elide the immeasurable human costs of the crime but to frame just how profitable a slave in various sectors can be to his or her exploiter. Knowing this information helps guide more effective policies, laws, and penalties intended to thwart the offense.

The global weighted average exploitation values of a slave in the primary categories of slavery found in the world today are:

Sex trafficking	$68,177
Labor trafficking	$5,825
Debt bondage	$2,545
Other forced labor	$9,173

These numbers represent conservative estimates of the expected profits that a slave exploiter's business would enjoy per slave (see appendix A for details). There are, of course, significant regional variations in these numbers. For example, the EV for sex trafficking ranges from approximately $28,300 in South Asia to approximately $141,700 in the United States. Similarly, a debt bondage slave in agriculture in Nepal would have an EV of approximately $850, and a debt bondage slave in construction in Dubai would have an EV of approximately $7,700. For labor trafficking and other forms of forced labor, significant variations are found from one industry to another, such as domestic servitude, manufacturing, and mining. The ranges of profitability are significant, and the reality revealed by these numbers is that slavery is a very financially rewarding business. Indeed, the global weighted average EV of all forms of slavery is $9,367 compared to the global weighted average acquisition cost of a slave of $550. These numbers paint a very clear picture of how profitable the business of slavery has become. When one supplements this fact with the reality that the crime is rarely prosecuted, and that when it is, the financial penalties for the offense are often a fraction of the profits generated by the business, the picture of why the business of slavery is thriving becomes even clearer.

Governments, industry, and consumers may express concern about slavery, human trafficking, child labor, and other labor abuses, but the kinds of sustained, aggressive, fully resourced antislavery tactics required to cleanse the world of slavery remain frustratingly elusive. The lack of risk in the business of slavery, conjoined with its immense profitability, promote an enduring and pervasive global system of human exploitation. The profits of slavery are becoming more clearly understood, but the chief reasons for the near risk-free nature of slavery receive less focus. The forces that promote the business of slavery and render it a relatively risk-free venture are discussed next.

TWENTY FORCES PROMOTING SLAVERY TODAY

During the course of my research, twenty forces emerged that promote slavery in the world today. Most of these forces are directly responsible for why slavery remains such a risk-free business venture. The most helpful way to frame these twenty forces is to hearken back to the initial "Three P" approach to human trafficking outlined by the UN Palermo Protocol and the U.S. Trafficking Victims Protection Act in 2000. The three P's to addressing human trafficking are prevention, protection, and prosecution. A fourth P was added later—partnership, which refers to coordination among key stakeholders in efforts to combat human trafficking. I would like to add a fifth P—progress, which refers to measurement and research.

Prevention

Efforts to prevent individuals from being enslaved or trafficked suffer from the following key deficiencies:

1. *Failure to provide reasonable alternatives to the most destitute and vulnerable populations.* Most cases of slavery I have documented were precipitated by a lack of reasonable alternative sources of security and income. Awareness campaigns meant to prevent slavery by educating potential victims to the risks of accepting offers from recruiters/traffickers meet with limited results when individuals face circumstances that place their daily survival in jeopardy. Families have no choice but to accept risky offers, embark on distress migration, sell a child, or make other heartbreaking decisions due to the lack of alternatives. With widening asymmetries in income distribution and other structural economic injustices inherent in the current governance of global capitalism, an ever-at-risk population of countless individuals will be pushed into slavery because of our collective failure to attend to the basic needs of human survival for all people.

2. *Failure to provide access to formal credit markets.* The inability of the poorest of the poor to access fair, formal credit markets drives countless people into debt bondage every year. This lack of access also places families at risk when they are faced with income shocks caused by illness, loss of life, or other catastrophes. Reasonable credit sources are vital for families to bridge the gap until these shocks subside, or to meet basic subsistence needs.

3. *Failure to protect displaced people in a postcrisis context.* The first responders to any crisis in the developing world are often human traffickers. These traffickers prey on the vulnerabilities of displaced people—whether resulting from environmental catastrophe or military conflict—who often have no reasonable alternative to the trafficker's offer for assistance. Crises precipitate countless cases of human trafficking every year as a result of failures to protect the vulnerable in the immediate aftermath of the crisis.

4. *General acceptance of the subjugation of low-class/caste groups and minority communities.* Across the world, there is general acceptance or apathy toward the subjugation, exploitation, and oppression of low-class/caste groups and minority communities. Exploiters have repeatedly told me that the slavelike conditions in which low-caste groups are being exploited are improvements for them. Even though the onerous truth may be that

the food and shelter provided by slave exploiters represent an immediate material improvement for the exploited individual, this fact does not justify slavery. Entrenched and anachronistic biases relating to caste, ethnicity, and gender remain a stain on the face of humanity. Until it is no longer deemed acceptable to exploit these communities, the world will not be rid of slavery.

5. *Failure to provide connectivity and information tools to foreign migrants.* Slavery thrives in isolation. In the modern world, information and social networks are more accessible than ever, but migrants who end up in labor or sex trafficking are often cut off from connective technologies that could otherwise prevent or end their exploitation. Simply having access to hotlines, local NGOs, family, friends, law enforcement, and other social networks can provide vital sources of information and potential assistance should migrants face exploitative scenarios.

6. *Imposition of up-front fees for labor migrants.* The imposition of up-front fees on labor migrants is the leading tool used to exploit these individuals in debt bondage and forced labor. The fees are often overstated and compel desperate migrants to mortgage their lives on a wage-earning opportunity that is crucial for their family's survival. Capitalizing on this desperation, human traffickers in destination countries impose debts through up-front fees that wreck the lives of labor migrants and are a leading cause of human trafficking around the world.

Protection

Efforts to protect survivors of slavery after they have been exploited suffer from the following key deficiencies:

7. *Penchant to see survivors as offenders.* Law enforcement and judicial regimes tend to see survivors of slavery as offenders. Usually, survivors are first assessed as offenders of migration laws, antiprostitution laws, or labor laws relating to a lack of permits or proper work documents, which results in their being detained, fined, or deported. Doing so allows countries to wash their hands of the problem rather than invest in the protection and empowerment of survivors. Doing so also plays right into the hands of slavers and traffickers, who often deliver their victims to the authorities hoping to have

them deported so they can avoid paying wages or truncate risks associated with having a victim form ties that could lead to assistance or escape. As if being exploited as a slave were not enough, being further victimized by the law enforcement officials who are supposed to protect the rights of the exploited makes the slave's journey all the more pernicious.

8. *Failure to provide long-term empowerment of survivors and break the cycle of slavery.* The foundation of true protection is long-term empowerment. Protecting survivors from being further victimized or revictimized for the duration of their lives means providing education, work opportunities, residency status, health services, and other support that will enable survivors to set their lives on a secure path. This benefits not just survivors but their families and future generations. The cycle of slavery can only be broken when survivors can truly survive. Freedom is not a one-time event but a process that must endure for a lifetime.

9. *Failure to protect survivors of slavery, as well as their families, from former exploiters pursuant to being witnesses in a prosecution.* Survivors are needed for successful prosecution of their exploiters, but they and their families tend not to be adequately protected in the immediate period after their exploitation ends, let alone for the crucial period of time required for survivors to be witnesses in a prosecution. Even though slavery survivors who agree to participate in legal proceedings typically receive more protections than those who do not, protections remain sparse, and the long-term risks faced by them and their loved ones remain largely unaddressed. Protections that extend beyond legal proceedings are also often very limited, and survivors more often than not become victims all over again.

Prosecution

In addition to failing to protect survivors, the following deficiencies hamper efforts to prosecute slave exploiters:

10. *Failure to prioritize slavery cases, except for the easy ones.* Slavery cases remain underprioritized around the world. The easier cases—those dealing with sex trafficking of minors in particular—tend to be most commonly prosecuted. Transnational human trafficking cases involving migration that

devolves into forced labor or forced prostitution of adults tend not to be prosecuted because they are understandably difficult to investigate, let alone win. Nevertheless, it is crucial that legal systems prioritize these prosecutions to invert the perception that slavery is a low-risk business with minimal consequences.

11.   *Laws that do not adequately penalize the economic nature of the crime.* In my first two books, I describe how in many countries the laws against slavery offenses prescribe only minor economic penalties; even if an exploiter is prosecuted and convicted, slavery remains good business.[45] I expand this argument in my law journal paper, "Designing More Effective Laws Against Human Trafficking."[46] Some exploiters may face prison time, but as long as their networks continue to benefit economically from the exploitation, the driving motivation of the offense remains intact. Some countries have begun to prescribe more robust economic penalties for slavery offenses that are aligned with the exploitation values of slaves in one industry or another, but for the most part the design of criminal law does not reflect the immense profits generated through the business of slavery.

12.   *Corruption and the failure to implement or enforce laws where they exist.* Even where good laws exist on paper, they remain poorly enforced almost everywhere in the world, especially in countries where corruption of law enforcement, government, and judicial officials are issues. Without enforcement, slavers and traffickers remain free to exploit the vulnerable with little to no risk.

13.   *Inadequate training of law enforcement, prosecutors, and judges to recognize the offense and prosecute it effectively.* The most well-intentioned police officers, prosecutors, and judges may nevertheless not be able to effectively investigate and prosecute, or even identify, slavery cases due to a lack of training. Despite some improvements, a substantial global gap remains in educating the criminal justice system about what slavery crimes look like, how to investigate them, and how to prosecute them effectively. Using technology to support investigations and prosecutions is also crucial.

14.   *Failure to effectively penalize the demand side of sex trafficking.* Male commercial sex consumers and sex traffickers are not punished severely enough to deter the demand-side forces of the most profitable form of slavery—sex trafficking. Doing so for consumers requires a system in which purchasing a female or child for commercial sex is a criminal offense, which

is not the case in numerous jurisdictions. There is heated debate on this point, but I believe the optimal response to eliminating sex trafficking must include the criminalization of the purchase of women and children for sex. Punishing traffickers and pimps is less controversial, but more severe and strictly enforced penalties are crucial components to any system that seeks to eliminate sex trafficking.

15.   *Failure to introduce sufficient cost and risk to corporations to motivate cleansing of global supply chains*. Efforts to introduce risk to corporate officers and board members for slavery in their supply chains have commenced, and I believe doing so is vital in order to motivate these companies to invest whatever is required to cleanse their supply chains of slavery and severe labor exploitation. Companies have every right to seek out low-cost production environments, but doing so comes with an associated obligation to ensure that decent labor standards are maintained. Risk to corporate officers is perhaps the most effective way to motivate these efforts. Pressure from consumers also may help to ensure that global supply chains are reliably cleansed.

Partnership

Although coordination and cooperation among antislavery stakeholders has improved, deficiencies in forging partnerships across borders continue to hamper antislavery efforts. Some of these lingering deficiencies include:

16.   *Lack of transnational cooperation with investigations and prosecutions*. Most countries struggle with transnational cooperation on investigation and prosecution of slavery cases, not to mention partnerships to help with the protection of survivors. Distrust, definitional differences, jurisdictional wrangling, and a lack of structures and mechanisms to support cooperation mean that survivors are underprotected and slavers are all but unpunished, allowing their criminal enterprises to thrive.

17.   *Insufficient resources and coordination among antislavery NGOs and shelters*. Most antislavery NGOs operate on minimal budgets and lack the capacity to coordinate with partners in other countries. Transnational partnership among antislavery NGOs and shelters is crucial for survivors, especially in the cases of children. The services these organizations provide to

survivors are crucial if survivors are ever to reclaim dignified and stable lives. In some cases, NGOs have become competitive with each other as they lobby for a shallow pool of donor resources. Although this is understand-able, the lack of cooperation is very much responsible for many of the defi-ciencies in survivor protection and empowerment, as well as shortcomings in leadership of the antislavery movement.

18. *Inadequate coordination between sending and destination countries of labor migrants.* Source countries for the world's migrant labor force and the destination countries that rely on these workers do not adequately coor-dinate on protective mechanisms to minimize slavery. Each side tends to point the finger at the other as bearing the brunt of responsibility, but both sides must invest and coordinate equally in predeparture and postarrival mechanisms that can help keep migrants protected, connected, and safe. In particular, these countries must coordinate to eliminate excessive recruiter/placement fees, wage deductions, abusive treatment, worker isolation, and other tactics used to transform a hopeful journey of labor migration into a dark descent into slavery.

Progress

Progress means measurement of what works and does not work as it relates to efforts to achieve the previous four P's. They key deficiencies in achieving progress include:

19. *Insufficient research and data gathering on all aspects of slavery.* Research must be conducted to establish baseline data and metrics on every aspect of slavery, be it the size and functioning of each type of servitude from one country to another or measurement of the efficacy of tactics to prevent slavery, increase prosecutions, or enhance survivor protections. How many victims of sex trafficking are there in the United States? What proportion of the Thai seafood industry is tainted by slavery? How effective would awareness campaigns be at minimizing labor trafficking from Bangla-desh to construction work abroad? How effective would expanding access to credit among the poorest of the poor in India be at preventing bonded labor? These and numerous other questions must be researched and mea-sured so that we can assess our progress in the fight against slavery.

20. *Lack of sustained and adequate resources to promote progress in anti-slavery efforts.* Donor support of antislavery NGOs, research, and policy advocacy remains insufficient and inconsistent. Governments, charitable foundations, and industry must coordinate more effectively to create larger pools of resources committed on a consistent basis if we are to make meaningful progress to end slavery. Part of the reason for the lack of resources has been the data gap, which can only be addressed if researchers and NGOs demonstrate that they can conduct the investigations required to populate the antislavery space with robust and reliable information that will in turn guide policy and motivate donors to invest in further initiatives.

TEN INITIATIVES TO ERADICATE SLAVERY

The ten initiatives outlined here are intended to address the primary forces that promote slavery around the world. Tackling these forces will simultaneously address other forms of servitude, such as child labor and severe labor exploitation, more generally. The details of these initiatives are discussed fully in chapter 8. I believe these ten initiatives provide the optimal opportunity to eliminate slavery and other forms of severe labor exploitation from the world.

1. Elevated scaling and effectiveness of global antipoverty programs focused on (1) massive expansion of microcredit, especially for non-income-generating activities; (2) a global economy integration initiative for the poor in rural areas; (3) achievement of universal primary school education for the poor, especially girls. (*Forces 1, 2*)
2. Rapid-response teams focused on prevention and protection in crisis zones. (*Force 3*)
3. Awareness and education campaigns dedicated to alleviating social and systemic biases against subordinated castes and ethnic groups. (*Force 4*)
4. A "Technology Trust" focused on creating innovative solutions to the current barriers in antislavery efforts, including connectivity for migrants, assisting with investigations, facilitating research, expanding credit markets, providing reasonable alternatives, and others. (*Force 5, and others*)

5. Redesign of the process and governance of labor migration, including (1) the prohibition of up-front fees and (2) new multilateral agreements between sending and receiving nations to prevent human trafficking, ensure access to assistance for migrants, and vigorous punishment of offenders. (*Forces 6, 18*)

6. Legal reform, including (1) minimum standards for effective survivor-witness protection; (2) a sharp increase in the economic penalties for slavery offenses; (3) severe penalties for consumers of commercial sex; (4) strict liability for corporate officers and board members for any instances of slavery or child labor in the company's supply chains; and (5) laws or strategic litigation that establish strict liability for owners/employers relating to all actions of labor subcontractors. (*Forces 9, 11, 14, 15*)

7. Policy reform, including (1) all migrants detained by law enforcement must first be screened for slavery abuses prior to consideration of migration, labor, or prostitution violations; (2) tax and tariff incentives for companies that credibly assure their supply chains are untainted by slavery; and (3) most-favored nation trading status for countries that enact and enforce rigorous labor laws that meet the criteria of the ILO core labor conventions, and denial of such status for countries that do not. (*Forces 7, 15*)

8. A mandatory UN Fund for Slavery capitalized by 0.1 percent of every nation's GDP to be focused on survivors, NGOs, and research. (*Forces 8, 17, 19, 20*)

9. International Slavery Courts. (*Forces 10, 12, 13*)

10. A transnational slavery intervention force focused on investigating cases, liberating slaves in coordination with local NGOs, and providing evidence for prosecutions. (*Force 16, and others*)

WHAT CAN ONE PERSON DO?

When faced with powerful and deeply entrenched forces that promote slavery around the world, it can seem daunting to any single person to contemplate how they can contribute to meaningful efforts to eradicate these crimes. There are at least seven steps any individual can take today to join the fight against slavery:

1. *Learn about the issue*: Read this book and share it with others who are interested in learning more about slavery.

2. *Financial support*: Numerous NGOs around the world are working assiduously with insufficient resources to address various aspects of slavery, from prevention to survivor empowerment and everything in between. Any financial or volunteer support you can offer is of tremendous benefit to them.

3. *Contact lawmakers*: Demand that your lawmakers do more to ensure that corporations do their part to certify that their supply chains are not tainted by slavery or child labor. Demand also that they promote policy efforts that are most likely to rid the world of sex trafficking—attack all facets of demand aggressively. Finally, demand that your government enacts and enforces a no-slavery policy in all its procurement, contracting, and purchasing of goods and services.

4. *Slavery-free institutions*: Demand that your city, state, county, company, university, high school, or any other major purchaser of goods takes every necessary step to become "slavery free." For example, universities can ensure that all food, garments, and other products they purchase are untainted by any form of slavery or child labor, all the way down the supply chain. Cities, counties, and other municipalities can all do the same. I believe that every university in the world should create a scholarship so that at least one survivor of slavery each year can receive a full education.

5. *Contact corporations*: Any company that sources raw materials or low-wage labor anywhere in the world must be pressured to investigate and certify that its supply chains are free of slave labor or other severe forms of labor exploitation. Consumers must also demand that companies whose products they purchase ensure that this kind of investigation and certification becomes a regular aspect of their operating models.

6. *Community vigilance*: Organize yourselves into antislavery community vigilance committees. Work with local NGOs and law enforcement to identify slavery cases and to promote the just and full empowerment of survivors. Push relentlessly for the effective prosecution of exploiters. Follow the guidance of NGOs on how you can be most helpful because they have great experience in this area.

7. *Media and technology*: Use the power of social media to contribute to the fight against slavery. You can use these tools to spread awareness, organize community efforts and protest campaigns, or pressure lawmakers

and law enforcement to do more. Make videos or documentaries that educate others on the issue; use GPS tagging on your mobile devices to record
areas in which you feel slaves might be exploited, then report these areas to
NGOs or reliable law enforcement. Find other creative ways to fight back
against slavery by using all forms of media and technology tools.

If you take some or all of these steps, we will be much closer to creating an
environment in which slavery can no longer exist.

For my part, it is and will remain my lifelong mission to see the end
of slavery. I will continue to research these crimes, advocate against them,
and do everything in my power to promote their permanent eradication.
To eliminate slavery is to rid the world of the most ancient and degrading
offense against the essence of what it means to be human—to be free. Freedom is not a one-time event; it is not a singular moment in which chains of
bondage and oppression are broken. Rather, it is a state of being that must
be preserved and protected across a full human life.

I did not foresee this journey as my life's calling when I took my first
research trip in the summer of 2000. I thought my venture would end with
the appropriate realization that I was neither equipped nor qualified to
make a difference. But the horrors I saw, the torment I witnessed, and the
injustices that ran riot like untamed beasts compelled me. I felt driven to
invest every measure of my energy, acumen, sweat, tears, and force of will
to learn as much as I could about slavery in an effort to make any positive
contribution at all. That anyone on this Earth should be denied basic dignity, freedom, and control of their bodies ignited a fire in me that burns
to this day. I am often asked whether I have lost faith in humanity after all
the horrors I have seen. Sometimes I feel have. I have choked many times
under a suffocating gloom of despondency. But the slaves I meet breathe
life into me. They have been chewed up by an unforgiving world and persist nevertheless with grace, strength, and no bitterness toward those who
betrayed them. Who am I to be deterred by paltry adversaries such as fatigue
or grief or a shortage of resources? Understanding slavery and promoting
more effective efforts to abolish it have become the fundamental preoccupa-
tions of my life. I will lead no other life. The slaves I met have humbled me,
inspired me, and driven me to pursue justice for them, and with them. No
matter how many times they are broken, no matter how much is taken from

them, and no matter how forsaken they feel, their will to be free transcends any force of human debasement I have witnessed. It is more powerful than the greed, the violence, and the barbaric qualities that are responsible for their enslavement. The indecency of slavery has stained humanity for far too long. May we be the generation that permanently buries this ignoble offense. And may all the slavers and traffickers shudder at the sound of our thunder, as we bear down with unyielding force to rid their pestilence from the world once and for all.

CHAPTER 2

SEX TRAFFICKING

The Case of Nigeria

Brute force, no matter how strongly applied, can never
subdue the basic human desire for freedom.
—Dalai Lama

INTO DARKNESS

I HAVE STEPPED into darkness many times, but none so dark as
Nigeria. To research slavery is to face the raw and unrestrained bestiary of
man. Those beasts are most fiercely unleashed in the dens of sex slavery,
and Nigeria is the most unleashed of them all. Other countries may have
more victims and other networks may be more sophisticated, but Nigeria
took everything I had experienced about sex trafficking and cast it into an
inscrutable abyss. It took all my fortitude not to fall into the abyss myself; for
once the creeping pall invades your mind, it never leaves.

I landed in Nigeria before dawn on January 2, 2010. Christmas car-
ols played over the speaker system as I waited in the immigration queue
at Lagos Murtala Mohammed International Airport. The tranquility of
the music and the calm before first light belied the extremes of violence,

hardship, and disarray I was about to encounter. It took years of planning before I felt I could travel to Nigeria and conduct research effectively and safely. I needed local fixers and trusted relationships deep in the field; I also needed considerable resources. Despite being one of the poorest countries in the world, Nigeria is one of the most expensive in which to conduct human rights research. The primary culprit is security costs. The moment one steps outside the airport, security is a pressing concern. The price of keeping safe within Lagos is steep enough, but once I left the capital for rural areas, those costs skyrocketed, as did the challenges of getting around and finding enough food to eat.

Lagos is a miasma that transcends description. The metropolis is built in a swampland stitched together by the longest bridge in Africa, the Third Mainland Bridge. Filth, smog, putrescence, and urban snarl exceed human tolerance in this steamy West African capital. The sky is narrow and stained, hanging wearily like mud-caked clothes. Beneath it lies one of the most violent cities in the world. Peril skulks in every shadow, preying on less vigilant souls. Roaming the streets at night is a death wish. Gangs known as "Area Boys" will mug you, abduct you for ransom, or just kill you for sport. Navigating the city by daytime is a trial by combat. In addition to unyielding traffic, Lagos is an oppressive nebula of ramshackle huts, run-down buildings, stockpiles of trash, hordes of people, and the thickest haze anywhere in the world. Yellow buses that look like they have been through war zones shuttle citizens around town, while the rich travel comfortably (when they leave their gated compounds) in stretched, bullet-proof sedans. It is a humid, dusty, heavily congested megacity that is difficult even for experienced travelers to traverse. To have a chance, one must rely on a trusted guide, and my guide in Lagos was Stanley. I arrived on a Sunday, and after a quick breakfast Stanley took me to church.

Church in Nigeria is unlike church anywhere else, and going to a Sunday service at the TREM Redeemed Evangelical Mission in Lagos was the first step toward understanding the power of spirituality to the people of Nigeria, a power that is central to the trafficking of women, girls, and boys from the country. The open-air church was draped in red and green streamers for the Christmas season. The ceremony was officiated by Bishop Mike Okonkwo, who wore a flowing blue and gold kaftan. Bishop Okonkwo officiated his service to more than four thousand people. He preached at the top of his lungs to a rapt congregation that cheered more loudly and more feverishly with each passing hour. By hour four, the energy of the gathering was electric. Bishop Okonkwo mesmerized the audience with an impassioned praise of God. His oratory was enthralling. As his sermon reached its apex, he suddenly fell to the ground and spoke in tongues. As if in mass hypnosis, the entire congregation fell to the ground as well, and everyone spoke in tongues. I cannot describe the cyclonic sensation of observing thousands of people in mass rapture, crying phrases that seemed to have no meaning. The congregation was in ecstasy. It was one of many experiences I had in Nigeria that defied comprehension. I watched intently as men, women, and children rolled on the ground with eyes transfixed on another dimension. I worried that my incongruous presence might somehow corrupt their experience, but I realized I was a nonfactor in the euphoria of the moment. It was a fathomless scene, both beautiful and alarming, a communion wreathed in wails of exaltation. At length, Bishop Okonkwo returned to himself and brought the congregation back with him. There was a mass release, followed by a calm that passed my understanding. The sermon concluded with praise for children, who are the innocent future of the nation.

After the ceremony, I was invited to meet with the bishop in his office. He was still wiping the sweat from his brow when I entered. Up close his presence was surprisingly soothing. Was this the same man who had just brought thousands of people to an unbridled frenzy? The bishop welcomed me with a gracious smile and spoke to me about his sermon. He explained that the people in his country need to feel that God loves them so they can have hope. "God's love gives every person a foundation that can withstand any storm," he explained.

I wanted to ask the bishop about the period of his sermon in which everyone was speaking in tongues, but I did not know how to formulate the question. I assumed he would simply say that the spirit of God entered the congregation and that they felt the ecstasy of his presence. What other explanation could there be? We spoke about various topics, then the bishop introduced me to his wife, Dr. Peace Okonwko, who would show me the church's shelter for victims of sex trafficking.

Dr. Okonkwo gave me a gracious tour of the shelter, which housed twenty-nine survivors at the time I visited, ages eleven to nineteen. The shelter personnel were going to great lengths to heal these survivors from the brutalities they had endured. This was one of the largest and most respected survivor shelters in Nigeria, operating in conjunction with the International Organisation on Migration (IOM) and the National Agency for the Prohibition of Traffic in Persons (NAPTIP), a Nigerian government agency formed in 2003 with the mandate of combating human trafficking in the country. All but three of the victims had been trafficked abroad before being deported and sent back to Nigeria. Several had been deported more than once. A young girl named Hope told me she had been to Italy, Spain, and France and was passed from one madam to the next before she was arrested and deported. "The madams in Spain are the worst," she said. "They beat us for fun every day." Fifteen-year-old Osa said, "I wanted to go to Europe so I could send money to my mother. She was sick and could not work because my father beat her. I had to be with men like my father. It was very bad."

I documented the stories of these children, one painful tale at a time. The shelter was striving to give them hope, healing, and a chance at a decent future, but there was no mistaking the brutalities they had endured. The stories they told of arduous journeys to Europe, the tortures of men and madams, and their fears of failing to repay their debts were identical to the narratives of the Nigerian sex trafficking victims I had documented in shelters across Europe several years earlier. These were the victims who first piqued my interest in traveling to Nigeria.

The first sex trafficking victims from Nigeria I met were in Italy. I describe some of these encounters in *Sex Trafficking*.[1] From Italy, my encounters spanned Europe, and eventually Thailand and the United States. All but two of the Nigerian sex trafficking victims I met were from Edo State, all were Yoruba and lived in terror of a juju priest who had taken control of their souls during a ceremony that almost none were willing to describe. These women and girls told impossible tales of traversing the desert by foot for weeks and months before taking a raft from north Africa to Spain, only to be deported and trafficked back again. They were tormented by their madams, brutalized by the men who purchased them, and refused to cooperate with local authorities for fear that the juju priest would curse them. This curse was no small matter—an evil spirit would possess anything that had been, or one day would be, born from their womb. If that were not enough, the juju priests typically worked in conjunction with the Nigerian mafia, which threatened the worst possible punishments to the victims and their families should the girls ever try to escape or fail to repay their debts. The juju ritual also serves the purpose of erasing the girl's identity. She is told she must forget who she is and be reborn as someone else, someone under the control of the oath. The level of control exerted by the juju ritual was beyond anything I had encountered. Chains and locked doors were nothing compared to the hold this curse had on the women of Edo State. The curse clutched their souls and did not let go. Few of the Nigerians I met were willing to speak about the ritual. One young woman who did so was named Gift.

I met Gift in Copenhagen at a Red Cross shelter for sex trafficking victims. She was from the Eshan village in Edo State. The name of her village means "place she ran to," based on an old story that the queen of the Benin Empire fled to this area centuries ago after a quarrel with the king. Today young girls cannot flee from Eshan village fast enough, and they search desperately for safety and income in faraway lands. Gift's father died when she was six, leaving her mother and three siblings to fend for themselves. They worked as day laborers in farming for the local landowner, but the wages were paltry, and the family could barely survive. Tribes and armed militia from the north also began raiding villages in the south and absconding with young girls, placing Gift and her sisters in considerable jeopardy. In this context, Gift was desperate to travel to Europe. This is what she told me.

> I took the juju oath when I was fifteen years old. The priest made me swear to repay my debt for arranging my trip to Italy. He said I would work as a cleaning lady. A few days later, some men took me from my village to Lagos and gave me a passport and plane ticket. I flew to Milan. When I arrived, a Nigerian woman met me. She wore beautiful clothes and jewelry. She took me to an apartment and said she had purchased me and that I would work in prostitution until I paid her forty thousand euros. I told her there was a mistake, but she beat me until I cried, then she forced me to be with men. She said if I did not obey her, she would tell the priest and he would curse me. She said the men who took me to Lagos would kill my mother and sisters.
>
> I worked in prostitution for this madam for eight months in Milan. The madam was evil. She beat us and made us do horrible things with men. One day I was arrested. I told the police what happened to me. They deported me back to Nigeria. At the airport in Lagos, the mother

of my madam in Milan picked me up and told me I had not paid
my debt. She made me work as her house slave in Lagos for six months
while they arranged to send me back to Italy. She beat me every day
and terrorized me psychologically. After six months, a man we call
a "trolley" said he would take me back to Europe. He drove me and
five other girls to Burkina Faso. We worked there for three months in
prostitution to earn money for the rest of the trip. After Burkina Faso,
two trolleys took thirty girls to Tunisia. Sometimes we traveled by car;
sometimes we walked. It took more than a month.

At Tunisia we went to the coast where we took a rubber boat called
a zodiac. We got lost on the way, and it took us four days to arrive
in Spain. There was very little food and water on the boat, and two
girls died. The trolleys threw their bodies into the sea. We landed on a
beach in Spain where tourists were drinking cocktails.

After a few days, the trolleys drove us to Italy. I returned to my
madam and worked three years in prostitution. I was arrested again
and deported back to Lagos. The madam's mother said I still had fif-
teen thousand euros debt. This time, I worked as a house slave to a
family on Victoria Island for almost one year, then they sent me on a
plane back to Italy. After two more years in prostitution, my madam
sold me to another madam in Denmark. I thought my debt was paid,
but she said I still owed five thousand euros. Some Arabic men took
me on a train to Jutland, and the new madam made me work in a
brothel. Men came from many countries to that brothel. After five
weeks there was a raid and I was sent to prison. The authorities con-
tacted the Danish Center Against Human Trafficking and they came
with me to court. The judge told me that since I was not trafficked
directly from Nigeria to Denmark, I did not qualify as a victim of
human trafficking for Denmark, so I was sent back to prison for immi-
gration violations. I was in prison eight weeks while the NGOs tried to
help me. They explained to the judge that if I was deported to Nigeria
I would be a house slave again and would be trafficked back to Europe
for prostitution. Eventually, the court granted me asylum and I was
taken to a shelter. Two days after I arrived at the shelter, I received
a letter from the juju priest on his stationery. He said if I cooperated
with the authorities or discussed my oath he would send someone to

kill me. My younger sister, Mercy, has taken the oath with the same priest. She wants to come to Europe because the conditions in my village are bad. I begged her not to come.

I blame myself for what has happened. I had ambitions for a better life, and God has punished me. Ambition is a sin. I learned my lesson.

Gift showed me the letter that was sent to her by the high priest of Edo State. (I will refer to him as "GT.") He is the head of the Cult of Ayelala. I read the threats he made; they were written in plain English on professional letterhead. When I looked back up at Gift, she burst into tears. "You tell me, what can I do? This man will kill me! How do I protect my sister?" I took Gift's hands and promised her I would go to her village, meet with her family, and do everything I could to persuade her sister not to travel to Europe. I also promised myself that I was going to meet GT.

The juju oath undertaken by thousands of women and girls in Edo State before they are trafficked abroad is shrouded in mystery. Many child soldiers take the oath as well, although it is primarily administered to females before leaving Nigeria for forced prostitution abroad. One component of the oath requires that the women must never discuss the ritual, let alone try to flee or stop working before discharging their debts. These debts, which can exceed forty thousand euros, are the highest levied against sex trafficking victims anywhere in the world. A few brave survivors like Gift, and a few juju priests in Edo State, discussed the ritual with me in pieces, providing just enough detail for me to piece together most of what happens.

The ritual typically starts late at night in a juju priest's shrine. It can last a few hours or go on for days. The priest takes some of the girl's menstrual blood, nail clippings, and hair, and places these items in a container with her photo affixed to the outside, upside down. The priest and the girl drink alcohol and drugs to achieve an altered mental state. As they chant, the young woman must repeatedly take several oaths: she will obey her madam, never try to escape, never discuss the ritual, never cooperate with authorities abroad, and will keep working until she is told that her debt is discharged. The priest marks the girl's body with cuts using a sharp stone or razor blade, then he smears the cuts with ash. The girl undertakes the ritual because she will not be transported abroad otherwise, and she also receives a blessing from the priest that her journeys will be safe and fruitful. A tray of sand and chicken bones is used for divination to predict the girl's future, and a pact is made with the earth so she can be controlled or cursed by the priest whenever her feet touch the ground, no matter how far away she is. The priest also takes control of the girl's womb, giving him the ability to curse any child that has been or ever will be born from it. The girl lives in terror of this curse and believes in its power completely. No amount of reasoning can persuade her that the curse is invalid.

Although the arrangements vary, many priests are paid by the Nigerian mafia to conduct the rituals. The mafia handles the travel documents and transportation to Europe. Madams in Europe purchase the girls from the mafia, then work them as prostitutes until they feel the debts have been repaid. The madams operate sophisticated networks across Europe to buy, sell, and exploit girls as sex slaves. Several madams I met were former slaves who had discharged their debts and "graduated" to exploiting other women, just as they had once been exploited. Many of these madams returned to Edo State to show off their material wealth, building big homes in Benin City, driving fancy cars, and wearing expensive clothes. Known locally as "Italianos," the madams are living advertisements of the riches that await the girls of Edo State if they take the oath and travel to Europe. They tell the girls that the only barrier that stands between them and a prosperous future is breaking their oath. Never do so, and prestige, wealth, and respect will be theirs.

EDO STATE

By the time I met Gift, I had built the ties I needed to conduct research in Nigeria effectively and safely. Although I was sincere when I promised her I would go to her village to do what I could to persuade her sisters not to travel to Europe, I knew that my task was likely to be futile because her sisters probably had no reasonable alternative other than to leave. Even if I managed to persuade them on the day we met, who is to say what might happen weeks or months down the road? The pernicious realities faced by the girls in Edo State were just as responsible for their exploitation as someone like GT.

The first step in my journey to Gift's village was to travel from Lagos to Benin City, the capital of Edo State. Traveling in Nigeria proved to be more difficult than travel in any other country I have visited. First, the environment is utterly toxic. There is a perpetual brown murk in the air from the burning of crude oil and vehicle pollution. To make matters worse, I arrived in Edo State at the time of the Harmattan winds, which carry fine sand from the Sahara desert across the entire country. As bad as the air was in Lagos, it was much filthier in Edo State, and in Delta State it was worst of all. Near Port Harcourt, the air was intolerable and the ground was covered in a toxic oil slick. Plant life was sparse, and I did not see a single bird in the sky. Hills of rubbish were everywhere, with a dead body or two lying next to them now and then. Land travel in Nigeria, even with security and a trusted driver, is unequivocally discouraged due to the certainty of being abducted for ransom or being forced to pay numerous "dashes" (bribes) at police check points along the highway. I was advised never to use plastic currency in Nigeria, or my credit card details would be stolen within minutes. Corruption runs rampant in the country, and most people reading this book will have received numerous emails from a supposed Nigerian barrister promising an inheritance of millions of dollars if the recipient's bank details are provided.[2] These emails are known locally as "419 Letters," referencing the portion of the Nigerian penal code that addresses fraud. The same scam artists prey on their countrymen as well, often selling another person's home or land without the owner's permission. As a result, hand-painted signs are often placed in front of homes across rural Nigeria that read: "This home and attached land are not for sale, by order of Jesus."

In addition to being the capital of Edo State, Benin City is the capital of the historic Benin Empire.[3] Unlike most of West Africa, Benin was not a slave-dealing empire, making it all the more disheartening that the region has become one of the primary sources of human trafficking from West Africa. The southern portion of Nigeria was dominated by the Benin Empire dating back to the fifteenth century, and it is said that the current Oba (king) of Benin can trace his line of royalty back to 1170. When the British arrived in Benin City in 1897 and discovered human sacrifice, they were so appalled that they burned down the king's palace and took control of the empire. Their next task was to civilize the "heathens" through the introduction of Christianity. Traditionally, the people of Edo State are Yoruba and follow an all-powerful God named Olorun or Olodumare ("owner of the universe"), along with well over one thousand other deities and spirits. The Yoruba tradition was mixed with Christianity upon the arrival of the missionaries, and it evolved into a unique Christian-Yoruba mix still practiced today across much of southern Nigeria. However, unlike other parts of southern Nigeria, Edo State clung more tightly to traditional beliefs, which have seen a resurgence since the chaos that ensued in Nigeria after independence in 1960. In this context, several cults to ancient deities in the Yoruba tradition have emerged. The primary one, the Cult of Ayelala, is responsible for all juju oaths taken by Nigerian girls prior to their trafficking abroad. This cult dominates the spiritual lives of the Yoruba people, and it is also the primary source of law and order in the state. Most people have little faith in the Nigerian police and justice systems.

Ayelala is a fascinating deity and her origin story reveals why she governs the juju oaths. Long ago, there were said to be two main tribes in the Yoruba lands, the Ijaw and the Ilaje. An Ilaje man fell in love with an Ijaw woman, and even though he was already married, he ran away to the Ijaw to be with the woman. This created strife between the two tribes, so it was agreed that an Ijaw slave woman would be sacrificed to atone for the sins of the adulterous Ilaje man. As the slave woman was being sacrificed, she uttered the word "Ayelala," which means "the world is incomprehensible," and this became her name. Before she passed away, Ayelala made a solemn vow to witness all agreements made under her name, and should they be broken she can be invoked to curse the oath breaker. Ayelala was deified, and a cult grew around her and spread across Benin. She instills fear in all believers and is the ultimate dispenser of justice and the protector of truth and morality.[4] Traveling to Gift's village meant traveling into the heart of the land of Ayelala—the land over which GT had complete control.

Gift's village was about 100 kilometers north of Benin City. Travel by car from the city to her village was unavoidable, even if highly inadvisable. I had several drivers throughout my time in Nigeria, most of whom were very cautious and professional. Finding a driver with a reliable car in rural Nigeria, however, was quite a challenge. A car breakdown deep in a rural area was not at all desirable. I did my best to find dependable drivers and cars through word of mouth, and although the results were mixed, the driver who took me to Gift's village turned out to be particularly helpful.

His name was Step-by-Step and he spoke pidgin English, which does not relate in any systematic way to normal English. For example, "hoy far" means "hello," "abeg" means "please," "chop" means "food," "how bodi" means "how are you," "butta my bread," means "God has answered my prayers," "go slow" means "traffic jam," and "so kin so" means "two-door vehicle," such as the one driven by Step-by-Step. I tried to memorize a few useful phrases before traveling to Edo State, but communication was still difficult without a guide who could translate pidgin English to English, and such guides were simply not available.

I set out with Step-by-Step from Benin City early in the morning for the drive to Gift's village. As we ventured deeper into the countryside, the landscape was a contrast of brick-red earth, pale-green foliage, and chocolate-brown haze in the sky. The land seemed to wheeze and groan under the strain of its defilement. The red color of the earth in Nigeria in particular caught my eyes, as I had never before looked down at the dirt and seen any color other than brown. It was as if the land was covered in a legacy of rust-dried blood.

Because of the language barrier, Step-by-Step and I could not talk to each other, so most of our drive was spent in silence. About half way to Gift's village, I phoned her at the shelter in Copenhagen to let her know I was almost at her home. We had stayed in contact during my journey, and she was both excited and anxious about my visit. She was very touched that I would be meeting her family, and she hoped that the voice of someone objective might be enough to persuade her sisters to pursue other options, such that they existed. However, I knew that no one short of the almighty would be able to change their minds. It was he, after all, who had left these children with no alternatives.

After I spoke with Gift, she sent word through a few people in her village who had mobile phones that I would be arriving. Gift's village consisted of a few dozen red clay houses with sheet-metal roofs. The clay was made by mixing the red dirt with water to form a bricklike substance that was sturdier than the mud huts in most of the villages I had visited in other rural settings. Gift's mother was named Joy, and as our car pulled up to her hut, she ran out, threw her arms around me, and erupted in tears. Like Step-by-Step, she only spoke pidgin English, so I could not understand what she was saying, but I understood her tears, her embraces, and her ardent gestures toward her children. I knew she did not want them to follow in Gift's footsteps, but I could see why she would not want them to stay in the village either. It was a place where people could barely survive. The only water came from rain, toilets were holes in the ground covered by a plank of wood, and there was no electricity. To make matters worse, kidnappings by militias heightened the risk of remaining. Though Boko Haram had not yet ventured this far south, it was rumored that they were coordinating with local sympathizers to abduct girls and take them north where they would be sold as sex slaves.

Joy was the mother of nine children, ages thirteen to twenty-five. Most of them spoke broken English, which they learned at a nearby government school when they were able to attend. Gift was the second oldest child. One of her younger sisters, Mercy, age sixteen, had recently taken the juju oath with GT and was preparing to leave for Europe. She was taller than Gift, with a very calm and reassuring presence that belied the harshness of her surroundings. Joy's only son, Promise, had recently been recruited to play in a junior football league in Greece, which I knew was little more than a trafficker's ruse to lure young African boys into forced labor in drug running, street begging, and petty theft in Europe. Even though Mercy knew she would likely by forced into prostitution, she was anxious to leave her village in the hopes that she would be the exception to the rule.

Joy invited me into her hut. Near the entry I noticed a wooden pole in the ground, with a dead pigeon tied to the top, hanging upside down. This, I later learned, had been arranged by GT, to indicate that Joy's home was cursed because Gift had broken her oath. No one in the village would step inside her home for fear that the curse would spread to them. The children's desperation to leave became clearer.

Inside, Joy's children huddled around me. The home consisted of two rooms, a main sitting room and one bedroom with dried grass on the ground. The main room had a phrase written with chalk on the wall: "There's nothing on Earth more precious than a loaf of bread." To be sure, a loaf of bread would have been a delicacy for Joy and her family; they subsisted primarily on boiled tree leaves and yams, three meals a day. Their weary aspects manifested all too clearly the toll taken by perpetual hunger. As with most of the people who lived in the village, work was difficult to come by, which meant income was minimal. During the agricultural season, there was farm work with a local landowner. The villagers were not called by the landowner every day, but when they were, Joy and her children woke at 4 AM and walked two hours to a farming area where they worked in day labor harvesting cassava and yam. They returned home around 8 PM. For their backbreaking work, they were paid the equivalent of $0.26 per day.

Joy apologized for having nothing to offer me to eat but boiled tree leaves. I told her she must not apologize; rather, I should apologize to her as all I had to offer her family were a dozen granola bars I brought for them. I handed out the granola bars, and the children tentatively ate them. Joy sat down on the ground next to me and started to cry. Mercy, whose English was relatively good, translated the conversation. "My mother says Gift is so far. We know she is in Europe, but we do not know where she is. She is so far."

Joy asked me if Gift was okay, and I said she was safe in a shelter. "Please tell Mercy not to go to Europe," she begged me. I looked at Mercy intently and considered my words. I wanted to come right out and tell her "Do not go!" However, once I stepped foot in Joy's home and saw the penury and perils of their existence, I did not feel it was my place to instruct them on what they should and should not do. Still, I had to give Mercy some level of warning, which I did. I explained the mistreatment Gift had endured, just like so many other children from Edo State who had embarked on similar journeys. I could not offer a reasonable alternative, so I knew that my warnings held little meaning. If someone is standing in a fire, you can warn them all you like that if they jump out they may land in the mouth of a crocodile—they still have to jump.

I spent the rest of the day and that night with Joy and her children. Light came by shrouded moon and cooking fire for a few hours, then impenetrable darkness. There was little more I could accomplish regarding travel to Europe, so we talked about their struggles in the village and their hopes that God would one day bless them with a better future. As the hours passed, my thoughts turned to GT and my hope to learn more about him and the juju oaths. I knew Mercy had recently taken the oath, so I asked her if she could tell me more about it and the priest who administered it. Much to my surprise, she pointed to Step-by-Step and said, "He is the one who took me."

I could not believe the coincidence, if that's what it was. Of all the drivers who could have taken me to Gift's village, I ended up with the man who had driven her sister Mercy to GT for her juju oath. Maybe there are not many drivers in rural Edo State, or maybe it was just dumb luck, but as it turned out, Step-by-Step had driven dozens of girls to GT through the years. Not many people know the way to GT's shrine, but Step-by-Step knew the way well. I asked Mercy to ask him if he would take me, and they both said it was not a good idea. Step-by-Step said that GT's shrine was far away in a rural area and that GT would be very suspicious if we just showed up. I tried to persuade Step-by-Step that it was important for me to see GT and his shrine, because I wanted to understand him and the power he held over girls like Gift and Mercy. Eventually, Mercy persuaded him by agreeing to come along with us under the guise of saying that she needed more guidance from him before leaving for Europe. She would say that I was a friend of her sister's who had come to visit and was interested in helping more members of the family migrate to Europe. It felt like a flimsy cover story that GT was not likely to believe, but it was the only way I was going to have a chance to meet the man who had terrorized Gift and countless other Nigerian sex trafficking victims around the world.

Two days later, Step-by-Step, Mercy, and I drove to meet GT. His shrine was located a few hours drive from Mercy's village, deep in the forested area down a remote dirt road. We did not talk much during the drive, and I could tell that both Mercy and Step-by-Step were very uneasy. When we were about a mile from GT's shrine, Mercy began to panic. She trembled and asked to be let out of the car. "I can't go," she said, "I can't go. Please leave me here. I can't go."

We pulled the car to the side of the dirt road, and I told Mercy I was not going to leave her on her own in the middle of the forest. She told me she would be fine and that she did not want to disrupt my research. I was very uncomfortable with the idea of leaving Mercy on her own and assured her I could always return another day, but she was adamant that we continue without her. She explained that if I tried to go back another time GT would likely be suspicious because Step-by-Step had asked permission for us to visit on that particular day. It was a difficult decision, and if anything happened to Mercy, I never would have forgiven myself. I knew I was crossing a line, but I calculated we would be back within an hour, maybe less, so I agreed to leave Mercy by the side of the dirt road. She stepped out of the car and took a seat in the shade under a tree. Before we pulled off, she told me, "Do not drink anything he gives you!"

As we continued down the path, I felt conflicted about leaving Mercy behind and contemplated going back to her. I was also quite anxious that without her I could not understand Step-by-Step and that our cover story was no longer plausible. Why on earth was I randomly, and without Mercy, showing up to visit GT? I ran through possible scenarios in my mind but could not come up with a clear answer to the dilemma. This would probably be my only chance to meet GT, but I did not want to cause harm or risk to anyone other than myself. The risks of leaving Mercy on her own in the forest for an hour were difficult to assess, as were the risks of carrying on with the meeting with GT without her. Indeed, not carrying on with the meeting with GT might also raise suspicions on his part that could put Mercy and her family at risk. Overcome by the complexity of the situation, I pushed on.

From a distance, the shrine appeared ominous and incongruous. As we got nearer, I saw a peach and green painted building with "Ayelala Spiritual Home" written on top. Outside, fenced off by a pile of mattresses, was a warrior statue, red with a white-painted face. A sign in front of the statue read, "Out of bounds for women under menses." Step-by-Step parked the car outside the shrine. He was tense and desperate to tell me something, but we could not communicate with each other. I pointed to the door of the shrine as if to ask, "Is that the way in?" He nodded, then pointed to the camera in my hand and shook his head no. I put the camera in my pocket.

We stepped out of the car, and I took a moment to take in my surroundings. Suddenly seven children rushed at us out of nowhere, hissing and shrieking. I looked at Step-by-Step nervously, and he made a "steady on" gesture. The children swarmed and howled ferociously. Eventually they scurried off. Later a colleague told me these were "witch children" who were possessed by demons as a result of the curse unleashed by GT on their mothers for breaking their juju oaths. Cast out from their homes, GT took them to his shrine and raised them as he saw fit.

At this point, the fear that Step-by-Step, Mercy, and thousands of girls from Edo State had felt became all too real to me. I am a rational person, but—here in the middle of West Africa amid customs and powers I did not understand—even I began to wonder what kind of world I was entering. What were the rules, and what kind of forces held power here? Step-by-Step gestured to me to wait where I was as he walked into the shrine. I stood alone outside, trying to take in as much as I could. I quickly pulled out my camera and snapped a few photos of the shrine and the surroundings. The front wall of the shrine was covered in dozens of framed photographs. I moved closer and saw that each photo was of a deformed female, some with distended bellies, others with disfigured faces and limbs. These were the women GT had cursed for breaking their oath, broadcast plainly for all to see. I imagined a sixteen-year-old village girl confronted by howling witch children and seeing these images upon entry to the shrine, and I began to understand the awful power of this man.

Step-by-Step emerged from the shrine and waved me in. I waited for a moment and thought one last time about whether I should proceed. When entering dangerous venues such as a brothel with sex slaves or a carpet factory with child laborers and armed guards, I always had an exit strategy. However, here there was no escape. The moment I walked through the door into the shrine, my fate was out of my hands. I could be walking into the kind of trap I had assiduously avoided so many times before. This was, after all, a cult whose priests were rumored to perform human sacrifice and eat human body parts during their rituals. I decided to proceed.

I followed Step-by-Step into the shrine. There were more framed photos of disfigured and deformed women on the inside walls, some white ceiling fans, piles of artifacts, clothes, and trinkets scattered about, and about a dozen red wooden benches facing an altar. There were at least two hundred small mirrors hanging from the ceiling on short strings (I later learned these mirrors held demon spirits that GT could unleash on any woman who broke her oath). The altar consisted of a small wooden table with various large bottles of alcohol on it, and the numbers "2" and "1" painted white in red squares on the floor. Beneath the altar were a dozen large yams painted with blue markings, and above was a framed photo of the king of Benin. A handful of priests in red robes sat on white plastic chairs on either side of the altar. Directly behind the altar, sitting on a red sofa and wearing a light green robe, was GT. He was a broad man, intense, with a penetrating gaze. I feared him the moment I saw him. It suddenly seemed all too plausible that there and then, in the dark heart of his realm, this man might actually have the ability to curse me just as he had so many Nigerian girls. I felt his eyes slicing me like knives, and I tried to assess whether I should push forward or leave.

"Welcome," GT said in perfect English, "I understand you are interested in our culture."

Step-by-Step looked at me nervously.

"Yes," I replied, "Thank you for allowing me to visit."

GT waved me forward, "Sit here. I can describe our culture to you."

I took a few steps forward, keeping my senses trained on my surroundings to catch any sudden movements. I took a seat on the front bench, and one of the priests in red robes entered from a side door holding an oatmeal colored beverage in a glass.

"Please have this drink," GT said, "It is a custom for us."

I nervously took the glass, remembering Mercy's warning not to drink anything GT offered me.

"I'm not very thirsty," I replied, "But thank you."

"Please drink, it will cool you down."

I did not want to drink the beverage, but I knew if I declined it could be construed as an insult to his hospitality. I tried to think quickly of a delicate way to avoid drinking the beverage.

"Actually, today is a day of fasting for me in my religion, so I can't have the drink. I hope that's okay."

GT nodded, "Of course that's okay."

I later learned I had been offered a malted beverage laced with intense and sometimes incapacitating hallucinogens, which GT gave most girls prior to beginning the juju ritual.

"Where are you from?" GT asked.

"I am Indian by ancestry, but I live in the United States."

"I have been to America many times," GT replied, "Just last month I was in Miami."

"What brought you to Miami?"

"I have business there."

I spoke with GT about his travels, the many cities in the United States he had visited, and my interest in understanding the local culture. I knew GT did not believe a word of my cover story. He was probing to ascertain the real reason I was visiting him, in his shrine, far off the beaten path in the rural reaches of Edo State. He was too sophisticated not to be suspicious, and I knew it was just a matter of time before the charade was over. I had seen enough, and I was not about to pry into areas that would raise his suspicions further. I felt increasingly apprehensive about remaining in the shrine and was desperate for a way to leave.

"I must apologize for coming in the middle of the day," I said to GT, "You look busy. Perhaps I could come back another time and we could speak more about your culture."

"We will be having an important ritual here tomorrow night," GT replied, "I will send a driver to bring you. You will be my guest. Where are you staying?"

I told GT the name of a village about a hundred kilometers away from the village where I was actually staying.

"Be ready at five."

"Thank you," I replied, "Perhaps I can leave a donation for you, as gratitude for your time."

GT nodded. I took out about forty dollars worth of Naira and placed them on the altar. Before leaving I wanted to do one last thing because I knew I would never return to this place.

"Would it be okay if I took a picture with you?" It was a brazen question, one that may have pushed matters one step too far. After a moment GT said, "Okay."

I stood where I was, on the opposite side of the altar in front of GT, turned around, and faced Step-by Step. I handed him my camera and motioned to him to take a photo. He shook his head no, but GT told him it was okay. I stood there, stiff as a board, and Step-by-Step took the photo. I thanked GT again and said that I looked forward to being his guest the next day. I walked out slowly, taking one last look at the deformed women, the markings in front of his altar, and the demon-prison mirrors hanging from the ceiling. After closing the main door of the shrine, I looked into Step-by-Step's eyes and said, "Let's go. Now!" He did not understand the words, but he knew exactly what I said.

Thankfully, Mercy was safe just where I left her. We picked her up and continued back to her village. I could tell that she was relieved to see me.

"How did it go?" she asked.

I took her hands and said, "I understand."

A few weeks later Mercy left for Europe.

THE MADAMS

My brief encounter with GT helped me understand the nature of his power. He is the counterpoint to Bishop Okonkwo. Both men govern with intense spirituality—the bishop rouses his congregation into an ecstasy of hopeful communion with the divine, whereas GT wields the divine for a grimmer purpose. The unrestrained faith of their congregants empowers both men to prophet status; however, one is a prophet of light and the other is a prophet of darkness. They are the two faces of divine power, two outcomes of fervent spirituality. No doubt, GT sees himself as a man who brings order to a chaotic world infected with corruption and the degradation of morality and law. That is the power he exerts, which he transfers to the madams, who act as extensions of his reach. This makes the madams the crucial link in the Nigerian sex trafficking chain. They purchase and exploit the trafficked Nigerian women, wielding power through physical and psychological force and the ever-present threat of the juju curse.

There have not been many studies on the madams of Edo State to explain how they operate and how they recruit sex trafficking victims from the region. One study conducted in Benin City in 2004 found that one-third of women surveyed had been approached by a madam who offered to help them get to Europe for work.[5] Roughly 97 percent of respondents knew what sex trafficking was, and 70 percent had relatives working in prostitution in Europe, most of whom had been recruited by madams.[6] The madams and the system they represent seem to be well known to the women of Edo State. Given their central role in the sex trafficking chain from Nigeria, I endeavored to meet as many as I could.

Most madams in Nigeria live in Benin City or in Lagos. It was relatively easy to meet them, and most were quite willing to speak with me. The conversations I had with the madams were remarkably similar to each other, and also remarkably similar to the conversations I had with *gharwalis* in the brothels of India. In both cases, the women saw themselves as doing a favor for poor, illiterate girls by providing them with opportunities for a better life. The concept of "sex trafficking" had little meaning to them, and they did not perceive any fault with what they were doing. Five of the six madams I interviewed in Nigeria were former sex trafficking victims themselves (not that they saw it that way). This was the natural progression, in their eyes, of hard-working, dutiful girls who keep their oaths and repay their debts.

The most extensive conversation I had was with a madam named Love. She was thin compared to the other heavy-set madams I met, and there was even a hint of kindness in her eyes. She was intelligent, practical, and quite at ease with her vocation. She explained that she first left Edo State after taking a juju oath at the age of sixteen. She worked for four madams across Europe for five years, after which she was told that her debt had been repaid. At the tender age of twenty, she was ready for her new life.

My madam threw a party for me when my debt was finished. She told me, "Now, you can be just like me!" She gave me one thousand euros as a gift, and I started working as a madam myself. It was the happiest day of my life. I made so much money you cannot imagine. I send money to my family every month. My parents are proud of me. They built a new house in Benin City, and they sent my two sisters and my brother to school. In this country, school requires fees, so who do you think is going to pay? I paid! I tell my girls that if they work hard, they can be just like me and help their families. Most of the girls are selfish and lazy and wicked. They want money without work. They lie and they steal. If bad things happen to them, they can only blame themselves.

I pressed Love on the issue that most of the girls she was talking about were probably too young to realize what they were getting into, and that they were too vulnerable to make a real "choice" to take the oath and go to Europe.

"They are not stupid. They know exactly what they are doing," Love retorted.

"Then why do so many try to escape?" I asked, "Why do most of them want to stop this kind of work and return home?"

"As I said, they are lazy. Once they realize they have to work to earn money, they quit. If you want a better life, you have to work for it. This is true for all people."

"Then why do they have to take the juju oath? Why make them afraid to stop working if they wish to be lazy, as you say. Why force them through fear?"

"Do you know how expensive it is to get them to Europe? They have to repay these debts, or they will run away after they arrive. We make an investment in these girls and they must pay us back."

"But it doesn't cost forty thousand euros to take them to Europe."

"We also have a right to our profit for housing them and teaching them and giving them this opportunity to be wealthy for the rest of their lives.

It's like an internship, you see. Don't they have this in your country? Why is this so hard for you to understand?"

Love and I sparred politely for a while. For every argument I made to point out the exploitative nature of her trade, she had a perfectly reasoned response. If girls tried to escape, it is because they were lazy. If the use of a juju oath applied undue coercion on the girls to stay in prostitution, it is required because the wicked girls will otherwise flee before working off the costs of their transport. In Love's mind, these girls were lucky to have the opportunities she afforded them. She had nine girls under her "protection" (as she put it), and she traveled back and forth between Italy and Nigeria regularly, so she could spend time with her family and recruit more girls. When she was away, other madams kept charge over her girls until she returned. There was not much that surprised me about my encounter with Love except that toward the end of our conversation she offered to arrange for me to meet several Nigerian girls in shelters who had been deported from Europe. Surely, I thought, most of them were sex trafficking survivors and would not have positive things to say about their experiences, let alone their madams.

"I know you are a good man," she said, "I want to help you even if we do not agree. Most people only want to help those they agree with, but in Nigeria we are not like this."

Love mentioned one shelter in Benin City and two in Lagos. I thanked her for her generosity and visited two of the shelters she mentioned in Lagos. They were home to girls whose stories were particularly devastating. They had all been trafficked for the first time between the ages of thirteen and twenty. Several of them were pregnant for the second, third, or fourth time when I met them. One of the "older" survivors I met was Sandra. She was thirty-one and had worked for several madams in Italy, France, and England. She had short hair that was gray beyond her years, and though her face was sallow, she was always smiling. Sandra was arrested in England a few years ago and courageously assisted with the prosecution of her madam. She was granted asylum, but after a few years she missed her family too much and wanted to return home. She thought by this time, it would be safe.

A few days after I came home, some men came in the night. They broke into my home, dragged me into the street, stripped my clothes, raped me,

and chopped off my left arm with a meat cleaver. They said this was my
punishment for breaking my oath.

Sandra was left for dead but managed to get to a hospital with the help
of neighbors. She was eventually fitted with a crude plastic prosthetic in
place of her left arm and has since lived in various shelters. The head of the
shelter, Anne, told me that the violence against Sandra had been particularly
inhuman because she is a lesbian.

"In Nigeria, it is better to be an animal than to be a homosexual," Anne
told me.

Traditional cultural beliefs across Nigeria, including in the Yoruba tradition, view same-sex preferences as dirty, unnatural, and pathological.[7]
Even secular law is set harshly against same-sex relations, which in the
southern states are punishable by up to fourteen years in prison,[8] and in
certain northern states that have adopted Shari'a law the punishment may
be stoning to death.

Despite the brutalities she had endured, Sandra remained remarkably
cheerful about her future. She had even recently started going to school.

"I am going to study law, so I can fight for justice for women like me,"
Sandra told me.

If Sandra's story were not harrowing enough, I heard stories from two
other young women at her shelter, Veera and Precious, that were even more
disturbing. They had both recently been rescued from a "baby factory" in
Lagos. They were eighteen and nineteen years old and had been locked
inside a building in the outskirts of the city for a few years, where they were
forcefully inseminated and kept imprisoned throughout their pregnancy.

"There was a nurse who fed us," Precious explained, "And a doctor came
to examine us and deliver the babies."

Veera and Precious both delivered two babies while they were held
captive. The babies were rumored to have been sold for international
adoptions.

"Some of the other girls in that place said the babies might be used for
sacrifice by juju priests," Veera added.

I asked how many girls were in the baby factory with them, and they said
there were over thirty. I had heard anecdotes about these factories but had
considered them to be an urban myth until I met two girls who had actually

been in one. News stories revealed very little in the way of corroboration, but I did come across a few instances, including a case in 2013 of seventeen girls in Imo State who were locked inside a baby factory, each impregnated by a single man. The girls gave birth to babies who were again rumored to have been sold for international adoption.[9] The conditions Veera and Precious described were impossible to imagine. The notion of being forcefully impregnated and held captive like a breeding animal left me nauseated. The rumor that some of these babies were used in black magic juju rituals was beyond reckoning. Precious insisted it was true and told me about a place, called Jankara Market, where items for black magic juju rituals could be found. She told me that at the southeast corner of the market I would find dried monkey heads, animal skins, insects, frogs, and, in very secret places accessible only to insiders, human body parts, including from babies. I went to the market, to the southeast portion, and I saw all manner of creatures for sale, but nothing human.

After meeting Veera and Precious, I tried vigorously to find one of the baby factories in Lagos, but I was not successful. Every lead I explored turned up empty. The Nigerian mafia is said to operate the factories, so there are considerable risks relating to how far one can push. To my knowledge, no one knows exactly how extensive this phenomenon is in Nigeria, or in other countries across western Africa where similar rumors persist. It is one of the most abhorrent forms of sexual slavery I have ever encountered, all the more so because the result is the birth of an innocent child who is either sold off to international adoption or, if the darker rumors are true, killed in blood sacrifices.

HOW DID IT COME TO THIS?

From the severities of poverty and desperation that motivate thousands of Nigerians to take juju oaths and embark on perilous journeys with traffickers to the merciless control exerted over them by priests and madams, Nigeria represents human trafficking in the extreme. The system is unrelenting, and I could not help but wonder how the country arrived at this bleak state. In my estimation, three socioeconomic factors in Nigeria's history hurled the country into a state of severe impoverishment and unrest, which ultimately precipitated its contemporary human trafficking crisis.[10]

The first factor of Nigeria's history that informs its present state of unrest is the religious divide between Muslims in the north and Christians in the South.[11] Islam arrived in West Africa around one thousand years ago, culminating in the creation of the Sokoto Caliphate in 1804, which consolidated the northern half of Nigeria under Islamic rule. At that time, the southern portion of the country was dominated by the Yoruba culture and the Benin Empire. Christianity, which was brought by the colonial powers, was also growing in influence. These religious divisions ossified, resulting in ongoing clashes and strife. The south controls the all-important oil ports, which further exacerbates tensions. Religious conflict has raged across the country for decades, leaving the poorest people of Nigeria desperate to find safety abroad, which fuels human trafficking. The raids, murders, and human trafficking activities of the Boko Haram, beginning in 2013, are the most extreme expressions of the clash of cultures between extremist Islam and the more moderate Muslims and Christians in the country.

The second factor of Nigeria's history that influenced the current state of violence and instability in the country was the discovery of oil in the Delta region by Shell-BP in 1957. This discovery preceded Nigerian independence by three years and has precipitated several decades of military strife among those seeking control of oil territories. The strife was exacerbated by the fact that the boundaries drawn at independence forced together three highly disparate and incongruous ethnic groups—Hausa-Fulani in the north, Yoruba in the southwest, and Igbo in the southeast—and forced them under a single governance in the south, where the oil was found. As a result, the first few decades of Nigerian self-rule were mired by strife among the disparate tribes and communities of the nation for control of land and oil. Major ethnic riots in 1962 and 1964 relating to regional land divisions and accusations of rigged elections rocked the country. In 1966, a group of Igbo army officials led by Major General Johnson T. U. Aguiyi-Ironsi overthrew the elected government and assassinated Prime Minister Balewa (a Fulani) and several senior officials in the government. Ironsi named himself president and instituted martial law. The Muslim community in the north naturally viewed the coup as a Christian attempt to undermine their customs and take control of the oil resources in the south, resulting in mob violence and thousands of deaths. Military leaders in the north staged a coup against Aguiyi-Ironsi four months after his coup, assassinating him and retaking control of the country. Ethnic violence between the north, south, and east raged for several years, culminating in a declaration on May 30, 1967, by the military leader of the eastern region, Lieutenant Colonel Odemugwu Ojukwu, that his territory was to be a separate nation called the Republic of Biafra. The military government in Lagos promptly responded with a declaration of war on the Republic of Biafra. Biafra was supported by France, and Lagos received support from Great Britain and the USSR. This postcolonial proxy war left 3 million Nigerians dead. On January 12, 1971, the Biafran forces surrendered, but the country was in ruins. The Biafran war remains one of the bloodiest postindependence civil wars in postcolonial history, and its crippling effects are felt by millions of Nigerians to this day.

With some semblance of stability under military leader Yakubu Gowon, the government's focus returned to capitalizing on the oil reserves discovered by Shell-BP prior to independence. The government forged a joint venture with BP and erected a state-owned oil concern, the Nigerian National Petroleum Company (NNPC). Nigeria joined OPEC, and the rise in oil prices in the early 1970s brought huge amounts of capital into the country, most of which was deposited in the accounts of a handful of oligarchs. Oil quickly became responsible for almost 90 percent of all government revenue, which meant that economic stability in Nigeria was highly dependent on the price of oil. The stability under Gowon did not last. There was too much oil at stake.

The third factor that contributed to Nigeria's contemporary human trafficking crisis involved a series of coups and riots throughout the 1970s and 1980s. Angered by the imbalanced allocation of the country's newfound oil wealth, Army Brigadier Murtala Mohammed from the north led a coup and took control of the country in 1975. The very next year, Mohammed was assassinated and replaced by a Yoruba military leader from the south. The country returned to civilian rule in 1979, but the oil bubble burst in 1981 and the country fell into massive debt, escalating inflation, and broad-scale unemployment. Riots followed, and thousands of people were killed. Those who had made their wealth during the oil boom of the 1970s took their money out of the country as quickly as they could. The 1980s were marred by one military coup after another, leaving the country in a constant state of disarray. The country's debt skyrocketed and per capita income fell to below $300 per year. In an effort to quell the strife between north and south, the capital of the country was moved from Lagos to Abuja in 1991. Nonetheless, corruption, coups, civil unrest, and the allocation of oil income to a small wealthy elite have typified Nigeria's political and economic realty for the last few decades. When oil prices boom, the money flows in; when prices bust, the country suffers from massive increases in debt and inflation. The most recent drop in oil prices in 2015 put severe pressure on the poorest in the country, increased ethnic violence, and pushed peasants to migrate abroad in search of income and security. All the while, violence between Muslims and Christians shows few signs of abating. The unfortunate truth is that disparate and incongruous ethnic groups were thrust together at independence, and oil was found in just one part of the country, leading to a series of devastating coups and clashes that have resulted in decades of suffering. This suffering is unquestionably more real and painful than the prospective harms most any Nigerian would face by accepting an offer from a human trafficker. In this context, millions of poor Nigerians remain eager to flee their country, and traffickers are only too happy to assist them.

ENSLAVED BODY, MIND, AND SOUL

The combination of political and economic instability, grinding poverty, social unrest, and powerful cultural forces of coercion conspire to ensnare countless women and girls from Edo State in sex slavery around the world. More than any group of sex trafficking victims I documented, these young women are enslaved body, mind, and soul. In Sex Trafficking, I provide details and metrics on the sex trafficking cases I documented around the world,[13] some of which are updated in appendixes A and B of this book. The uniqueness of the journeys of the Nigerian sex trafficking victims, especially their levels of debt, merits a closer look. In total, I documented the cases of sixty-six Nigerian sex trafficking victims in full. Here are some of the summary statistics of these cases:

- 100 percent females
- 16.7 years: average age at time first trafficked
- 98 percent involved debt bondage
- $30,528: average debt to repay

- 95 percent from Edo State
- 93 percent took a juju oath prior to being trafficked abroad
- 82 percent trafficked to Europe, 13 percent to Asia, 5 percent to the Americas
- 54 percent trafficked more than once
- 50 percent had another family member who had previously migrated abroad/been trafficked

Some of the most striking data to emerge from these cases relates to the high proportion of victims forced to repay debts (98 percent), as well as the average level of the debts ($30,528), which are five to ten times greater than the debt levels of sex trafficking victims I documented from other countries who were held in debt bondage. No doubt, the powerful spiritual hold placed on these girls by the juju oath plays a pivotal role in the coercive extraction of large amounts of money from the victims. Indeed, many Nigerian sex trafficking victims will retraffic themselves if they are deported out of fear of failing to discharge their debts. It is also worth noting that the average age of the Nigerian sex trafficking victims at the time they were first trafficked (16.7 years) is a little higher than the average of all the sex trafficking cases I documented (15.4 years), but most were still minors at the time they were first trafficked. Just slightly more than half of the victims were trafficked more than once, and half were not the first members of their family to migrate or to be trafficked abroad. Beneath these numbers, there is immeasurable torment, misery, and woe. The system of Nigerian sex trafficking assaults the totality of the human *being* of its victims with unyielding violence and debasement. Most disconcerting of all, very little is being done to protect the women and girls of Nigeria from the monsters who devour them—domestically or abroad.

BADAGRY

My extraordinary time in Nigeria drew to a poignant close in Badagry, a town about a two-hour drive west of Lagos. In the late fifteenth century, the Portuguese were the first Europeans to arrive on the West African coast in search of new trading routes and access to the Saharan gold trade. The most important consequence of their arrival was the commencement of the trans-Atlantic slave trade, in which Badagry played a central role. Africans were initially taken as laborers on Portuguese ships crossing the Atlantic, and they were subsequently sold into slavery on sugar plantations in the Caribbean Islands. Once Pope Leo X gave permission for slaves to be taken from Africa in 1513, the number of African slaves trafficked by European powers to the Americas grew rapidly. By the end of the sixteenth century, the Dutch, Danish, Swedish, French, and British had all arrived at the "Slave Coast" of West Africa to trade in slaves and traffic them to the Americas. Much has been written about this trade and little needs to be added here beyond the fact that during its precolonial period (1500–1800) and during several decades of British rule (1800–1960) Nigeria was a primary source of trafficked African slaves for European powers. Estimates are that around 3.5 million of the 11 million Africans trafficked into slavery across the ocean during the course of the trans-Atlantic slave trade emanated from Nigeria. Of these, approximately 550,000 passed through Badagry.

Most of the slave museums and historic buildings in Badagry are located on Marina Road, which runs parallel to the coastline. The first historic site I visited was the Vlekete Slave Market, build by the Portuguese in 1502. The market was named after a local deity, Vlekete, goddess of the sea. The original structure was destroyed in 1852, but it was subsequently rebuilt and turned into a two-story museum that chronicles the slave trade that took place at the market for 350 years. Indeed, Vlekete was one of the first and largest slave-trading markets where Europeans bartered with African slave dealers who brought slaves from the inland regions. At its peak, it was open for business seven days a week, with 150 slaves typically sold each day. Europeans inspected each slave prior to negotiating a price. Were they young, fit, and healthy or older and diseased? Once prices were agreed upon, the buyers paid in spirits, guns, silk, beads, cannons, cotton, and other commodities. The slaves they purchased were taken to holding cells, called baracoons, where they were crammed fifty or more into a 9 foot by 9 foot room, forced to defecate, urinate, sweat, sleep, and agonize on top of each other. They could spend months in these cells, waiting to be shipped to the Americas, branded with the name of the slave trader who purchased them. There were once several baracoons in Badagry, but only one of the buildings stands today: the Seriki Faremi Williams Abass Brazilian Baracoon. It is a yellow-painted building with a rusted tin roof, built in 1840. Seriki Abass was a former slave from Yorubaland who was sold as a child to a Portuguese slave trader and trafficked to Brazil. His owner taught him to read and write, and Abass learned several languages, including Portuguese. Years later his owner told him he would set him free on condition that he work for him as a slave dealer back in Africa. Abass agreed. He returned to Badagry, where he built his slave baracoon and began dealing with African slave traders to acquire slaves to sell to the Portuguese. Rusted chains, shackles, and mouth muzzles used to restrain the slaves were on display when I visited the Brazilian Baracoon. Each restraint came in smaller sizes as well, for children. Abass went on to become a very wealthy and powerful man, with 128 wives and 144 children. He died in 1919 and is buried at his Baracoon compound at Badagry, haunted no doubt from every direction by the boundless wails of despairing slaves.

When the European slave traders were ready to depart with their cargo, they took the slaves from the baracoons across a narrow lagoon to a peninsula just off the coast of Badagry. I hired a boat to take me across the lagoon to the northern edge of the peninsula, just as the slaves were ferried centuries before. From there, the slaves trudged in shackles to the southern shore, where the larger seafaring ships awaited them. I walked that same path, through the brush and the coconut trees. With each step I tried to imagine their dread. Did they have any understanding of what was happening to them? Did they try to bargain with their captors? Did they fear they would never see their family members again? Did they have any sense of where they were going and the fate that awaited them? It was a walk of miserable imaginings. I peered down at my unshackled feet and reflected on the hundreds of thousands of shackled ankles that walked these same sands centuries before. What separated my free steps from theirs other than flukes of time and birth? I could feel the searing distress of the slaves walking across these very sands, swelling with panic, frenzy, and horror. Just when I thought the terror of this walk could not get any worse, my spirits collapsed when I came upon a sign that read "Original Spot, Slaves Spiritual Attenuation Well."

Next to the sign, I found a small, red-stone well tucked inside a hut. There was a poem hanging on a wall written in English and Yoruba. Centuries earlier, each slave would drink from the well, and recite these words:

I am leaving this land,
My spirit leave with me.
I shall not come back now,
My shackles do not break.
It is the shackles that hold the ship down.
My ancestors bear me witness,
I shall not return.
This land shall depart,
My soul do not revolt,
My spirit go along with me.
I depart to that land unknown
I shall not return.

I fell to my knees. It was too much to bear.

Slaves bound for the Americas recited this *oath*, that they were leaving their land and that they would never return. They prayed for their spirits to go with them, and not revolt. They were to be slaves forever, for the shackles do not break.

How was this oath any different from the juju oaths Nigerian slaves take today before departing for servitude abroad? They too leave their land and pray that their souls stay with them, remain safe, and do not revolt. They too know they will be slaves forever, for the "shackles" that ensnare them do not break.

After I read the oath at the Slaves Spiritual Attenuation Well, I understood slavery more clearly than I ever had before.

Slavery is the erasure of humanity.

I drifted off the slave path toward the coconut trees. I sat, knowing not where to go. The whispering palms held no solace. The salty smell of the ocean brought no comfort. After all my years of research, it was as if I understood slavery only for the first time—and that understanding devastated me.

I completed the slave walk to the beach at Badagry, where I was greeted by a sign that read "Point of No Return." Here slaves passed through two pillars, like a portal, into the lowest rungs of hell. They boarded the slave ships and never returned, other than a handful like Abass. The ocean ferried them to an unknown land of torture and slavery. The beautiful blue never looked the same again.

CHAPTER 3

LABOR TRAFFICKING

Slavery at Your Dining Table

Enslave the liberty of but one human being and the liberties
of the world are put in peril.
—William Lloyd Garrison

SLAVERY INSIDE AMERICA'S BREADBASKET

ONE OF MY favorite snacks is almonds. I enjoy them plain, roasted, salted, slivered, and smoked. I take my cereal with almond milk and my toast with almond butter. I believe my hand cream even has almonds in it. Around 90 percent of the world's almonds are grown in California, to the tune of $5.9 billion in production during the 2014–15 crop season. Indeed, almonds have quickly become California's second largest agricultural commodity behind only dairy ($9.4 billion) and ahead of grapes ($5.2 billion), cattle ($3.7 billion), and berries ($2.5 billion). As with all of California's agricultural products, almonds are grown in the state's Central Valley, a 22,500 square mile region that spans from Bakersfield in the south to Redding in the north. The valley has a width of between sixty and eighty miles all the way between the two cities. It is an arid zone whose suitability for agricultural production was vastly enhanced in 1933 with the inception of the Central Valley Project. The project was created to provide irrigation and municipal water to the Central Valley by storing water in twenty reservoirs in northern California and distributing it across the valley through a vast series of canals and aqueducts. The project has not been without controversy, especially during California's most recent drought. Almonds, in particular, have been at the center of a fervent water allocation feud because they require a substantial amount of water to produce. These important water allocation and preservation matters notwithstanding, the Central Valley Project has helped California become home to 76,400 farms with a total of 25.5 million acres, producing agricultural products worth $54 billion in 2015. California is not only the largest agricultural state in the United States but one of the most productive agricultural zones in the world. California is home to more than 99 percent of the U.S. stock of fourteen crops including grapes, figs, olives, pomegranates, pistachios, walnuts, and almonds. The state exports most of these products abroad as well, with the top foreign markets being the European Union, Canada, China, Japan, and Mexico.[1] California may be best known for Hollywood and Silicon Valley, but its agricultural sector is an economic behemoth; as with all such behemoths, it requires a substantial amount of labor.

The Central Valley is one of the easiest places to research that I have explored. In most every respect, aside from air quality, it is the exact opposite of Nigeria. The region is safe and smoothly traversed thanks to Interstate 5 and State Route 99, which run roughly parallel, north to south, across the valley. Aside from lung-burning smog, a persistent layer of dust on my car, and an unpleasant bouquet of odors always worse at night, there were not many obstacles to my research in California. In fact, the agricultural region can be quite beautiful. The symmetry of perfectly parallel lines of almond trees in white bloom stretching for miles in every direction offers a soothing order that contrasts with the chaos and disarray I encountered in other regions. Each day I spent in the valley drew to a close with a splendid sunset, thanks paradoxically to the excessive levels of air pollution—horrible to breathe but brilliant for painting the last moments of the day with thick and enduring hues, red-blushed and enflamed.

It is no mystery that California's agricultural sector is heavily reliant on low-wage migrant labor. During the peak of the agricultural season, thousands of migrant workers can be seen toiling away in the fields. Most of these workers travel to the United States from south of the border. A smaller number arrive from East Asia, primarily Thailand and China. The formal channel for migration and seasonal work in the agricultural sector is provided through H-2A visas,[2] or the "guest worker" program. In addition, many thousands of migrants arrive each year and work on an irregular and undocumented basis. Whichever channel migrants use to enter the United States, labor trafficking is more prevalent in the country's agricultural sector than I had anticipated. An individual is a victim of labor trafficking under U.S. and international law if he or she is (1) recruited, transported, transferred, or harbored (2) through force, fraud, or coercion (3) for the purpose of forced labor, slavery, or debt bondage. I met more than a thousand migrant workers in the Central Valley during the course of my research, and using highly restrictive criteria I documented the cases of 303 victims of labor trafficking. These victims can be divided into two categories: irregular migrants and H-2A visa seasonal guest workers. The labor trafficking victims I met told me extraordinary tales of exploitation and degradation similar to the experiences of agricultural slaves in the United States centuries ago. I cannot comprehend how, in some very important ways, so little has changed in the American agricultural labor system during the last two centuries, at least for the workers trafficked into its unforgiving clutches.

Figure 3.1 provides a basic picture of the labor supply chain from Latin America into the U.S. agricultural sector. The bottom of the chain is populated by the workers who migrate through regular (H-2A visas) or irregular channels into the United States. Both regular and irregular migrants often are recruited to travel to the United States for agricultural work by a labor recruiter called an *enganchadores* (literally, "down payment"). Many irregular migrants make their way north across the border without formal recruitment by engaging a *coyote* on their own. In most of the cases of irregular migration I documented, the coyotes facilitate the border crossing for the migrants because they know the best routes for entry on any given day that will minimize the chances of interception by the U.S. border patrol. Coyotes are usually in league with the enganchadors, and in many cases they are the same person.

Once the migrants have crossed the border, they are handed off to a labor broker, also known as a farm labor contractor (FLC). This person might

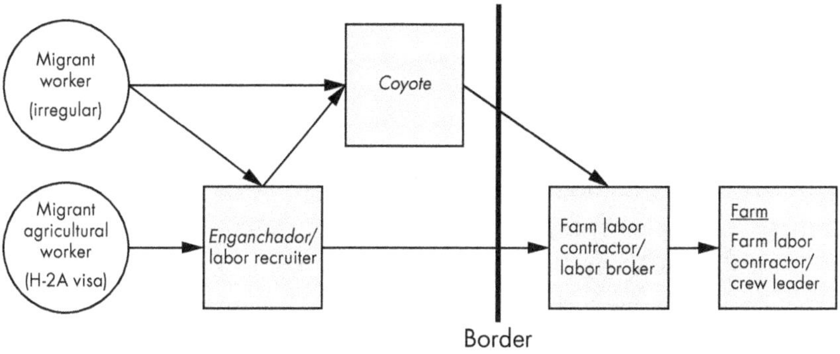

FIGURE 3.1 Agricultural labor supply chain from Latin America
to the United States

be part of a different network from the recruiters, or the entire process may be vertically integrated into one network. The FLC takes control of the migrant's work life and manages the contracts, housing, wages, food, and other needs on behalf of the primary employer, the farm owner. Crew leaders on each farm manage the daily work routines and assignments of the workers on behalf of the FLC. Sometimes FLCs act as crew leaders. For the most part, farm owners have little contact with their migrant workers and are only vaguely aware of the particulars relating to them. The FLCs manage everything.

When labor trafficking occurs, it is almost always exacted by the FLCs or by the crew leaders. The coercive labor conditions forced on migrant workers by the FLCs are exacerbated and reinforced by debts accrued from fees charged by the enganchadores, who arrange the work opportunity, and by the coyotes, who arrange the border crossing (for irregular migrants). When I began my research, I suspected I would find forced labor to be more prevalent in the irregular migrant population of California's agricultural sector due to the inherent vulnerability of their migration status; however, I was surprised to find that slavery and other exploitative conditions occurred almost equally in the population of regular migrants who arrived on H-2A visas. An exploration of some of the cases I documented reveals exactly how and why labor trafficking occurs in the U.S. agricultural system.

Labor Trafficking—The Irregular Migrant

It is surprisingly easy to find irregular migrants working on farms in California. I simply had to spend enough time forging local ties and trust in the worker communities, after which access was relatively straightforward. There was no need for security, bribes, or other complexities—just a translator. The most conducive locale for interviews was in the barracks, apartments, shacks, and other facilities where the workers slept at night. I met Enrique at one such worker residence in the summer of 2014. He was short, had an angular face, and hailed from southern Mexico, not far from the border with Guatemala. We sat in the shade under a tree outside the dormitory he shared with more than twenty other farm laborers, and he told me a harrowing tale of forced labor that stretched from his hometown right to your dining table:

> I am from Chiapas. When I was nineteen years old, I left my parents and younger sister to travel to America for work. A man we call enganchador said he can arrange the work for a fee of 20,000 pesos [~$1,400]. My parents offered our land on loan for this fee. The enganchador took us to Nogales by bus, and a coyote met us there. His name was Antonio. We knew he worked for a cartel. I was nervous to cross the border with him. Antonio led us to a house, and he said we had to pay 10,000 pesos [~$700] to cross the border. After we cross, he said he can arrange farm work in California. I told him I already paid the enganchador to get the work, but Antonio said this was not his problem and I must pay him or return to my home. None of the men in the house had the money, so we had to work for the cartel until we earned enough. I do not want to discuss the work I did. Five months later Antonio took us across the border.
>
> We walked for two hours and somewhere in the desert we came to a truck. Some men who were friends with Antonio drove us to an avocado farm in California. This was in 2009. From that time . . . what can I tell you . . . I have worked on five different farms . . . avocado, oranges, almonds, lettuce, and walnuts. Sometimes I am in the field picking the vegetables, or sometimes I am packing the boxes. In the beginning, I objected because the work was too difficult and I was not

being paid what they promised, but the boss said if I complain he will make me deported. He said my parents' land would be taken by the enganchador to repay the loan. I was very sad about the situation, but I had to keep working.

This place we live in here is not for humans. We sleep on dirty mattresses and share one toilet, all of us. We have no phone here, and we are far away from the city. If we want to go to the city, like if we want to go to the bank or buy supplies or maybe call our families, the boss charges $50 to drive us.

From dawn until dark we work. Usually we work six days a week. In the beginning, Antonio said we would earn $1,000 each month. I thought this was so much money I could not believe it. I thought I would send money to my family to help their circumstances. But it was a lie. I never earned this amount. Sometimes I am paid by the bucket; sometimes I am paid by the month. I never earned more than $500 in a month, and this is barely enough for my rent and my food. So I have nothing. After five years of work I have nothing.

I feel trapped because if I make problems I know I will be deported. I keep working because I hope one day I will go to a good farm where I will earn enough money to help my family. Until that day, at least I am alive. I am grateful for this, I know.

Please tell people there are thousands of Mexicans on these farms just like me. We share the same experience. We are forced to work like this because of poverty. I do not think the Americans realize where their food comes from. If they knew, they would not be happy.

Enrique was twenty-four years old when I met him, but like so many slaves I have documented, he looked old beyond his years. His body was worn, his face was haggard, his eyes were weary, and his hands were coarse and weathered like leather gloves. Life for him had been reduced to little more than a corrosive struggle to survive. I asked Enrique about physical ailments or injuries he had suffered, and he offered a wry smile: "You should ask which part of my body is not broken. That will be quicker." Enrique's vision was failing him, and he had chronic respiratory ailments. He suffered from heat exhaustion and frequent diarrhea. I asked if he ever received medical care, and he said the boss brought a doctor if workers were too sick to work or had a serious injury, but otherwise they had to toil through their ailments. They were charged $200 for the doctor's visit and additional costs for any medicines they required, all of which compounded their debts. This arithmetic made them much less likely to ask for medical assistance, even if it was needed.

Toward the end of our conversation, I asked Enrique about his time working for the cartel, but he said again that he did not want to discuss it. I did not push further; I knew all too well from other interviews I had conducted along the Mexican border with California and Texas what kind of "work" migrants were forced to do by the Sinaloa, Gulf, and Zetas cartels. From back-breaking day labor, to being drug mules, to burying dead bodies or dissolving them in acid, to forced prostitution, the cartels exploit migrants with medieval brutality. I could see in Enrique's sallow eyes that he had probably been forced to perform acts that would likely haunt him for the rest of his life.

I documented eleven other workers at Enrique's farm, all of whom told similar stories. Each one of them was ensnared in multiyear conditions of slavery. Eight were from Mexico, three from Guatemala, and one from El Salvador. Nine were recruited by enganchadores in their hometowns. All of them migrated north with the hope of earning enough income to send money back to their families, and all of them expressed a wish to return home one day with enough money to start a small business or get married and start a family. The same nine workers who were recruited by enganchadores had all offered family land as collateral for the up-front fees charged by the enganchadores. The threat of having their families evicted from their homes or land if the loans were not repaid was a powerful force of coercion that kept the victims working year after year in the hope that they would one day be free of the debt. As Rodrigo told me, "All we have is that land. If we lose it, my family will not survive."

In addition to the recruitment fees charged by the enganchadores, Enrique and the other eleven workers had all been assessed additional fees from coyotes: some fees had to be worked off prior to crossing the border, and some fees were added to the fees charged by the enganchadores. In the latter cases, the enganchadores and the coyote were usually the same person or part of the same network. Only two of the eleven workers I documented at Enrique's worker residence had been able to send small amounts of money home across the years (through Western Union). For the most part, they worked day and night just to survive, with no opportunity to leave, do other work, or return home. Their movements and employment options were completely restricted, and they had no way to break free of this chokehold. In truth, I could tell little difference between these men and prison laborers other than that physical incarceration is more obvious for prisoners, and their living conditions might actually be better.

During the course of my research, I documented a total of 175 labor trafficking victims who worked in California's Central Valley by way of irregular migration channels. Their journeys were fraught with peril, debt, and servitude. They were exploited at almost every step in the process, from recruitment by enganchadores, to border crossing with cartels and coyotes, to their work in the agricultural sector in California. Although my research was restricted to the state of California, cases of irregular migrant agricultural workers who end up in forced labor conditions have been documented across the United States in Texas, Florida, North Carolina, Georgia, Colorado, Washington, Maine, Nebraska, and Idaho. Almost anywhere agricultural products are grown, you can find these exploited workers if you look long enough. Another interesting fact that emerged from my research is that almost half (84 cases) of the irregular migrants I documented in forced labor on farms in California were not recruited by an enganchador. Instead, they made a decision to migrate north without a job opportunity awaiting them and found their way across the border with the help of a coyote. Fees for crossing the border in these cases skewed higher, ranging from $1,000 to $2,000. For these individuals, the forced labor exploitation typically began at the coyote stage, often in the form of harsh servitude for a cartel such as Enrique had endured. In other cases, the exploitation commenced after arrival in the United States when the migrant liaised with an FLC or other labor recruiter, who then exploited the vulnerability inherent to their irregular status to coerce them into forced labor. In every case of agricultural labor trafficking I documented in California, the FLC or other labor recruiter was reported to me to be directly involved in the exploitation, be it with irregular or regular migrants.

Precise estimates for the number of irregular migrant labor slaves being exploited in the U.S. agricultural sector are difficult to calculate, but there are easily tens of thousands of such individuals toiling in servitude in plain sight. I cannot stress enough just how accessible these slaves are; they were right there, being exploited in broad daylight. I had but to build trust and start speaking with them to document their cases. There were no guards, barriers, threats, or other blockades. One by one I documented these slaves, and with more time and resources I could have easily documented hundreds more—the broken bodies that pick, process, package, and supply us with the food we eat every day. They endure unimaginable perils to migrate to the United States in search of a decent life, only to find slavery and degradation instead. No matter the circumstances through which an individual enters this country, he or she never deserves to be a slave. That is, however, exactly what many migrants find, whether they enter through irregular channels or with pristine paperwork.

One of the last irregular migrant slaves I documented was a man named Mateo. He was working on a berry farm not far from Redding, California. In a desperate bid to escape poverty in El Salvador, he ventured north, managed to cross the border into the United States, and connected with a labor recruiter known to other people from his hometown. After three years of exacting forced labor and a complete inability to leave the farm despite a pressing desire to do so, he had been paid roughly $6,180 in wages (~$171 per month), sending home as much as he could. With a very gentle, accepting voice, he said to me, "We are the people no one wants, but everyone needs." The wisdom of his words astounded me. When the powerful do not want the people they need, they invariably find ways to subjugate, debase, and diminish them. That is the caustic formula that drives the culture of slavery. The millions like Mateo are discarded, unprotected, and exploited by the societies that cannot seem to function without them but do not ever want to recognize them as equally human. These migrants do not brave the immeasurable hazards of irregular migration so that they can take something from us; they do so because we pull them here, into a system that operates on levels of misery we would not accept for "our" people but are all too content to accept on Mateo's behalf. Some justify his exploitation by citing his offense against migration laws (which I reject), but migrants who abide by those same laws are often just as exploited as those who are unable to do so.

Labor Trafficking—The H-2A Guest Worker

Those who travel to the United States through an H-2A visa can be just as vulnerable to slavery as those who arrive without visas. Their push to migrate is derived from the same motivation—the dream of elevating their families or desperation to escape violent and insecure environments. For those who migrate through regular channels, the perceived up-front risks are much less. They are entering the United States through legitimate means and believe they will have a wage-paying job waiting for them. Nonetheless, many of these individuals end up as labor trafficking victims, and for them the dynamics are similar to those of irregular migrants. Paradoxically the H-2A program offers additional distinctive avenues for servitude that are often exploited by the very people providing the visas—namely, the FLCs.

An H-2A visa allows a foreign national to enter the United States as a guest worker for temporary or seasonal agricultural work. The program was specifically established to provide a means for agricultural employers with a shortage of farmworkers to bring foreign workers into the United States on a temporary basis to meet short-term labor needs. It is difficult to know exactly how many H-2A agricultural workers there are in the United States in any given year, but the number has been increasing every year for the past decade, with estimates of H-2A workers in the United States in 2016 ranging from 100,000 to 130,000.[3] These workers are supposed to be covered by most U.S. wage and labor laws. They also are meant to be provided with free housing for the duration of their contracts, the same health and safety protections as U.S. citizens performing the same work, workers' compensation benefits for medical costs and time off work for medical reasons, free legal services relating to their employment under the visa program, and reimbursement of the full costs of their travel to the job site once they have completed 50 percent of their contract period. Despite these important protections stipulated in the H-2A visa program, I found that forced labor was often present among the guest workers in California's Central Valley. The primary reason for coercing a guest worker into forced labor appears to be related to the cumbersome requirements on the employer for bringing in migrants under the program, which makes it desirable to keep the workers for more than one season rather than reapplying each year.

A young man named Felipe, whom I met at a farm near Bakersfield, explained his situation:

> There is a recruiter in Mexico who works with the brokers in Califor-
> nia to make the H-2A visas for us. His name is Luis. The cost is 30,000
> pesos [$2,000] to arrange the visa and transportation to the farm in
> the United States with guaranteed work for the season. Luis says we
> will be paid 150,000 pesos [$10,000] for the season if we work hard.
> Most of us did not have money for the fees, so Luis said the fees can be
> deducted from our wages. He said that 10,000 pesos [$667] was for the
> cost of transporting us to California and that we would be reimbursed
> this amount after we finished our contract. I received my documents,
> and we came to Calexico in a bus where a man named Fernando
> drove us to a farm. He took us to these apartments and said we would
> rent these from the broker. Fernando took our visas and said he will
> return them at the end of the season.
>
> I worked on a farm in Mexico before I came here, so I was familiar
> with the work. We work on the soil and do construction, and when
> it is time we pick the vegetables by hand. Fernando did not give me
> a wage the first three months. He gave me a pay slip in English, so I
> could not understand it. When I asked him why there was no money
> left for me, he said it was because of the deductions for my transpor-
> tation from Mexico. He said they also took money for the apartment,
> food, transportation to the farm, and also for a lawyer to process our
> visa. I asked him to show me my wages and these expenses in Span-
> ish, but he did not. At the fourth month, I received a wage of $200.
> It seemed too little, so I asked the crew leader to explain the wage to
> me. He said they had to do repairs on one of the trucks they used to
> transport us, so this was deducted from our wages. I did not think this
> was fair. They said if I did not like being at the farm, they can send
> me back to Mexico. I did not want to do this because I have no money
> after all this time.
>
> Our crew leader is very strict. They have beaten some of the work-
> ers, including me. If we ask too many questions, he says we should be
> happy we have a job. He says we are lucky and there are lots of people
> who can take our place.

We are not allowed to leave the farm during the day, and we have to stay in our apartment at night. The apartment is crowded and it is not in a good condition. It is very hot so we asked for fans. They brought two fans and charged us for them. There are rats in the apartment. The only good thing I can say is that we have enough food to eat.

At the end of the first season, they told us that if we want to stay, they can help us. The broker said he would keep our documents and we could stay on the farm, and we can earn $400 or $500 each month. This is not as much money as I hoped, but it is more than I can earn in Mexico. I have been on the farm for four years. I would like to do other work where I can earn more, but if I leave, I will be deported for staying past my visa. Now I think I might never leave this place.

That is my situation. I know some workers who have a much worse situation. These days I can send some money to my family. They charge us $40 to take us to the money transfer office, but it is worth it.

Felipe's situation was complex, but he was clearly in a condition of forced labor at the farm, and I believe he had been recruited and trafficked from Mexico for that purpose. His documents were confiscated on arrival, and his freedom of movement and employment were completely restricted. He worked for paltry wages (about $1.50 per hour) in a system of unfair and excessive wage deductions and the ever-present threat of deportation. Even if he wanted to leave the unfavorable employment situation and search for another option while his H-2A visa was legitimate, the visa stipulates that it is only valid as long as he works for the employer listed on it, so he never really had an alternative. He was resigned to his situation and was trying to see the best in it. The only time his face showed any signs of life was when he told me how he sent money to his family, however little it might be. This seemed to be the primary driving force that kept him going. Otherwise, he knew that he was being exploited each day as he slogged on the farm in harsh circumstances. When I asked him about his plans, he said he expected to work on the farm until he died . . . or maybe one day he might try to run away and return to Mexico.

Other guest workers I met throughout the Central Valley told me similar stories. They had all been recruited by labor brokers near their homes in Mexico. Interestingly, 42 of the 128 labor trafficking victims in the guest worker program I documented found their jobs through websites. All 128 had their contracts and documents confiscated for the duration of the season. A total of 73 of the 128 victims stayed past their initial visa terms and were in the midst of multiyear forced labor. Of the remaining 55 cases, 42 of them were exploited in forced labor conditions during their first guest worker term in the United States, and the remainder were exploited in forced labor conditions during subsequent years in the United States. Wage deductions were rampant, especially for the initial transportation fees. These fees were either overstated when linked to a wage deduction, or they were not reimbursed when the worker paid them out of pocket, even though the guest worker program stipulates that they should be reimbursed in full after the worker has completed 50 percent of his contract. The fees the workers were charged by labor brokers or FLCs for the arrangements made under the H-2A program (transport, documents, etc.) ranged from $2,000 to $5,500 in the cases I documented. The higher fees were typically for workers from farther south in Central America, and even a few from the Caribbean. For those workers who ventured back and forth under the visa program across different seasons, the fact that they were not allowed to switch employers during their work periods was used by the more unscrupulous FLCs to exploit them in conditions of slavery. Physical abuse was common. Illness and injury were also the norm, including heat stroke, respiratory ailments, vision impairment, urinary tract infections, lacerations, and broken bones. Every individual I documented lived in housing provided by the FLCs that was quite a distance from the nearest city. The housing areas were the only venues in which I was able to interview the workers, typically during the night hours, or on Sunday, which was their only day off. The houses and apartments I saw were in terrible condition. Paint was peeling, toilet and kitchen facilities were insufficient, and there was no air conditioning, which made sleep very difficult during the stifling summer months in the Central Valley. The workers were all given enough food to eat in terms of calories, but the quality and nutritional value was quite poor (usually canned or processed bulk foods). It is a painful irony that these farmworkers live and work in the midst of one of the most plentiful agricultural zones in the world, yet they are forced to subsist on substandard and processed foods. As one worker, Juan, whom I documented at a farm near Fresno, told me,

"In Mexico we can eat the food from the farm. Here we cannot touch our mouths to it."

Aside from obvious greed, I was perplexed as to why farm owners or their FLCs would resort to extracting slavery under the H-2A program. Their primary motivation appeared to be to avoid the complications of going through the tedious application process year after year, but it seemed to me that attorneys could handle this without too much expense, especially relative to the revenue streams the farms enjoyed. In an effort to explore this question further, I spoke to Douglas, a man who owned more than 1,100 acres of farmland in the Central Valley. He explained exactly why some farms in the valley resort to exploitative tactics.

THE H-2A GUEST WORKER PROGRAM: A CLOSER LOOK

Douglas's land is green-striped, with thousands of parallel rows of almond and pistachio trees stretching beyond the horizon not far from the city of Lost Hills, California. He inherited the land from his father and takes great pride in his stewardship of the portion of the earth allotted to him. Douglas invited me to his home, and we sat on his covered patio under ceiling fans. He was a fourth-generation farmer in the Central Valley and an avid supporter of the H-2A program. He described the process and procedures of the program in detail:

> First off, we have to apply at least 45 days before we want the worker to receive the visa. I also have to try to recruit U.S. workers with newspaper and radio advertising and first give the job to any U.S. citizen who applies before I can give it to an alien. Americans don't take the jobs, so that part is not an issue; it's just a hassle really. The filing fee is $320 per application. For each alien I hire, I have to pay another fee of $10 up to a hundred workers. Those are the fees, so all in all it's pretty cheap from my perspective. Each visa I get is valid to 364 days. That covers one full season of work. The lawyers handle the rest, but they aren't too expensive either. They have to file petitions every year with the Department of Labor that we certify there are not enough U.S. workers who are willing and able to do the work, and that if

aliens are hired it will not have a negative impact on the wages of U.S. workers in the area. Let me tell you point blank that part is bullshit. They are just covering their asses. Even though I pay the same wages to my aliens as I do to my U.S. workers, most farms out here don't, and that brings wages down without a doubt. No one with a straight face who knows what they're talking about will tell you otherwise. Wages go down because of all the alien workers from across the border. That's the way it works, and that's the way people want it to work. Yeah, it means U.S. citizens are less likely to take the work, which means we need more aliens. It's a system, and everybody knows it. They count on it. That's been the way out here for a long time, and that's how it'll be long after I'm gone.

I asked Douglas whether there were any efforts by the authorities to ensure the guest workers receive the same wages as U.S. workers.

"What did I just tell you? They don't want them to get the same wages. It's all in the paperwork. We keep logs of wages and all that information is in our filings, but people can file whatever they want and nobody is going to ask past that. Even if they did, the government doesn't have the resources to audit all those records. You can forget about that."

"What about wage deductions, for things that are supposed to be provided to the workers under the program for free, like housing or medical care?" I asked.

"A lot of the farms exploit the aliens. Let's just get that straight. They know nobody is going to do anything about it."

"I've also seen a number of cases where the workers are charged large up-front fees and go into debt trying to pay them back, or they have these fees deducted from their wages, far in excess of what they should be."

"The rules of the visa say that recruitment fees are our responsibility, but it also says that we can charge 'reasonable' fees to the worker for help in arranging their documents and transportation. That's where the aliens get hosed. The brokers charge them these crazy fees and deduct from the wages whatever they want. What are those aliens going to do?"

I talked to Douglas about some of the other cases I had documented in which workers had been told they could stay past their visas to earn real money because most of the first year's wages had been deducted for fees. Douglas said this situation happens often and is part of the system in the valley. I next asked him about housing and pointed out that many of the worker domiciles I had seen were in terrible condition.

"Housing has to meet OSHA standards," Douglas replied, "They do on my farms. I can have someone show you."

"You mean like having a minimum number of cubic feet per person?"

"Yeah, it's all regulated—the number of people per toilet and per shower, hot water, ventilation—they go into detail on that stuff."

"But nobody seems to be monitoring that this is actually being done."

"Honestly, if it's done like the law says, the aliens would be better off than U.S. workers. I think that's why some people feel it's okay to slack on the rules."

After speaking at length with Douglas about the specifics of how his farm operates, I asked him what his primary concerns were about the farming system in general in the Central Valley. Without a moment's hesitation he replied, "Water."

"You mean the drought?"

"I mean, we're running out, and it's no joke."

I had seen billboards on highway 99 and the I-5 freeway throughout the Central Valley pitching both sides of the water debate—conservationists pointing out how much water it takes to produce one pound of almonds or an ounce of cheese or eight ounces of beef, and other billboards blasting politicians for mismanaging the state's water supply and being more worried about preserving indigenous fish stocks then supporting local farmers. Douglas had firm opinions on the matter.

People are upset about the almonds around here. It's true they suck water all year round, unlike other crops, but the fact is one mature almond tree can produce 2,500 pounds of almonds in a year, and right now almonds wholesale at $3.50 a pound, so you do the math and tell me that a farmer doesn't have the right to plant more almond trees if he wants to. Hell, I enjoy a good steak as much as any man, but you can bet beef takes just as much water as almonds, but you don't hear anyone talking about giving up steaks to save our water supply.

I was curious about the comparison, so I asked Douglas just how much water beef requires, and he said anywhere between 800 to 900 gallons of water for one eight-ounce steak. The ratio astounded me. Douglas explained further that eight ounces of chicken requires closer to 150 gallons of water, and eight ounces of eggs less than 100 gallons. As for almonds, they require around 100 gallons per ounce, roughly the same as beef. The statistics Douglas shared made me appreciate more clearly just how water-intensive the agricultural sector was. I thought that being a vegetarian might have absolved me from some of the water wastage, but my predilection for nuts made me just as culpable.

Douglas had a lot more to say about California's water supply. I listened to his concerns, then returned the conversation to my research into labor issues and asked him if there was anything else about the farm labor system in California that he thought was a source of the abuses.

"There is one other major problem I would point out," Douglas said. "Until a few years ago, the FLCs were paid by a percentage of the worker wages. You can bet this led to a lot of abuse because the corrupt ones would take more than they were supposed to. So the state switched to a fixed fee per worker recruited. I think they thought this would solve the wage problems, but it made things worse."

"How so?" I asked.

"Now the FLCs recruit more workers than we need just to get those fees, and a lot of those aliens just get sent back with debts from the fees they paid the recruiters, or they sit around here doing nothing, earning nothing. That's when they end up in bad situations."

Douglas went on to explain that there is no annual limit on the number of H-2A visas that can be granted by the government, and this feeds right into the racket of exploitative brokers and FLCs recruiting more workers than are needed and pocketing the large, up-front fees they charge for arranging the visas. Because many migrants have accrued huge debts to make it to the United States, they are willing to accept almost any work opportunity they are offered to try to repay their debts, and those offers often involve slavery.

My conversation with Douglas helped me understand the inner workings, and failings, of the system of labor recruitment in the Central Valley. He identified many of the crucial gaps and loopholes that allow labor exploitation and slavery to persist in California's agricultural sector: a lack of oversight and auditing of wage records; a lack of adherence to the policies of the guest worker program; H-2A policies that promote exploitation; and a system that, according to Douglas, thrives on low-wage, expendable migrant labor and hence is not really motivated to do anything about the abuses.

Toward the end of our conversation, Douglas spent a few minutes talking about the history of the Central Valley. He felt very connected to the land because of his ancestry, and I could see that he tried to manage his farm in an honest way. Douglas mentioned a few other farms belonging to friends that I could visit, which I managed to do. I thanked him for his time, and as I got up to leave he said, "I have to be honest. Sometimes my crew may take shortcuts. I don't condone it, but I know it happens."

FLCS

Everything I learned from the farmworkers and farm owners throughout the Central Valley made it clear to me how, why, and where forced labor occurs. In virtually all cases, the FLCs were involved, so I set myself to the task of learning more about them. The California Department of Industrial Relations defines an FLC as:

> Any person/legal entity who, for a fee, employs people to perform work connected to the production of farm products to, for, or under the direction of a third person, or any person/legal entity who recruits, supplies, or hires workers on behalf of someone engaged in the production of farm products and, for a fee, provides board, lodging, or transportation for those workers, or supervises, times, checks, counts, weighs, or otherwise directs or measures their work, or disburses wage payments to these persons.[4]

The California Labor Code section 1683 requires that anyone acting as an FLC must be licensed by the California Division of Labor Standards Enforcement and must be certified at the federal level by the U.S. Department of Labor. As of May, 2016, there were 350 FLCs registered in California, out of a total 810 FLCs registered across the United States.[5] This means that roughly 43 percent of all licensed FLCs in the United States are in California. The average wage of an FLC in California is $60,040, which is roughly three times that of a properly paid farmworker, and more than eleven times the average wages received by the labor trafficking victims I documented in California's agricultural sector. FLCs in California come in all sizes, from one-man operations to large companies such as Valley Pride, Inc. and Tara Picking, which have more than one thousand employees between them. The majority, however, are small operations of one to three people. Many of these one-man operations were started by former farmworkers.

I began my investigations into California's FLCs with the state's Farm Labor Contractor Association. Only willing to speak off the record, a high-level member of the staff described the duties of the association to me and the issues it faces with improper behavior with some of the licensed FLCs. The first thing this official told me (let's call him "Jim") is, "Most of the problems with improper payment of wages or treatment of workers happen with FLCs that are not licensed." Jim assured me that the licensed FLCs go through a rigorous licensing process, including nine hours of coursework, a written examination, and extensive training on sexual harassment, which Jim said was one of the biggest problems among California's FLCs. The other problem he deals with regularly is "the lack of enforcement of OSHA heat stress regulations," which leads to numerous cases of heat stroke and even deaths each year.

I asked Jim whether any efforts were made to crack down on FLCs that operate without a license, if this is in fact where most of the abuses occur.

"We don't have as many inspectors as we need," Jim replied. "That's because of budget cuts from the state. But if we do find an FLC operating without a license, they can be fined up to $10,000."

"Only up to $10,000?"

"That's the maximum fine."

I pointed out to Jim that if exploitative FLCs can make ten or twenty times per year the amount of the fine by putting workers in forced labor, then the fine is not terribly deterrent.

"That's the law," Jim said.

"What about the recent change in FLC compensation from being paid a percentage of the worker's wages to being paid a one-time fee for each worker recruited? Won't this lead to overrecruitment, which leaves a lot of workers here with no job or income, which ultimately ends up with them being exploited as they try to find a way to repay all the up-front fees they were charged?"

Jim needed me to repeat the question, then break it down into parts, but he eventually told me that there can be abuses either way the FLCs are paid. I asked Jim if he could think of any other means of FLC compensation that might help minimize abuses, but he did not have any ideas. Neither did I, aside from better monitoring.

Jim's overall perspective was that the California Farm Labor Contractor Association does as good a job as possible at monitoring FLCs given its resource constraints, and that most of the abuses take place with the non-licensed FLCs. He conceded that if a licensed FLC were shorting workers on wages or putting them in substandard housing or exacting conditions akin to slavery, there were simply not enough inspectors in the state to do much about it. The federal government also has a role to play because FLCs must receive federal registration to operate. At the federal level, FLCs are monitored by the Department of Labor Wage and Hour Division, which can revoke their licenses for infractions. To date, a total of 672 FLCs across the United States have had their registrations revoked; almost all of them were individual operators.[6] There are, however, bound to be numerous duplicate entries in the list of revoked FLCs because people often reregister with a new name or use a family member's name. The lack of accountability in the system at the federal and state levels frustrated me, especially because it was clear that this was a major factor in allowing abuses to take place. The lack of accountability was partially a function of insufficient enforcement, but even more a function of the absence of visibility and liability for farm owners relating to the actions of their FLCs. If farm owners faced serious and tangible liability for worker exploitation, the system would surely have far fewer abuses.

As I pieced together the labor supply chain in the Central Valley, it became clear to me that FLCs in essence function the same way for American farm owners as foreign manufacturers (like Foxconn) do for U.S.-based companies (such as Apple). They are a means of outsourcing the recruitment, treatment, and management of labor that severs legal liability between the company and the conditions under which the workers live and work. Farm owners can point a finger to the FLC and claim ignorance of any abuses that may be committed. They can say they do as much as possible to require decent working conditions, just as a U.S. multinational can claim the same for workers they use through subcontractors abroad, but that the ultimate responsibility lies with the FLC or labor subcontractor. In the case of California's agricultural sector, FLCs serve as intermediaries that provide the owner with the cheap labor pool they want, while simultaneously severing the legal, but not the ethical or moral, liabilities associated with the treatment of those workers.

The more I thought about it, the more I realized that the FLC system in California reminded me quite clearly of the *jamadar* system of labor recruiting in India that also severs the employer's liability for labor abuses. In this system, labor recruiters also operate in the same country as their employers, which one would hope might tighten the link of vicarious liability between owner and worker via the subcontractor. However, in *Bonded Labor* I outlined exactly how the jamadar system of labor recruitment in South Asia ends up being a primary driver of slavelike labor conditions in numerous sectors across the region's informal economy, thanks to the absence of vicarious liability.[7] The FLC system in the United States works exactly the same way as the jamadar system in India: an employer has labor needs and outsources fulfillment and management of the laborers to a subcontractor (the FLC or jamadar). The FLC or jamadar recruits workers, transports them to the worksite, manages their working conditions and wages, and in many cases exploits the imbalance of power between them and the workers to exact slave labor. The lack of vicarious liability between the primary employer and the FLC or jamadar means that the employer is not legally responsible for abuses committed by the contractors.

This lack of liability leads to a key thesis about global labor trafficking:

> Systems that sever liability between primary employers and migrant laborers through labor subcontractors are responsible for a significant proportion of slavery and child labor in migrant worker populations around the world.

This system must change, either through a direct legal relationship between the primary employer and the laborer or through the extension of the principle of vicarious liability to include the relationship between primary employer and labor subcontractor. In *Bonded Labor*, I call for either new statutes or strategic litigation to extend liability from the jamadar to the employer through a broadening of the reach of vicarious liability, and I believe the exact same needs to be accomplished in the United States vis-à-vis FLCs and the farm owners who engage them. Doing so would lead to a considerable decrease in abuses because farm owners would have a vested interest in maintaining compliance with labor laws and in ensuring that they work with fully licensed FLCs, if in fact most abuses are committed by the unlicensed ones.

My efforts to conduct interviews with FLCs were not as productive as I had hoped. I managed to have conversations with just three small-sized FLCs in California, and they largely corroborated what I already knew. They were fully licensed, and each maintained that they adhered to all stipulations of the H-2A visa program. Of interest, one of the FLCs told me, "There are a lot more unlicensed contractors out here than people realize. That's where you have the problems." The FLCs also told me that when abuses occur it is at the hands of the crew leaders who manage the workers directly at the farms and not the FLCs. Many crew leaders are former farmworkers who have climbed up the ranks. Although they often are the same person/entity as the FLC, they also may be hired by FLCs (as was the case with the three FLCs I interviewed) to manage labor on their behalf. The FLCs stressed that unlicensed FLCs, in particular, relied on crew leaders that they did not monitor at all. This was yet another level of subcontracting complexity to explore, but I was slowly narrowing the scope of where the abuses in California's agricultural labor supply chain were occurring, from farm owners, to (mostly) unlicensed FLCs, to (possibly) the crew leaders. I spoke to them next.

CREW LEADERS

After several forays and enquiries, and quite a bit of time building trust, I had several conversations with crew leaders on farms where I had documented cases of labor trafficking. The crew leaders had significant latitude in how they managed the migrant workers. No one was regularly monitoring them as long as the workers were productive. If the crew leaders wanted to (or were instructed to) squeeze labor costs, they knew exactly how to do it, and how to get away with it. The migrant workers were vulnerable, frightened, and lacked any will to think seriously about pursuing an alternative employment opportunity or enforcing their rights, and few even knew what their rights were. The conversations I had with crew leaders were at farms in the San Joaquin and Sacramento valleys. Nine out of the eleven crew leaders I interviewed were Mexican. There were strong racial and class divisions between the crew leaders and the farmworkers they managed. The Mexican crew leaders saw themselves as a higher class of individual than the migrants from El Salvador, Honduras, and Guatemala, and they also saw themselves as superior to the other Mexican workers, even though most of them were once in the same position themselves. It was a similar dynamic to what I documented with gharwalis in India or madams in Nigeria, who were all once "lowly" prostitutes but in their new roles of power took on airs of superiority, having survived long enough (and been trusted enough) to be promoted to becoming exploiters themselves. These new positions came with an elevation in status, power, and self-worth that most of the crew leaders, madams, and gharwalis reinforced at every occasion.

The most interesting conversation I had with a crew leader was with a heavily opinionated man named Elias on a walnut farm not far from Jacinto, California. In a matter-of-fact tone, Elias outlined his job responsibilities: "I handle the farmworkers. I keep them housed and fed. I transport them from the apartments to the farm. I drive around the farm most of the day. I make sure the farm runs smooth. If something breaks down, I fix it."

I asked Elias about some of the cases of labor exploitation I had documented. He responded firmly: "You don't understand how things work here until you live out here for a whole season on these farms. This is good work for the migrants. Most of them are hard workers. They know how lucky they are to be here because they have nothing back in Mexico. America gives them opportunities, but not all of them have been trained to work hard the way we have. We have to be firm with the workers who are not as experienced, but that's only to help them be better."

Elias' response made me feel as if I were speaking to Love (the madam) back in Nigeria. Like her, Elias did not feel that he was abusing or exploiting the workers under his charge; rather, he was giving them a once-in-a-lifetime opportunity to earn a better life. According to him, many of the migrants did not know how to work hard (i.e., they were lazy), so he had to be firm with them and train them to work harder so that they could succeed in the opportunities he was giving them. What he called "training" I called "slavery," and that is the essential perceptual difference responsible for much of the servile labor exploitation around the world. I asked Elias what he meant by having to be "firm" with the workers.

"A lot of them want to run away because the work is too hard," he replied. "They think they can find some other job where they don't have to work."

"Do you really feel they are all trying to run off and cheat you?" I asked.

"They're gone the minute you turn your back."

"So you feel you have to keep them under guard or keep their documents so that they don't run away, that's what you're saying?"

"In some cases."

"I can't say that's consistent with what I have seen, but I suppose you would know better than I would."

Elias looked at me with a wry smile, "What do you think you've seen?"

"I've seen hard-working men who are put in situations of severe exploitation, not paid the wages they were promised, charged excessive fees for rent and food, forced to live in subhuman conditions, sometimes charged excessive fees to arrange their visas or jobs in this country, and they end up trying to work off these debts for years, with little income to show for it. That's what I've seen."

"If that's what people are telling you, they're lying."

"Why would they lie?" I asked.

"Because they think you'll help them."

"Why would they need my help?"

"Because they don't realize how much better they have it here than back in their homes."

"I don't think they see it that way."

"They're better off than I am too."

"I don't think they see it that way either."

"That's because you don't know how things really work out here."

"So tell me."

"No, you tell me, how do you think they work?"

I thought about it for a moment then replied, "Well, I think compared to you, the workers would say the fact that you can come and go freely and are able to change jobs if you want to makes your situation much better, not to mention that you are probably paid the wages you are promised."

"What makes you think I can just come and go as I please?" Elias asked.

"Can't you?"

"Where am I going? I have bills to pay. I can't leave this job any more than they can leave theirs."

I tried as patiently as possible to explain to Elias that although his options may be constrained due to his financial situation or the lack of alternatives for someone with his skill set, no one was restraining him or preventing him from leaving with threats of deportation if he wanted to leave.

"No difference," he curtly replied.

"I think there's a big difference."

"That's because you don't understand."

"Maybe, but I'm trying."

Elias and I grew increasingly frustrated with each other, and I could sense that he was growing skeptical of my intentions. He told me he had to return to work, so I thanked him for his time. Before I left, he asked, "Are you going to write some report or something?"

"Probably a book," I said.

"I hope you don't get it wrong, about the situation here. People who come here and work hard can get ahead, just like I did. People who take short cuts are going to have a bad experience. You can tell everyone that's what I said."

I thanked Elias for his thoughts. Despite his arguments that the only issues the migrant workers faced in California's Central Valley were their own laziness and treachery in abusing the H-2A system, I had documented more than enough cases to persuade me that the migrant workers were by and large honest, hard-working men whose vulnerability and desperation invariably placed them on the wrong end of an exploitative arrangement. Perhaps some might try to game the system, but most had mortgaged so much and undergone such onerous ordeals to make the journey to California and have the opportunity to work on a farm that they were only too grateful to have the job and persisted in the hope of one day being paid the wages they had been promised. In fact, the labor trafficking victims I documented were exploited at both ends of their journey, first by the recruiters who charged exorbitant fees that placed many in levels of debt that they could never discharge, then by the FLCs/crew leaders who imposed excessive wage deductions that meant the workers had almost no money left with which to repay their debts, not to mention the fees that were added for the irregular migrants at the border. Many of the farms in the Central Valley seemed to run on well-oiled systems of servitude and bondage that were akin to almost every other migrant labor trafficking sector I documented around the world, from domestic workers in South Asia, to construction workers in the Middle East, to seafood workers in East Asia. Across the globe, including in the United States, numerous industries operate on the backs of a subclass of vulnerable labor migrants who are recruited, indebted, and coerced to work in subhuman conditions at minimal to no wages under threats of abuse, deportation, or other penalties. After years of research, I could not help but wonder just how much of the global economy operates on this feudal system of migrant enslavement. The precise answer may never be known, but the abuses inherent in the worldwide system of migrant worker trafficking and slavery must be properly assessed and addressed because this system has been woven into much of the global economic order for centuries.

A HISTORY OF LABOR TRAFFICKING

The undeniable truth is that labor trafficking is nothing new to the American agricultural system.[8] As far back as the early 1600s, indentured workers were brought to the colonies by the British to work in agricultural fields under systems of peonage and serfdom. As the agricultural economy in the colonies grew and outpaced the available pool of indentured laborers from England, the Atlantic slave trade commenced to meet the labor shortage. The slave trade lasted until the Slave Trade Abolition Act of 1807 was passed in the UK Parliament. Slavery in the United States persisted as an institution until the Thirteenth Amendment to the U.S. Constitution was ratified in 1865. The shift from slaves and indentured workers from overseas to migrants from Mexico began in earnest about two decades prior at the end of the Mexican-American war in 1848, at which time tens of thousands of migrant workers from Mexico began arriving in the United States. Most of these migrants moved freely back and forth across the border for seasonal agricultural work; others were ensnared in various forms of forced labor for years at a time. This period of Mexican migration beginning in the mid-1800s coincided with the industrialization and expansion of the U.S. agricultural sector. Indeed, agricultural growth was so brisk that it even exceeded the available supply of Mexican migrant agricultural workers, so the United States resorted to importing Asian farmworkers from the 1860s to about the 1930s. By the end of the nineteenth century, roughly seven out of eight farmworkers in the United States was either from China, Japan, or the Philippines. This led to a xenophobic backlash in the form of the Chinese Exclusion Act of 1882, which banned the employment of Chinese workers. Jim Crow laws beginning in the 1890s then systematized the segregation and oppression of the descendents of African slaves, which pushed many to enter into sharecropping arrangements with white landowners. World War I stymied migration to the United States, causing a new farmworker shortage. In response, the first "guest worker" program focused on Mexican farmworkers was created, and it lasted until 1921. The flow of Mexican migrants went the other way after the Great Depression and the Dust Bowl of the 1930s, and 500,000 Mexicans were deported to Mexico due to a glut of farm labor. Eventually, the labor market stabilized. As the agriculture sector recovered, the United States faced another labor shortage, which led to passage of the Emergency Labor Program in 1942, also known as the Bracero (literally "one who works using his arms") Program, brokered between U.S. President Franklin D. Roosevelt and Mexican President Manuel Avila Camacho for an initial five-year term. As a precursor to the H-2A visa program, the Bracero Program allowed for seasonal or temporary labor by Mexican migrant workers in the agriculture and railroad sectors of the United States. Workers under the program were promised equal treatment and wages as those of U.S. citizens. Though the railroad part of the program ended with the conclusion of World War II, the agricultural program continued due to ongoing labor shortages in the sector. Treatment of the braceros was nearly identical to that of many H-2A workers today: extended hours, poor living conditions, underpaid or unpaid wages, physical violence, debt bondage, coercion of labor under threat of deportation, and other abuses. Even the U.S. Department of Labor officer in charge of the program, Lee G. Williams, described it as a system of "legalized slavery."[9] Bracero strikes spread across the country until Congress eventually ended the program in 1964. During its twenty-two-year run, over 5 million braceros came into the United States, making it the largest foreign worker program in U.S. history, larger even than the 3.5 million African slaves brought into the United States during the entire time of the Atlantic slave trade.

The end of the Bracero Program was hastened by the rise of Cesar Chavez's National Farm Worker Association, founded in 1962, which later merged with the Agricultural Workers Organizing Committee to become the United Farm Workers (UFW) in 1966. The UFW has been drawing national attention to the struggles of migrant farmworkers across the United States for decades, and it has helped to inspire the creation of numerous farmworker unions and organizations. Though not as prominent today as it was during the 1970s and 1980s, the UFW continues to organize and advocate for the rights of migrant farmworkers in the United States. In 2016, the UFW lobbied ardently in support of the passage of AB 1066 in California, which for the first time requires that overtime wages be paid to farmworkers in the state when they work more than eight hours per day. The fact that the bill required more than a few minutes of debate is astonishing. Nonetheless, it was passed by the state legislature and was signed into law on September 12, 2016, stipulating a phased-in approach that would culminate in farmworkers in California being paid overtime wages when they work more than eight hours per day, by the year 2022.

Although most Americans do not realize it, their nation's agricultural system has relied heavily on migrant laborers and slaves from Africa, Asia, and south of the border for the last four centuries. The country's agricultural sector has functioned to varying degrees on bondage and servitude from the beginning, which is no different from agricultural sectors elsewhere in the world. From feudal times to the present day, the arrangements that characterize agricultural work have been remarkably resistant to change, including in the United States. Laws are passed, awareness is raised, workers protest, and lives are lost—but trafficking for slavery and bondage in America's agricultural sector remains far more prevalent today than almost anyone cares to admit. Although some laws are now in place in the United States that are meant to protect migrant agricultural workers, based on what I have seen, they are not remotely getting the job done.

LEGAL PROTECTIONS

Labor laws in the United States have become more protective of migrant workers in the last several decades, but gaps in rights and in enforcement continue to hamper efforts to eliminate severe exploitation in this sector. The most important law that provides protection to all workers in the United States is the Fair Labor Standards Act (FLSA) of 1938. This act guarantees minimum wages, overtime pay, and other rights and standards for workers, but the act did not originally cover most farmworkers. Almost three decades after its original passage, in 1966 the FLSA finally included farmworkers, but only on large farms, and only related to certain minimum wage provisions. To this day, small farms are not covered, and overtime wages still do not apply to farmworkers on farms of any size. This lack of wage protection is heavily exploited by crew leaders and FLCs, who extract excess labor under the guise of working off debts, meeting quotas, or paying for rent and food. To make matters worse, the Portal-to-Portal Pay Act of 1947 further limits the scope of compensation to farmworkers by stipulating that travel time to and from the workplace as well as incidental activities performed before and after principal work activities, which can add up to several hours per day, are not subject to compensation. Although the FLSA sets the minimum age for hazardous work at sixteen years, for farm work the age is set at twelve years as long as the work is in the morning or at night. Thankfully, I did not document many cases of child labor on farms in the Central Valley, and certainly not anyone as young as twelve or thirteen years of age. Finally, farmworkers remain excluded from the National Labor Relations Act of 1935, which prohibits firing any worker who joins, supports, or organizes a labor union.

The Migrant and Seasonal Agricultural Worker Protection Act of 1983 is the primary federal legislation relating specifically to migrant farmworkers. The act prescribes certain protections related to payment of wages, record keeping, decent housing, safety standards, antidiscrimination, and written agreements between employers and workers prior to the commencement of work. Crucially, there is no minimum wage provision in the act. Initial violations of the act can be penalized with fines of up to $1,000 and up to one year in prison. Subsequent violations can result in fines of up to $10,000 and up to two years in prison. Neither penalty is an effective deterrent. Inspections and monitoring related to the law are supposed to be conducted by investigators at the Wage and Hour Division of the U.S. Department of Labor, but from what I saw in the field their capacity to adequately monitor adherence to the law in the Central Valley of California is severely deficient. Interestingly, the law includes a private right of action for claimants, but enforcement of the law remains anemic. There is not even a centralized database anywhere in the U.S. government reporting the number of cases that have been filed under the law.

The United States Trafficking Victim Protection Act of 2000 provides a basis to punish labor traffickers in agriculture or any other sector. I asked the Department of Justice how many cases had been filed under the act relating to labor trafficking in the agricultural sector, but no centralized data are available. Finally, many of the provisions of the Occupational Safety and Health Act (OSHA) of 1970 also apply to migrant farmworkers, but as I saw time and again, OSHA standards are at best inconsistently adhered to and at worst completely ignored. The consequences of the broad-based lack of enforcement of these and other laws and regulations relating to migrant labor in the U.S. agricultural system is that the invisible migrant workers continue to be coarsely and systematically exploited as they have been for centuries. It is unfathomable that these archaic modes of servitude have persisted in the United States agricultural sector for so long, focused squarely on whatever vulnerable migrant population is trafficked into the country to harvest the food we serve at our dinner tables. To visit farms in certain parts of this country is to go back in time to an era of sharecroppers, serfdom, and slavery. How much longer will this disgraceful time warp be allowed to persist?

THE INDECENT EQUATION

After spending several months conducting research in the Central Valley of California, it was clear to me that I had barely scratched the surface of labor trafficking and slavery in the region. However, the research I conducted was more than sufficient to demonstrate that people around the world eat slave-made food exported from the United States every day. Those same almonds I enjoy in my home are enjoyed in homes in the United Kingdom, Germany, India, China, Japan, Canada, Mexico, and numerous other countries.

Although I was not able to gather a sufficient number of cases to express a prevalence rate of labor trafficking in California's agriculture sector, I documented more than enough cases to know that the problem is real, serious, and significant. Some of the findings from the 303 cases of labor trafficking I documented in California's agricultural sector include:

- 100 percent males
- $426.30 per month: average wage ($16.40 per day; $1.31[10] per hour as compared to average hourly wages of $12.30 for all U.S. agricultural workers)[11]
- 22.8 years: average age at time first trafficked
- 206 workers from Mexico, 37 from Guatemala, 28 from El Salvador, 32 from other countries in Central and Latin America, and the Caribbean
- 175 workers without documentation; 128 workers on H-2A visas
- 253 cases of debt bondage
- 20 cases of children under the age of eighteen years

The individuals I met lived in highly unpleasant circumstances and suffered numerous health ailments. Exposure to extreme heat, pesticides, and other injurious conditions took an irreparable toll on the workers' well-being. Most disconcerting of all, the migrant workers shared a near universal sense of fatalism. They felt they had no place to go, no other employment options, and no way to disentangle themselves from their oppressive situation. This mix of exploitation, harm, and resignation left me in an intense quandary I have not yet been able to resolve. Almost everything I eat comes from these farms. As a vegetarian, dairy, nuts, and vegetables are essential to my diet, but it is impossible to know which cheese, almond, strawberry, or tomato is tainted. I contemplated eliminating foods from the specific farms where I documented labor trafficking, but it is impossible to know from which farm the nuts or fruits in my grocery store are sourced. Sometimes the farm is listed, but more often it is not, and with derivative products such as almond milk the producer typically sources from numerous farms. Further, on any given farm spanning thousands of acres, there will invariably be cases of severe labor exploitation mixed with unexploited laborers. Do I reject an entire farm and all its produce because I found a handful of labor trafficking cases on it? One might argue that one case is enough to taint the entire business, but one could also argue that there would always be a small number of infractions on farms even if they do their best to uphold labor standards.

My findings of labor trafficking in California's agricultural sector have been some of the most challenging for me to reconcile with my desire not to contribute to slavery as I go about my daily life. It has become impossible not to taste suffering with each bite of an almond, oppression in each mouthful of strawberries and degradation with each sip of milk. Every morsel is a reminder of the bitter misery of the slaves I met, transformed into the sweet enjoyment of my nourishment. This indecent equation has persisted for much of human history, and I wonder sometimes if it simply must be so. Perhaps we must to some degree always be sustained by the suffering of others. This possibility gnaws at me because it suggests not only that there must always be a subclass of people in this world whose lives are reduced to bondage and woe but that my entire antislavery career has been pointless. On certain days, this realization shatters me. I endeavor to suppress feelings of helplessness and despondency. I search for signs, for encouragement, for decency, and I cling to the fading hope that there might be a way for me to exist that does not necessitate the degradation of another.

I hope, but I do not know.

CHAPTER 4

ORGAN TRAFFICKING

Sold for Parts

Slavery is such an atrocious debasement of human nature,
that its very extirpation, if not performed with solicitous
care, may sometimes open a source of serious evils.
                                          —Benjamin Franklin

SHROUDED IN SECRECY

NO FORM OF human trafficking proved more challenging to research than human trafficking for organ removal, also known as organ trafficking.[1] The trade is shrouded in secrecy and is most often the province of dangerous organized crime groups, such as the Zetas and the Sinaloa cartel in Mexico, the Nigerian mafia, the Albanian mafia, and organized crime groups across South Asia. The issue is mired in complex ethical quandaries, and many upstanding physicians and even religious leaders feel that facilitating the sale of organs for transplantation is a noble deed that saves lives on both sides of the transaction: the recipient, who needs the organ to survive, and the donor, who is able to lift his or her family out of poverty by selling an organ (usually a kidney). Individuals who promote a market for buying and selling organs typically ask the following question: "Is selling a kidney any different from an individual's selling sexual services to make ends meet or a young woman selling her eggs to couples struggling with infertility?" Indeed, the trade in human bodies and body parts for economic consideration raises numerous moral questions without easy answers. When is it okay to sell oneself, or parts of oneself, if ever? Would not any loving parent sell a kidney if it meant his or her children could have food, an education, and enjoy better lives? If we are all owners of our bodies, can we not transact with them as we choose? Or are there broader social contaminations that invariably fester and spread when we allow individuals this freedom? Is there a categorical difference between selling an organ and selling sexual services, and if so, why? Why do only two countries at present—Iran and Singapore—allow the legal sale of organs, whereas numerous countries allow the legal sale of sex?

In search of answers to these questions, and to understand exactly how human trafficking for organ removal functions from one region to another, I conducted research in several countries, including Moldova, Kosovo, India, Nepal, Bangladesh, Singapore, Mexico, and the United States. In none of the cases I documented did I find a single instance in which the full theoretical benefits to the seller were realized. As with prostitution, the theories of self-determination and open markets for transactions suggest that in the right circumstances the transaction can be a win-win for all parties and that people should have the right to sell whatever parts they wish, but these theories did not bear out in the real-world cases I encountered.

I should note at the outset that a foundational question is whether organ trafficking is a form of slavery. It is certainly a form of human trafficking as specified in the Palermo Protocol (but not in the U.S. Trafficking Victim Protection Act), and many cases of organ trafficking are born out of debt bondage. Whether it is slavery—the condition or status of a person who is treated like property—is a separate question that can have opposing answers. I believe the phenomenon is too intricately linked to other phenomena we label as "slavery" to categorize it separately, but I appreciate the argument that this violation may not amount to forcing a person into a condition of slavery even though it may be a gross and unconscionable violation of human rights. The cases of organ trafficking I have documented are not included in the summary metrics on slavery I present in chapter 1 and in the appendixes because the economic data were insufficient and inconsistent.

Nevertheless, I do consider organ trafficking to be a form slavery that is every bit as dehumanizing, exploitative, and ruinous as any other.

I conducted a modest amount of research on human trafficking for organ removal in the Balkans and in East Asia; however, the majority of my research on this issue focused on South Asia and North America. Trying to track down and trace cases of organ trafficking and document each participant in the organ chain proved arduous, debilitating, and dangerous. There was no way to avoid brushing perilously close to major organized crime networks, and the exceedingly clandestine nature of the crime made it all the more difficult to collect comprehensive economic data on cases or piece together the nature of the organ trafficking networks from one region to another. Finding victims alive to tell the tale was also a significant obstacle to the research. The cases I managed to document have sharply influenced my thinking about the ethical questions related to organ sales and have reinforced the general thesis of my broader research on slavery—the poor, vulnerable, disadvantaged, and outcaste people of the world are chewed up and sold for parts by those with power, rights, and resources, with little consequence. Organ trafficking took this thesis to the extreme.

SOUTH ASIA: HARVESTED AND DISCARDED

Organ Villages in West Bengal

South Asia is ground zero for most forms of slavery, and organ trafficking is no exception. My first encounter with the phenomenon was during research I conducted in the summer of 2001. I traveled to several villages in West Bengal where *adivasis* (tribal people) had been recruited by *dalals* (traffickers) to sell kidneys. The people in the villages were beyond poor and almost completely disenfranchised from mainstream Indian society. A soft-spoken man named Debjeet described his experience:

> *The dalals come to our villages and offer 50,000 rupees [~$1,100] if we donate a kidney. We have almost nothing in this place, so many people accept these offers. I was only paid 10,000 rupees [~$222] after they took my kidney. The dalal said I will have medicine and the doctors*

will care for me, but no one gave me any care or helped me when I became ill. They left me here to die. I am always sick, and I cannot work. Now my wife must sell her kidney or we cannot eat. I knew there was a risk they will not pay me the full amount, but even 10,000 rupees is more money than I have seen. I am tired all the time. I have so much pain. I know I will die soon.

Debjeet was very unwell when I met him—gaunt, weak, and huddled under a tree, scarcely able to move. He had been continuously ill since his kidney was removed the previous year, and he had received virtually no postoperative care. He looked old beyond his years, as did many of the other young men in his village, and a few of the women, too. It felt as if his entire village had been systematically harvested for kidneys. Debjeet's surgery took place at a hospital in Kolkata. I asked him if he could tell me which hospital it was, but he did not know and could only describe it as a large building with hundreds of rooms for patients. After his kidney was removed, he was stitched up and sent on a bus to return home the following day. The bus only took him part of the way; he had to walk the final twelve kilometers under the baking sun, just one day after his kidney was removed. His life had been a bleak ordeal every since. He did, however, receive a lavish dinner the one night he spent in the hospital, "They gave me daal, aloo-gobi (potato and cauliflower), baingan (eggplant), luchi (puri), and for sweets I had two pieces of sandesh. It was the most food I ate in my life."

After Debjeet made it home, he was left to fend for himself. He had basically been used for his kidney then discarded like so much refuse. He showed me the nine-inch scar on his left abdomen where the surgery had been performed. The kidney had not been removed laproscopically, which added to his pain and left a glaring reminder of the loss he had suffered.

I documented a total of fifteen men and women in Debjeet's village who had undergone the same nightmare. Their misery left me infuriated. They had been carved up one by one and left to die. These were not one-off cases but part of a well-developed system of organ trafficking that stretched from remote villages straight into major hospitals in some of the largest cities in India. Unfortunately, the tales of impoverished villagers in India being carved up and sent packing with a handful of rupees did not end there. Across northern India I documented the same scenario time and again.

Desperate, poor villagers were promised life-changing amounts of money for kidneys, paid only 10 to 30 percent of what was promised,[2] then discarded to suffer a slow and agonizing demise. I documented a handful of cases of partial liver transplants, but most of the cases involved kidneys. The majority of the organ harvesting surgeries took place in what the victims described as proper hospitals, but some took place in small, nondescript clinic settings as well. A few hospitals were identified by name, including one of the largest hospital chains in the country—Apollo. I spoke to personnel at a few of the Apollo hospital branches in India, and they described the situations I documented as rarities and more the fault of predatory brokers who dupe everyone, including the hospital. My conversations at Apollo in New Delhi were just a few months before the hospital was in the local news for being used in a major organized crime organ trafficking operation that included two hospital employees who forged papers to facilitate the harvesting of organs from exploited peasants for use in transplant procedures in the hospital.[3] Despite increasing awareness of the risks and likelihood of fraud, many peasants still accept the offers out of desperation for any amount of money they might receive. Many peasants told me they were aware they would not live very long after the organ donation should they not receive adequate care, but even 10 percent of the promised payment would help their families in ways they could not otherwise provide. Such is the moribund calculus of the poor—sell a body part for ten cents on the dollar and know you will suffer an agonizing death, because this outcome may still be preferable to the alternative.

A second scenario I documented across India with alarming frequency was the offer to discharge a debt in exchange for a kidney. Many bonded laborers had become so indebted that they felt no hope of ever being able to repay their debts no matter how hard or how long their families worked. In Uttar Pradesh, Punjab, and Rajasthan, I encountered numerous families working in brick-making, carpet weaving, agriculture, mining, and construction who had been attempting for several years to work off loans that ranged from fifty dollars to a few hundred dollars. The debts grew year after year, no matter how hard they worked, then a crisis struck and the landowner or contractor told them they could not extend additional loans, but they could extinguish most or all of their debts if the debtor parted with a kidney. This barter was almost always accepted, and the debts were largely extinguished, but within a few years the family was back in debt because the male head of household who parted with the kidney could no longer work due to illness or death. The wife of one such man who had died just a few weeks after selling his kidney beat her chest and wailed as she described her pain:

> See what they did to my husband! They cut him like an animal. He came home, and he knew he was going to die. He was vomiting all night. He told me he was sorry he did this because he knew he made me a widow. See my two children there. They are sick. We have no food. I cannot buy medicine. They have killed us!

Somewhere, an upper-middle class Indian had received a new lease on life in exchange for the destruction of a peasant family. I have no doubt that the wealthy Indian was unaware of the harm to his poorer countrymen that resulted from saving his life, but I am not convinced that he, or the system that facilitated the transaction, really wanted to be aware.

The phenomenon of bonded laborers parting with organs to discharge their debts took an even more disturbing turn in Bangladesh.

Organs and Loans in Bangladesh

Deep in the southwestern fringes of Bangladesh, just above the Sundarban mangroves, waterlogged villages are perpetually at risk of flooding and of devastation by cyclones. It is a highly impoverished region that was once rich farmland. However, landowners saw more profit in saltwater shrimp than in farming and transformed hundreds of thousands of hectares into saline shrimp farms, devastating the local agricultural economy and displacing hundreds of thousands of peasants.[4] Many of the villagers who remained behind entered into debt bondage with their landowners, taking loans to operate the shrimp farms with the idea of repaying the debts with each year's shrimp harvest. The economics predictably disfavored the debtors, and they entered into cycles of perpetual debt. This drove many peasants to other moneylenders such as microcredit institutions, which operate extensively across Bangladesh. Peasants took loans from microcredit banks to repay other loans from landowners, or to supplement the original loans because they were unable to maintain basic survival. Traversing the rural reaches of southwestern Bangladesh, I encountered scores of families that had taken two or three microcredit loans each. The repayment requirements for these loans are strict, and in some cases debt collectors can be aggressive in pursuing outstanding payments. When peasants are unable to discharge their debts (either to the landowner or to the microcredit institution), many resort to selling organs to repay the loans that were supposed to lift them out of poverty. M. Hossein's story was typical:

> I took my first loan from Grameen Bank[5] three years ago. I was not able to pay the loan, so I took another loan from BRAC.[6] Then I was not able to pay this loan, and I had to keep taking loans because the interest was too much and I did not make enough income from my fishing business. When my loans passed one lakh taka [~$1,430], I became desperate. The debt collectors would harass me, and one of them beat me because I could not repay my loans. Some time later a man came to our village and promised we will be paid four lakh taka [~$5,720] for a kidney. I did not know what a kidney was, but this man told us we could live a very long time after the operation and that we would be doing a noble act to save another man's life. I did not know what else I can do, so I agreed. They took me to a hospital in Dhaka and removed my kidney. I have this long scar here. I was very sick after the operation and could not see out of one eye. My left arm is paralyzed. I cannot work at all. I was only paid fifty thousand taka [~$715] after the operation, so I still have debts. I wish I had never done this operation. It ruined my life.

Like so many organ trafficking victims I documented, M. Hossein looked like a skeleton, old beyond his years, barely surviving. His breathing was labored, and his face was shrouded in anguish. He was twenty-eight.

Other men in M. Hossein's village had made deals with the same recruiter, all to repay microcredit loans. Most had their operations in Dhaka, but others were sent to India and three were flown to Singapore. I was astonished at the level of coordination in the network of recruiting desperate and indebted Bangladeshis for organ transplants being conducted by doctors in hospitals in several countries. It was one of the most polished human trafficking networks I came across in South Asia, and I wanted to trace it in more detail. To do so, I needed to speak with the organ recruiters directly.

The organ-trafficking victims with whom I spoke offered a handful of names and phone numbers for the recruiters, all of whom were based in Dhaka. When I returned to the capital, I rang nine recruiters and managed to speak with three. I told them I was an Indian in need of a transplant and heard they could help me. Two of the three were willing to meet with me, Hasan and Iqbal.

Hasan asked me to meet him at the Radisson Blu hotel at six in the evening three days after we spoke. I arrived on time and waited in the lobby. After twenty minutes, Hasan had not arrived. I rang his number, but it went straight to a busy signal. I thought that perhaps he had arrived at the hotel, seen me, and decided something was amiss. I was preparing to leave when a man approached me and asked, "Siddharth?"

"Yes," I replied.

"I take you Hasan."

"He's not coming here?"

"Please."

The man headed out of the lobby. I surmised that he worked for Hasan and was probably taking me to meet him at a less public place. Perhaps this was part of his security process, or perhaps I was being set up. Either way, I had a choice to make. I could pass on the meeting with Hasan and try my luck with Iqbal, but that might lead to a similar result. For all I knew, Hasan and Iqbal were known to each other, and word could get around that I was not to be trusted.

I followed the man out of the hotel to a car. As we drove through the manic streets of Dhaka, I was not able to keep track of our course and was unsure to which part of town he was taking me. The driver spoke virtually no English, so there was little I could gain by trying to converse with him. I sipped on my water bottle and worked through a possible escape plan should the evening go in the wrong direction. Eventually, we arrived near a dimly lit alley between fairly dilapidated residential buildings. The driver parked the car and pointed toward the far end of the alley at a man. I could see that the man in the alley was chatting on a cell phone, smoking. There did not appear to be anyone else with him. There was no way out of the alley once I walked into it. I considered canceling the meeting because there was a good chance this was an ambush. As I ran through the possible outcomes in my mind, the driver pointed again to the man in the alley and said, "Hasan."

I surveyed the alley and deduced that there were bound to be people in the residential buildings, should I need to call for help, but that was no guarantee that help would arrive, or would arrive in time. I had to make a decision.

I walked toward Hasan with a firm gait. He was well groomed and well dressed. He also spoke perfect English.

"You are Siddharth?" he asked.

"Yes. Why are we meeting here?"

"You need a kidney?"

"I was told you could help me."

"You look healthy."

"Can you help me or not?"

"You are Indian, why are you in Bangladesh?"

"I tried in India for a few months," I replied, "I was told it would be quicker here."

Hasan took a long look at me, then started typing on his cell phone.

"If you can't help me, just say so," I told Hasan, "I have other options."

I heard footsteps from the far side of the alley. Two men were walking in my direction.

"What's going on?" I asked.

"I don't think you need a kidney," Hasan replied, "I want to know why you are here."

Within moments I was surrounded. I stayed calm.

"This is very unkind," I told Hasan, "I don't know what you think you will accomplish by trying to frighten me."

"Tell me who you are," Hasan commanded.

"I told you already."

Hasan smirked. His men closed in. They stank of cheap booze.

"Are you a journalist?" Hasan asked.

"Tell your men to back away, and I will walk out without any trouble."

"You will not go anywhere until you tell me who you are."

Hasan spoke to his men in Bengali. One of them shoved me.

"Speak," Hasan said.

"Okay," I replied, "Before I stepped out of that car, I took a photo of you with my cell phone and sent it to my wife. If I do not check in with her every twenty-four hours, she will contact my friends at the U.S. Embassy in Dhaka. Let me go, or you will be hunted."

Hasan took a moment to process my statement.

"Show me your phone," he said.

"If you touch me, you will be sorry. Your choice."

Hasan locked eyes with me. I locked back. He muttered at his men, and they backed off. Hasan spat on the ground not far from my feet, "I know all the brokers in Dhaka. No one will talk with you."

Hasan and his men left in the car that brought me. I was fortunate he did not call my bluff because there was no picture of him on my phone. I collected myself and started walking toward the nearest main road to hail a taxi. I was upset that I had put myself in a dangerous situation, but I had also been researching human trafficking long enough to know which traffickers were to be feared and which were petty thugs who would back down with a show of strength. I knew Hasan was a coward the moment I saw him. Despite his warnings, I was even more committed to getting a meeting with Iqbal.

My meeting with Iqbal was more informative, although not terribly satisfying. We met near the Sadarghat Ferry Terminal and found a relatively quiet place to talk. Iqbal was from Dhaka and had studied medicine in India before returning home to be a doctor. For reasons he did not explain, his medical career did not work out, so he found another way to help patients. He told me that most of his patients were Bangladeshis who lived abroad and came back for kidney transplants because the waiting lists abroad were too long. He explained that the longer they wait while on dialysis, the more damage is done to their bodies, so they are eager to have their transplants arranged more quickly. I asked Iqbal how patients from abroad found someone like him. He told me that prospective patients could find him through numerous informal channels, including social media and word of mouth. Once a patient decided to employ his services, several surgeons he worked with in Dhaka could perform the operation. The patient paid $75,000 to $100,000 for the procedure. Upon arrival in Dhaka, all of the patient's needs were met: accommodation in a nice hotel, surgical pretesting, transplant surgery, full recuperation, and discharge to travel home. I asked Iqbal how much he gets paid, and he told me he received 5 percent of the fee. He said he typically arranges two or three procedures a year, sometime more. I asked him how much he pays the donors, and he said they receive a fixed fee of one lakh taka (~$1,430). I told Iqbal that I had documented numerous peasants who were promised a certain payment but only received a fraction of it. Iqbal said he always paid his donors in full. I asked him about aftercare for the donors, and he said this was a problem because they usually returned to their villages soon after the operation and not many physicians traveled to rural areas to provide adequate care for them.

"You realize that even if these donors receive all the money they are promised but do not receive proper after care, their lives are ruined," I explained.

Iqbal did not respond.

"Do you think it is it fair to exploit poor people in this manner, just so the rich can survive?" I asked.

"Some people are worth less," Iqbal responded, "That is the reality in our world."

I was taken aback by Iqbal's harsh statement and asked him if he really felt that way.

"It's not my feeling, it's the truth. If you don't see this, that is your pity."

I wanted to argue with Iqbal to persuade him that the worth of all human beings is equal despite their life circumstances, but I knew it would be a pointless discussion. One of the great frustrations of my research has been continually encountering the reality that, for all practical purposes, the disadvantageous circumstances of billions of people in the world make them worth less than the rest of us. Add cultural and religious biases relating to gender, caste, ethnicity—all of which have for centuries reinforced the devaluation of certain groups of people around the world—and there is little practical merit in a philosophical argument for the theoretical equality of all people, especially in a country such as Bangladesh were it is painfully obvious that people are not at all equal. The real-world devaluation of the poorest people in the world provides logic for their exploitation, which in turn perpetuates their devaluation. Iqbal was simply the mouthpiece of an ancient system of human stratification based on arbitrary allocations of resources, rights, and type (gender, caste, etc.), which somehow persist into the modern age. This randomness was at the heart of almost every case of slavery I encountered, and it is perhaps the chief quality that makes the system so challenging to eradicate.

The numerous cases of organ trafficking I documented in Bangladesh that were catalyzed by the seller's need to repay microcredit loans led me to speak with the two largest microcredit lenders in the country: Grameen

Bank and BRAC. Officials at both banks informed me that they were aware of the issues. They stated that they always endeavored to ensure that their prospective loan recipients did not have other loans outstanding. However, there was no centralized system for microloans in Bangladesh, so it was challenging to determine the debt load of a prospective recipient. I asked about local agents who pressure or intimidate debtors into repaying their debts, which can cause them to take desperate measures, but officials at Grameen and BRAC said that their agents never resorted to any sort of aggressive tactics. They argued instead that these practices were more an issue with smaller, unlicensed lenders who prey on the poor, although this is not consistent with many of the cases I documented.

After several months of research, it was clear to me that the organ recruiters in South Asia were the glue that made the system work. The process began and ended with them; they were the link between hospitals and patients on one end and vulnerable donors on the other. The recruiters were supposed to pay the donors out of the fees they received, but they typically pocketed most of the cash and paid the seller a fraction of what was promised. As near as I could piece together, if a patient in Dhaka paid a hospital between $75,000 and $100,000 for the transplant, roughly $7,500 to $10,000 of this went to the recruiter, and perhaps $400 to $500 to the organ seller, or 0.5 percent to 1 percent of the total amount paid by the patient for the transplant. The ratios in India were closer to 1 percent to 2 percent. Transplant surgeons did not occupy themselves with securing donors (nor should they), and wealthy recipients did not really wish to know the details of the donor beyond assurances that the organ was disease-free and a proper match. The organ brokers made the system work across India and Bangladesh, allowing everyone else to look the other way. These brokers were even more crucial to the system I uncovered in Nepal.

Preying on the Oppressed in Nepal

The first time I visited the National Kidney Center in Kathmandu several people were outside the main entry begging for kidneys, either for themselves or for loved ones. Their faces were drawn with fear and desperation. Inside the center, patients were hooked up for dialysis in a relatively clean and modern facility. The mood was somber, but some of the patients kept a cheerful demeanor and believed their prayers for a kidney would be answered.

"I believe God will help me," a forty-year-old father of three named Madhav told me. "If I pray and do penance every day, God will help me."

Supriya had been undergoing dialysis for four years, since the age of fifty, due to renal failure attributed to type 2 diabetes. Her husband passed away several years earlier. She had two daughters, both were a match for donation, but Supriya refused to accept organs from them. "They are just starting their lives and have to take care of their children," Supriya explained, "I will not sentence them to an early demise by taking a kidney from them. Maybe their husband or children will need it one day. I would give all my organs to keep my children alive, but I will never take from them."

Although she spoke in a calm and reflective voice, I could sense the pain of Supriya's predicament deeper within her. I could well imagine that her children were exceedingly desperate to save her life, just as desperate as she was to preserve theirs. It was not hard to see why, in similar situations, some may resort to less orthodox measures to obtain a kidney.

Staff at the center informed me that patients like Supriya can expect to wait ten to twelve years for a kidney transplant in Nepal. Similar to most countries, demand for kidneys far outstrips supply. A nurse at the center named Rupa explained, "Because Nepal has fewer transplant physicians per patient population than other countries, our patients must wait longer for their transplant procedures and many cannot survive this long." Rupa told me that many patients who can afford to do so travel to India where they can secure a transplant more quickly. I was sure that in these cases the swiftness of the procedure was facilitated by duping peasant donors such as Debjeet. However, Nepalese patients like Madhav and Supriya cannot afford this option, so they wait . . . and pray.

Insufficient organ supply and a lower per capita level of transplant physicians are among the primary factors that create a flourishing black market for organs in Nepal. A sophisticated network of organ brokers has developed to recruit donors from the country's poorest areas for donation in hospitals in Kathmandu, as well as across the border in India. I spoke with staff at the Human Organ Transplant Center and the Grande International Hospital in Kathmandu, both of which had reasonable, albeit easily circumvented, checks in place to ensure organs had not been purchased or coerced from vulnerable peasants. The transplant teams seemed understandably focused on availing of any healthy organ that was donated to save their ailing patients. Some of the most disheartening cases I documented involved donors from the Makwanpur district of Nepal.

Makwanpur is a poor, rural district southwest of Kathmandu. Research in this area is arduous, as roads can only take one so far. I traveled by foot to get from one village to the next, usually several hours or a full day's hike up one side of a mountain and down the other. During the monsoon season, flash floods and rockslides can cut off travel for days. The region is isolated and poor, but given its proximity to the capital (as the crow flies), it is heavily sourced by sex traffickers, labor traffickers, and organ traffickers. The recruiters who travel to Makwanpur meet with villagers and promise more money for their organs than they can earn in several years. The villagers I met in Makwanpur were especially ignorant of what it meant to donate a kidney, and it was clear that the recruiters fully exploited this ignorance.

Raj, a weary and listless man, invited me into his small wooden hut and explained, "The recruiter told me my kidney would grow back." Raj showed me a 10-inch scar on his abdomen. "He lied to me. Nothing grew back. I am sick all the time. My family is in a very bad condition because I cannot work."

Vishal, from the same village, said, "They kept saying 'kidney,' 'kidney,' I had no idea what this was. I thought they would take some flesh from my stomach. If I had known what they were doing, I would not have agreed."

Vishal and Raj were both paid about 20 percent of what they were promised (~$450 each). Neither received any postoperative care after their kidneys were removed, and they were both sent back to their villages within two days of their operations. The harvesting of their organs, however, did not take place in Nepal. Both men were trafficked to India to have their organs harvested for transplant into Indian patients. I knew quite well how sex and labor trafficking from Nepal to India worked, but I was curious to learn how Nepali men were brought to hospitals in India and had organs removed and transplanted into Indian recipients without anyone raising concerns. Out of twenty cases of organ trafficking (all males) I documented in Makwanpur district, thirteen had gone to India and seven to Kathmandu. I followed the trail of these thirteen men to find out how the system worked.

One of the pitches used by the Nepali organ traffickers is that the donors will receive better medical care in India after their kidneys are removed than they would in Nepal. They are told the procedures will use the latest technology, that many of the surgeons have been trained abroad, and that they will be well taken care of at the hospital until they are strong enough to return home. Most of the Nepali donors are taken by bus across the border to Kolkata for the transplants. A smaller number are taken to Delhi. I did not document any victims who were taken to other cities, but I am sure they exist. Prior to the journey, the traffickers arrange a "No Objection Certificate" through the Nepali embassy in New Delhi. This certificate states that the Nepali donor is a relative of the recipient in India and has made the altruistic choice to donate an organ, without duress or payment. The certificate is provided to the hospital in India where the transplant will take place. Policy requires that a picture of the donor be included with the certificate, but photos are often not included. Either way, the procedures continue. Once at the hospital, the Nepali donor presents himself as a relative of the recipient. In none of the cases that I documented did the donor actually meet his supposed relative. A victim named Gopal told me what happened when he arrived at the hospital in India:

> *The night before the procedure I was given new clothes and taken for a very nice meal. There was so much food I wish I could take some to my family. I remember I thought that with the money they will pay me we can eat like this for the rest of our lives. The next morning I went for the procedure. The man who brought me from Nepal was named Hitesh. He spoke to the doctors in Hindi, so I did not understand them. They told me I would go to sleep, and when I woke up the procedure would be finished. After the procedure, I was in too much pain. Hitesh was gone. He left 18,000 rupees [~$360] for me, not 100,000 rupees [~$2,000] that he promised. The hospital discharged me that same day and told me where I could find a bus to take me home. I was very confused. I thought, what has God done to me? I had to urinate constantly, so it was impossible for me to sit in the bus for long periods. It took me four days to return home. I confronted Hitesh when he came back to my village, but he told me the hospital charged fees and that is why I received less money. Now I am so*

ashamed. I tell others not to give their kidneys, but people are so poor they will do anything.

When I followed up with hospitals in India about the Nepali cases I documented, the transplant units informed me that they relied on the Nepali embassy in New Delhi to verify that the donor is a relative of the recipient and is making an informed and altruistic choice. I asked the hospitals why they did not bother to have the supposed relatives meet each other prior to the procedures, just to be sure they were actually relatives. I was told that this can lead to stress, and it is better to keep the donor and recipient apart. I tried to speak with officials in the Nepali embassy in New Delhi, but I was brushed off. I also tried to speak with personnel at the Organ Retrieval Banking Organisation (ORBO) in India, but they too were not terribly sympathetic to my inquiries. I received an official statement that read:

> We are aware of the shortage of organs for transplant in India and are actively trying to address the same. The Indian Health Ministry has recently implemented a new systematic allocation system of cadaver organs to counter abuses. Allocation of cadaver organs shall be based on a city waiting list, followed by the state, followed by other states through a Regional Organ and Tissue Transplant Organization. We are taking additional steps to set parameters for kidney allocation across India and rule out the illegal trade involving organs.

Beyond this technocratic jargon, no one in India or Nepal was willing to answer my questions. Hospitals, embassies, and regulatory bodies all pointed their fingers at each other as being responsible for properly vetting each donor. They also seemed to have the impression that the exploitative scenarios I described were uncommon; hence, there is no pressing need to address them. After several years of research, it was clear to me that far more must be done across South Asia to screen supposedly altruistic donors more effectively, be they Indians or Nepalis or Bangladeshis, to ensure that they are not being exploited for their body parts. Once they are carved up and sent packing, their fates are sealed.

As Gopal from Makwanpur district told me, "After they took my kidney, my heart became too heavy to bear. I wish they had taken it instead."

Summary of Organ Trafficking Cases
Documented in South Asia

Although I cannot provide precise estimates and prevalence rates, I am confident that there are thousands of victims of organ trafficking in South Asia each year. Many are trafficked for organ removal inside national borders, and others are trafficked across borders (primarily to India). Patients also cross borders in significant numbers, seeking the quickest and most reliable possible transplant rather than abiding by the excruciatingly long waitlists that often extend well past their ability to survive. The poor also are desperate to survive, and the meager income they receive can be the difference between life and death for their families, at least in the short run. Enter the traffickers, who prey on the desperations of both parties and bridge the transaction between them. Because patients are being saved and the harms against the donors are pitched to be minimal, hospitals and regulators look the other way. In cases of organ trafficking, victims can do little to nothing to seek redress. Most are weak, unwell, and stigmatized; they are simply biding their time until death.

The following data summarizes some of the key metrics from the organ trafficking cases in South Asia that I documented:

- 104 cases of organ trafficking: 41 in India, 33 in Nepal, 30 in Bangladesh
- 91 cases of male victims; 13 cases of female victims
- 100 percent of victims belonged to low-caste or minority ethnic communities
- 63 percent of cases involved sale of a kidney to discharge a debt
- 42 percent of cases involved transnational trafficking
- $355: average sum received by victims
- 21 percent: average sum received as a percent of promised payment
- 1.18 days: average number of days after organ removal to discharge
- 24.5 years: average age of victim at time of organ removal

Beneath these numbers resides immense misery and the destruction of peasant families. The system of organ trafficking in South Asia thrives in the shadows of regulatory and enforcement loopholes at the grave expense of the poorest and most downtrodden people of the region. However, this kind of predatory viciousness is not found solely in poorer regions of the world. I found it thriving in the West as well, including in the United States, despite robust regulations meant to prevent any such abuses from taking place.

ORGAN TRAFFICKING AND THE UNITED STATES

Understanding the System: Cadavers and Live Donors

The United States has numerous laws and regulations relating to organ donation; nevertheless, human trafficking for organ removal is a serious and potentially growing problem in the country. I assumed it would be very challenging for anyone to introduce trafficked organs into the transplant system in the United States, but my investigation uncovered the loopholes traffickers are able to exploit.

As with all countries, there are two sources of organs for transplant in the United States: cadaver organs and living donors. Cadaver organs constitute roughly three-fourths of all transplant surgeries in the United States.[7] Harvesting and transporting cadaver organs for transplant is strictly governed by fifty-nine Organ Procurement Organizations (OPOs) spread across the country. Each OPO is required to be a member of the national Organ Procurement and Transplantation Network (OPTN), which was created by the National Organ Transplantation Act of 1984 and administers the national organ recipient waitlist. As of May 2017, approximately 120,000 Americans were waiting for an organ transplant, 97,000 of whom were waiting for a kidney.[8] When a patient in a hospital becomes brain dead and is a candidate for organ donation, the local OPO is contacted and goes to the hospital to make an assessment. They attempt to secure consent from the patient's family, but consent is typically secured in only half the cases.[9] If consent is received, the organs are tested for contagions and infections diseases. Once the organs are approved, all data are uploaded to a national computerized system called UNET, which is operated by the United Network for Organ Sharing (UNOS). A list of potential recipients, called a "closed sheet," is generated by an algorithm, and the organ is allocated first locally, then regionally, then nationally until a match is found.

This is akin to the new procedures described to me in the official statement I received from the ORBO in India. Data are sent to the recipient's physician for the first potential match, and if accepted, the OPO transports the organ to the recipient's hospital. Considerable coordination between donor and recipient hospitals is required. Hearts require the most coordination because the extraction and transplant must be performed by two teams in the same place, one right after the other. Lung, liver, and pancreas can last up to twelve hours outside the body; and if properly cared for, a kidney can last up to twenty hours, providing more flexibility between extraction and implantation. Because the OPO manages and monitors the entire process from donor to recipient, it is very difficult to introduce a trafficked organ into the cadaver organ system in the domestic United States. I conducted interviews at several hospitals, OPO offices, and with UNOS, and there was no reasonable way for a trafficked organ to enter the cadaver transplant system. At most, there could be one-off cases involving egregious levels of corruption either at an OPO office or by a transplant team.

Unlike cadaver organs, the living donor system opens a few loopholes through which trafficked organs can enter the system. The process of living organ donation in the United States is regulated by the Revised Uniform Anatomical Gift Act of 2006 (the original act was passed in 1968). The law outlines the mechanisms through which individuals can altruistically donate their organs and the processes hospitals should undertake to ensure the donation is truly altruistic. The process can be manipulated, however, and I documented several cases in which the "living donor" turned out to be an exploited migrant across the border in Mexico.

The process of altruistic organ donation in the United States is fairly straightforward. First, if an individual indicates that he or she would like to make an altruistic donation of an organ (usually a kidney) to another person, the person goes through a rigorous intake process at the recipient's hospital to ensure that the individual is making a fully informed decision, is not being paid, and is not under any form of duress. Duress can be particularly tricky when it comes to family members donating to each other. Would a child or a spouse donating to a family member out of love not also possibly be doing so out of a sense of obligation or pressure? As with sex trafficking, the line between "willing" and "coerced" can become quite gray. To minimize these scenarios, the altruistic donor is assigned a separate screening team from that of the recipient. This team is headed by an intake coordinator who is charged with ensuring that family members are not making the donation unwillingly. However, it is rare for a hospital to turn down an altruistic donor from within the family. Assuming the donor passes the intake process (as most do), they are tested to see if they are tissue and blood type matches for the recipient, followed by independent counseling leading up to the procedure. Most hospitals in the United States follow both the donor and recipient with regular medical checkups for at least two years to ensure optimal health after their respective procedures.

Despite their best efforts, the transplant units at several hospitals in Boston, Los Angeles, New York, Chicago, San Diego, Dallas, San Antonio, and Houston acknowledged that it is possible for a donor to pass the intake scrutiny and still be offering an organ out of duress or because of a financial payment. Websites such as ineedakidneynow.org and matchingdonors .com and Facebook pages such as Facebook.com/findakidneycentral create marketplaces for donors and recipients to transact with each other. These and dozens of other online marketplaces have sprouted up in recent years, and many of the sites specifically offer tips on how to pass the intake process at hospitals. These cases typically do not involve organ trafficking but rather illicit markets in organ selling. However, another category of living donor case is more likely to involve trafficked organs—those in which the living donor is (allegedly) a relative or dear friend living across the border in Mexico. This is the most common scenario used to introduce trafficked organs into transplant hospitals in the United States, especially in Texas, Arizona, and California, all of which are within reach for transporting a kidney via vehicle in the viability time frame.

On the Trail of Trafficked Organs

In my efforts to investigate organ trafficking in the United States, I followed two leads to identify hospitals that might be using trafficked organs from Mexico: (1) hospitals that consistently show a higher than 40 percent proportion of living donor transplants (25 percent or less is the norm) and (2) hospitals with disproportionate insurance billing for codes CPT 50547 and 50320, indicating that a higher number of transplants were performed than the number of organs they could possibly access. I followed these threads of investigation and found several hospitals in South Texas and a few in the San Diego area that appeared suspicious. I visited each of them in person.

The first thing I noticed at most of these hospitals was that organ brokers were operating outside the dialysis units. The brokers were well-dressed and respectfully solicited patients who were leaving after their dialysis sessions with offers that they could arrange a transplant in a short time frame. Most of the solicitations fell on deaf ears. I had detailed discussions with the nurses at several transplant units in hospitals across Texas and in San Diego. Only one transplant team, at the largest transplant unit in South Texas in McAllen, just a few miles from the U.S.-Mexico border, was unwilling to speak with me.

The nurses and coordinators with whom I spoke at the hospitals in Texas and San Diego were all well aware that there were organ brokers outside their dialysis units who promised they could arrange transplants within a few weeks. "Those brokers work with surgeons in private clinics on either side of the border," one nurse at Houston Methodist Hospital explained to me.

I asked about the issue of fake altruistic donors who are either under coercion or are being paid, and each unit told me they screened heavily against this, but they also said that other hospitals looked the other way. "They want to save lives," one nurse at the Christus Transplant Institute in San Antonio told me. "So as long as they have someone who says they want to donate, they proceed." Another nurse told me, "Just do a Google search for 'I need a kidney'; you will see a ton of sites that promise transplants for the right price. Most of those people go across the border, but some of them have the procedures in the United States. I'm pretty sure you would find organ trafficking with those cases."

One scenario described to me repeatedly in Texas and California was an alleged family member who lived across the border in Mexico and was said not to have immigration papers. This alleged family member would indicate that he wished to donate to the recipient at the U.S. hospital. In these cases, the U.S. hospital relies on a hospital in Mexico to perform the necessary testing, screening, and matching, and to send a letter attesting that the donor is not being paid or under duress. Once these formalities are accomplished, the organ is driven across the border for implantation. The system is very similar to the "No Objection Certificate" provided by the Nepali Embassy in New Delhi that attests that the Nepalese migrant is a willing donor or relative of the recipient. Unlike in India and Nepal (which share an open border), in the United States and Mexico the migrant does not cross the border because he claims not to have valid immigration papers that would allow him to do so. Without a border crossing, it is impossible for the intake team at a U.S. hospital to determine if something is amiss. Several transplant nurses told me candidly that they had no idea where the organs really came from in these situations and that they could possibly be cases of organ trafficking. As long as the tissue and communicable disease testing is performed at reputable hospitals across the border and the results are acceptable, they proceed. Assuming that many or most of these cases could involve organs that are fraudulently or coercively harvested, I wanted to understand exactly where the organs were coming from.

To probe the circumstances behind the alleged cross-border altruistic donations, I conducted interviews at migrant shelters in the border towns of Matamoros, Reynosa, Nuevo Laredo, Mexicali, Tecate, and Tijuana, as well as at the corresponding border towns on the U.S. side. In several shelters, I found individuals who had suffered fraudulent organ extractions and lived to tell about it. All of these Mexican border towns also have extensive medical, dental, and pharmacological clinics for Americans who prefer to cross the border for cheaper procedures and prescription drugs. The welcome centers in these cities provide maps with listings and locations of all the available medical facilities. There are also rumored to be off-book medical clinics that offer quick, but expensive, organ transplants. I was not able to track any of these down, primarily due to limits on the amount of time I could spend in Mexican border cities due to security issues.

Arranging for a security team was compulsory due to the risks of abduction by drug cartels. The Gulf cartel controls the border in the South Texas region; the Zetas own Central Mexico and portions of the Texas border; La Familia controls the border between Guatemala and Mexico; and the Sinaloa cartel owns territory between Baja California and California. The Gulf, Zetas, and Sinaloa cartels were of primary concern to me because I was conducting research in their territories. Each cartel operates sophisticated drug, human, and organ trafficking networks, and abduction of high-value targets for ransom is a key component of their business models. The brutality of these cartels needs little discussion; they skin people alive, behead them, dismember and scatter the body parts of politicians and informants across city streets, and dissolve bodies in acid. No one is off limits, least of all investigators poking around in cartel business. Because of the high level of risk, the only security teams willing to cross the border with me were private military contractors, typically veterans of the U.S. military involvements in Iraq and Afghanistan. Their main source of income following their tours of duty was to provide security for U.S. businessmen who cross the border for meetings or to inspect manufacturing facilities. The price for this kind of security is steep, but I was able to arrange a "human rights" discount with each of the teams that assisted me.

Each team had its particular operational style, but the basics were similar. Defensive tactics were of paramount importance because it is illegal to take firearms into Mexico. If we were arrested for having done so, we would probably spend the rest of our lives in a Mexican prison. Each team consisted of a primary vehicle (PV) and a chase vehicle (CV). The PV carried the executive protector (EP) and me. The chase vehicle consisted of two additional security personnel. The PV was typically a jeep, and the CV was usually a sedan. Each vehicle carried a first aid kit, trauma bag, and IV kit. The security teams developed specific driving tactics to avoid being boxed in or disabled. If the PV suffered an attack, the role of the EP was to get me to the CV for an immediate retreat across the border. I met with my security team to go over the tactical plan for the day each morning that we intended to cross the border. The latest cartel movements were reviewed, and if the team received intelligence that there was going to be too much attention near the border, that day of research was called off.

I made a total of nine forays across the border for interviews in shelters with my security teams in Texas and California. Three times we called off the trips the morning of departure due to security concerns. I was treated with the utmost respect by my teams, and I developed deep admiration for their professionalism and courage. At no point were we in serious danger (as far as I could tell), although on two occasions we had to return to the United States earlier than planned to avoid cartel movements. The security teams taught me how to spot the cartel *halcons* (hawks) just across the border. They were usually young males operating a taco stand, or just circling around on their bicycles looking for high-value targets for abduction. They used handheld radios to communicate through a private system of thousands of antennas and repeaters across Mexico to avoid tapping by the government on a cellular network. I was the only noncorporate client my teams had protected, so they were intrigued by my research. The days ended with a few drinks and dinner, during which I described the work I had been doing around the world, the kinds of tragedies I had documented, and some of the slaves I had met. The security teams had harrowing stories to share about their experiences in Iraq and but the tales that most astounded me related to the cartels. The EP with whom I most bonded, Rodriguez, told me "What you see in the media is just a fraction of what really happens down here." "This place is worse than Iraq."

The stories my security teams shared about cartel violence did not help calm my nerves when it was time to cross the border. With each foray, I felt that I was stepping into a highly unpredictable, hyperviolent world, which exceeded anything in my previous experience. Repetition eased my anxieties, but each trip was an excruciating experience, with senses heightened and an irrepressible feeling of dread. The first trip was one of the most stressful days of all my research, surpassed perhaps only by the anxiety I felt stepping into GT's lair in Edo State. Every minute that we were across the border, I was convinced we would be attacked. Every car that swerved near us felt like an attempt at abduction; every awkward glance was a possible assessment of me as a target; and everything I did not see and hear filled my imagination with scenarios of impending disaster. Why were that car's windows so tinted? Is that shifty fellow on his phone reporting me as a target? The steel nerves of my teams helped ease my stress when we crossed the border, and thanks to them I gathered invaluable information from the people I met in the border town migrant shelters.

At a shelter in Nuevo Laredo in 2011, a nineteen-year-old girl named Juanita told me a jarring story of migration and exploitation that began when she left her home in central Mexico:

> By the time I came to Nuevo Laredo I had already been raped several
> times. At the bus station in Nuevo Laredo the police arrested me. I did
> not understand the charges. After three nights in prison they sent me
> with a man named Alfredo. He was with the Zetas. They locked me
> in a house with other migrants. They told us if we wanted to cross the
> border we had to pay $600. No one had that money, but some people
> had relatives in the United States who sent money for them. The rest

of us had to work for the cartel. The women were raped by the guards
every night. I saw two people killed in that house for no reason. The
cartel sent me to Boys Town for prostitution. After a few weeks, they
sent a doctor to the house, and I thought he would give us medicine
because we were sick, but he did tests on us. After a few weeks they
took eight of the migrants to remove their kidneys. They were in a lot
of pain when they came back. One of them died. Thank God they did
not take my kidney. They made me take drugs across the border. I
could not believe I made it to America, then they forced me to come
back and bring drugs again. When we crossed, we were in groups of
three or four, that way if one group was caught the others got through.
My life was like this for more than a year. The cartel would not let
us go. One day there was a police raid. We were arrested. I cannot
explain what happened. After two weeks in prison they sent me to this
shelter. The cartel comes here to recruit the migrants, but I will never
go with them.

I heard numerous stories like Juanita's at the shelters I visited. Migrants
from across central Mexico and Central America survived the journey to
the U.S. border but were then raped, killed, exploited as drug mules, had
organs harvested, or worse. I met a few migrants whose organs were forcibly
removed, but most people I interviewed could only report that they saw this
happening to other migrants, as many of the unwilling donors did not survive. Several of the migrants from Guatemala also reported seeing or hearing about large numbers of bodies turning up along the Guatemala-Mexico
border with their organs removed. As many stories as I documented, and
as many people as I interviewed who had organs forcibly removed, it was
impossible for me to trace where these organs ended up. The cases were in
the past, and I discovered no leads to how or where the organs were used.
The organs might have been used in living donor transplants in Texas from
alleged altruistic donors in Mexico or for transplants in medical clinics in
Mexico for transplant tourists who traveled south for their procedures, or
they might have been sold to hospitals for medical testing. I realized I was
never going to be able to follow an actual trafficked organ from the point
of harvesting to the point of implantation, so the only remaining avenue
I could explore to try to piece together more of the network would be to

engage directly with an organ broker, such as those I saw operating outside the dialysis units of the hospitals I visited.

Meeting an Organ Broker

To go undercover as a prospective transplant patient and engage with an organ broker, I needed a credible cover story. For this, I turned to a few transplant surgeons who had been advising me throughout my organ trafficking research. They told me that I would need to indicate that I had just discovered that my kidneys were failing, but that I had not yet started dialysis. If I were to say I had already begun dialysis, the brokers could investigate to determine whether this was or was not the case. As a generally healthy young man, I could also explain to the brokers that I did not go for regular medical checkups and that the first time my problem was discovered was when I felt sick and went to the emergency room with nausea and vomiting, at which point I was told I had renal failure. I was also advised to pick a kidney disease that typically left most patients appearing to be otherwise healthy, such as focal segmental glomerulosclerosis (FSGS), the same kidney disease suffered by NBA players Alonzo Mourning and Sean Elliot. This disease would allow me to appear to function somewhat normally up to a few months before a transplant was required, and many FSGS patients attempt to secure a transplant before they have to begin dialysis, which also fit with my cover story. I was advised further that I would need to tell the brokers that I had no viable living donor, that my family members suffered high blood pressure and other ailments that disqualified them, and that I had the financial means to work with them if they could find me a kidney match. Luckily, my blood type is A-positive, which is the easiest to match. Finally, I was advised that the broker would ask for my glomurelar filtration rate (GFR), which is a measure of kidney function. A reading between 15 and 20 meant I could live without dialysis for a short period of time, so I was told to say that my reading was right around 20 and that the doctor was not able to tell me yet how fast my disease was progressing.

Armed with this information, I prepared to approach the organ brokers. Before doing so, I took some time to consider the moral legitimacy of what I was planning to do. People in my family had suffered terminal renal failure, and I knew all too well how debilitating the disease could be, including dialysis treatment and the daily anxiety of wondering how long one has to live. I felt revulsion at the prospect of pretending to be someone in this position, a feeling similar to times I feigned to be a customer in search of young girls to purchase during my sex trafficking research. But something about this was different. It cut right to the fundamental desire to live, to be forced to come to terms with the reality that your body had failed you, and the desperation to do whatever it took to survive. I spent some time reflecting on whether I was crossing lines that I would later regret, and whether I was justified in proceeding simply to conduct my research. In the end, I made the difficult decision to proceed.

As unpalatable as the research was going to be, I wanted to understand as much as possible about this grotesque trade in human body parts. I was told to be confident, to insist on being told from where my kidney was being sourced, the age of the donor, the full medical history, where the surgery would be conducted, and how I could be certain that the kidney being implanted was the one I asked for. "Be demanding," one transplant surgeon in Chicago advised me. "You are theoretically going to pay up to $200,000 to save your life. Act entitled. That's how someone in your shoes would behave."

During the course of my explorations as a prospective kidney transplant patient, I spoke to six organ brokers outside hospitals in South Texas and San Diego. Transplants were promised at "private clinics" on the U.S. side of the border or at hospitals in Monterrey or Tijuana. The furthest I pursued the process was with a broker in San Diego, Juan. He and I first exchanged emails, then spoke on the phone, then set a meeting in San Diego—all within three days. Juan wore a suit and tie to our meeting and spoke professionally. I kept to my story of a recent FSGS diagnosis and a GFR of around 20. Juan advised me that he could arrange a transplant in Tijuana with the same standard of care and sophistication as any hospital in the United States. He showed me glossy pamphlets with testimonials and said I could speak to previous patients. I told him I would prefer to have the procedure done in the United States, and he said he could arrange the same operation at a private clinic, but it would cost more. I asked him how much? "In Tijuana, the price is $200,000. In the United States we charge $300,000."

I asked Juan the important questions about the donor, matching, viral testing, and assurances that I would be getting the exact organ I purchased.

Juan gave me all the right answers. He said that the organ transplant system was "broken" and that his network was trying to save lives. I told Juan I wanted to see the clinic before the transplant, but he said this was not possible.

"Why not?" I asked.

"That's the policy."

"I'm putting my life in your hands. I need to see the clinic, and I want to speak with the donor."

These were nonstarters for Juan (and every other organ broker I spoke to).

"Then what's the next step?" I asked.

"You wire half the funds into an escrow account. Once we know the funds are clear, we will proceed with your match. If anything goes wrong, you may withdraw the funds at any time up to the surgery. The day before the procedure, you pay the second half, and we proceed with the transplant."

"What about after care?"

"The fee includes two years of postoperative care."

"Does the donor receive postoperative care as well?"

"Of course."

"And there is no way I can speak to him or meet him?"

"I'm sorry, no."

I had to decide how much further I was going to push down this path. Obviously, I was not going to put $150,000 into an escrow account just to see how far my research would go, and it was clear that Juan was not going to let me meet my supposed donor or visit the clinic or even meet the doctors until the last minute.

I told Juan that I had heard stories that some of the organs used in clinics are taken from migrants under false pretenses. I asked him how I could be sure this would not be the case with my surgery. "You are paying money so that you don't have to worry about these things," Juan replied. "I promise the donor will be paid fully. His life will be better. So will yours." In those few sentences, Juan encapsulated the essence of the contemporary organ trafficking phenomenon. Those who can afford to do so pay money to save their lives, *and* so they do not have to worry about the (human) costs associated with the transaction.

I was unable to proceed any further with my research into organ trafficking in the United States and Mexico. In total, I documented seventeen migrants whose kidneys had been forcibly or fraudulently removed, and I heard stories of scores of other migrants to whom the same had happened but who did not survive. I identified the loopholes in the altruistic donation regime that were evidently being used to introduce trafficked organs into the system, and I went as far as I could with an organ broker to explore how an actual case worked. I was unable to trace the networks from the point of organ harvesting to the point of transplantation in any particular case. Limited resources were one constraint, but untenable levels of risk presented a greater obstacle.

As I found in South Asia, vulnerable people in the Americas are being carved up for parts so that the wealthy can survive. As long as the severe market imbalances between supply and demand in transplant organs persist, the organ trafficking market is likely to thrive. Therefore, one must ask, "Are there any policies that might help rebalance the system and abrogate some of the pressures that lead to these exploitative black markets?"

CLEAR POLICIES, UNCLEAR RESULTS

The severe market imbalances between the supply and demand for transplant organs that give rise to illicit organ sales and human trafficking for organ removal have received the clearest policy response of any facet of human trafficking. Only two countries in the world—Iran and Singapore— have responded to these market imbalances by legalizing the sale of kidneys. No other countries sanction organ sales, and numerous international conventions and policy instruments staunchly advocate against legalized organ sales being a valid response to the crisis. The results of this near-unanimous policy approach do not, however, appear to have helped remedy the imbalances that motivate black markets in organs and organ trafficking.

The "Guiding Principles on Human Cell, Tissue and Organ Transplantation" was issued by the World Health Organization (WHO) in 1991, and it includes nine principles intended to prevent abuses in the organ transplant system that can lead to illicit organ markets and organ trafficking.[10] Article 3 of the Palermo Protocol includes organ removal as one of the forms of exploitation captured by the definition of human trafficking. Article 3 of the United Nations Optional Protocol on the Sale of Children,

Child Prostitution and Child Pornography was added in 2000 to the UN Convention on the Rights of the Child and states that the sale of children for the purpose of transferring their organs for profit should be a criminal offense. In 2000, the World Medical Association issued a statement that financial incentives for organ donation should in all cases be prohibited.[11] Article 22 of the European Convention on Human Rights and Biomedicine, ratified in 2002, prohibits organ and tissue trafficking, and Article 21 of the convention prohibits financial gain from the selling of organs. Organ trafficking was most directly addressed by the Declaration of Istanbul on Organ Trafficking and Transplant Tourism in 2009,[12] which outlined four principles to help address the supply–demand imbalances that lead to organ trafficking, including: (1) maximizing the use of deceased donor organs, (2) encouraging countries with established deceased or living donor programs to share their knowledge with countries that lack these programs, (3) protecting vulnerable populations from abusive acts, and (4) ensuring the equitable allocation of donor organs based on sound ethical principles. Article 6 of the declaration also specifically states that "organ trafficking and transplant tourism violate the principles of equity, justice and respect for human dignity and should be prohibited." Despite these and other conventions and guidelines, illicit organ sales and organ trafficking remain serious issues around the world.

As a result of the deplorable levels of exploitation and abuse in many organ transplant markets, some scholars have argued that a regulated system of organ sales would help eliminate exploitative practices, akin to those who call for legalizing and regulating prostitution as a way to eliminate abuses.[13] These scholars typically argue that bringing organ sales out into the open with careful monitoring and strict regulation will allow sellers to benefit financially without being exploited. Monitoring and regulation also will help ensure that poor sellers of organs receive adequate postoperative care. Proponents of regulation further argue that a transparent system that is carefully monitored to prevent deception and coercion will remove pernicious brokers and traffickers from the equation and ensure that the donors are not exploited. In the end, financial incentives, strict monitoring, and proper postoperative care for sellers will increase supply and help balance the transplant market. Not to be overlooked, a more balanced system will save more lives.

On the other side of the debate, scholars argue that regulation will not work because it is impossible to achieve adequate levels of monitoring and postoperative care, primarily due to funding deficiencies and corruption.[14] Black markets will inevitably arise to exploit a legalized organ sale system. The sellers will disproportionately be poor and vulnerable, and as a consequence they will inevitably suffer exploitation, will not be paid the promised sums, and will have little access to justice to enforce their rights. In addition to negative health results, they will suffer stigmatization and early demise that perpetuate cycles of poverty and exploitation. Finally, placing a market value on the body parts of the poor dehumanizes them and will reinforce the legitimacy of society's monetization of the labor, bodies, services, and body parts of the downtrodden. One study in India has confirmed many of these statements; researchers found that 86 percent of organ sellers suffered a decline in health, 36 percent suffered a decrease in income, and 79 percent stated they would not recommend selling a kidney to others because of the ill effects they suffered.[15]

What about Iran and Singapore? Do the regulated systems of organ sales in these countries work? Research in Singapore is limited because the country only legalized organ sales in 2008. In Iran, organ sales have been legal since 1988. Two studies in Iran found that 85 percent of sellers said they would not sell their kidney if they could go back and reconsider the decision, primarily due to ill health and lack of postoperative care.[16] The studies also found that 80 percent of donors suffered negative health effects after the donation and that 76 percent strongly discouraged others from selling.[17] With more resources and better enforcement, Iran or other countries that create legal systems of organ sales might be able to achieve better results, but the available evidence does not appear promising.

The research I have conducted in almost every aspect of slavery leads me to conclude that systems that legalize and attempt to regulate markets that involve the purchase of the bodies or body parts of the poor will inevitably lead to exploitation and misery for the sellers. Whatever is being sold—be it commercial sex, cheap labor, or body parts—the poor are inexorably reduced to expendable and dispensable resources for the wealthy. Theoretical enforcement of protective regulations and punishment of abuses consistently fail because of one glaring truth—we don't really care about the poor as much as we care about ourselves. They are "those" people from "those" communities, and that makes them disposable.

At the end of the first chapter, I offered ten initiatives that I feel provide the optimum opportunity to eradicate slavery. Most of these initiatives would also address the issues that underpin the organ trafficking market. Specific supply–demand dynamics promote organ trafficking, however, and powerful forces feed into these black markets, such as profit (for traffickers) and the will to live (for sellers via income, and for buyers via an organ). Policy responses customized to organ trafficking issues must accompany the ten broader initiatives I outlined in the first chapter. Some of these policies could include:

1.   An organ draft—all cadavers can be harvested for organs unless there is a specific religious objection by the family of the deceased. This is an aggressive policy proposal, but it would help alleviate some of the supply–demand imbalances by increasing the available supply of cadaver organs.

2.   Presumed consent—all individuals at death are donors unless they actively state otherwise before perishing. This policy is similar to the organ draft but provides individuals with an opportunity to opt out of being a candidate for organ donation at death, whether for religious or other reasons. This policy also increases the supply of available cadaver organs.

3.   Limited compensation—the deceased's family members are given a small financial benefit for allowing organs to be used for transplantation. This may help alleviate some of the financial strain on the deceased's family and motivate an increase in cadaver organ supply. The exact amount of the financial benefit would need to be determined so that it does not amount to the same as purchasing a human organ.

4.   Futures markets—provide a small financial benefit today to an individual who agrees to make his or her organs available at death. Again, the compensation would need to be thought through so that it does not amount to the same as purchasing an organ, but a modest financial benefit could help increase cadaver organ supply.

These and similar policies might help attenuate the supply–demand imbalances in the transplant organ system, but they will probably not succeed in balancing the market fully. The most promising effort to do so may come from 3-D printing technology. Forecasts are that 3-D printing technology should be able to produce human organs for transplantation by around

2030,[18] and if so, this might very well mean the end of black markets in organ trade or organ trafficking, assuming it is financially feasible for, and accessible to, all patients.

For the time being, the market imbalances that lead to organ trafficking continue to widen. Organized crime groups are heavily involved in organ trafficking from Asia to the Americas, primarily because of the substantial profits they are able to generate from the illicit harvesting and sale of body parts. These groups have developed highly organized systems that rely heavily on brokers to facilitate the transactions between sellers and buyers. Disrupting the operations of these brokers is one important step to take to combat organ trafficking markets, but it will not solve the broader problem. Data on organ trafficking is difficult to come by, in no small part because of the clandestine nature of the offense and the heightened perils associated with conducting research in this area. Nevertheless, research must be done, and new preventions and interventions must be attempted, or the poor, migrant, indebted, disenfranchised populations of the world will continue to be pressured, duped, and harvested for their organs, with just the shell of a person remaining.

BORDERS AND BLOOD

Borders play an important role in many aspects of slavery, and they are particularly enmeshed with the phenomenon of organ trafficking. Patients cross borders as transplant tourists in search of quick procedures, sellers are trafficked across borders to have organs removed for wealthy recipients, and migrants make their way to the borders of more affluent countries in search of a better life, only to be chewed up by cartels for sex, labor, and organs. In every case, the borders involved in organ trafficking networks are painted with blood, including the southern border of the United States.

On what turned out to be the last day of my research along the Texas-Mexico border, Rodriguez told me at our morning briefing that I had garnered the interest of at least one cartel. He advised that it would be too risky for me to cross the border. I called off our research that day, and I never conducted additional research along the border in that area. It was not, however, a completely unproductive day. Rodriguez told me that he had been working on a lead and managed to track down a surgeon who had conducted four transplants for high-ranking cartel members. The doctor was not willing to meet, but he had agreed to speak on the phone.

I rang the number the doctor gave Rodriguez several times, and he finally answered in the afternoon. I asked him if he was willing to answer a few questions. He sounded jittery but agreed. The doctor confirmed that in the last three years he had performed four transplants for high-ranking cartel members at two different clinics. He was not willing to disclose the locations of the clinics, or even the cities in which they were located. He had a team of physicians and nurses who assisted him with the harvesting and transplanting procedures.

"Where did the organs come from?" I asked.

"Migrants," he answered.

"All four?"

"*Sí.*"

"Did the migrants offer the kidneys willingly?"

"I am sure."

"Were they paid?"

"I don't know."

"Do you know where they are from?"

"Mexico."

"Are they still alive?"

No answer.

"Were they alive when you took the organs from them?"

No answer.

"Okay, maybe you can tell my why you did these surgeries for the cartel members?"

"I have no choice."

"Why not?"

"When they ask, you do it."

"Did the migrants have a choice, or were they pressured as well?"

"This is all I can tell you. Good luck."

The surgeon hung up. This was the only conversation I had with a physician who appears to have conducted transplants with trafficked organs from migrants. Though I could not confirm the details, I was reasonably certain the migrants whose organs were removed had not offered them willingly and were probably no longer alive. I wondered why the surgeon was open to speaking with me if he really was not going to answer any of my questions, but I appreciated that I probably pushed too hard too quickly. Rodriguez told me that he had leads on where the surgeon operated, but he warned me it was deep across the border. I was not willing to put myself or Rodriguez's team at risk, and I was left frustrated that I was not going to be able to gather more research across this part of the border.

Before I left South Texas, I spent the day driving around the area, taking it all in one last time—the white sun, the feverish breeze, the restless desert dust that tastes bitter in the mouth. About an hour northwest of Laredo along Mines Road, I found a dirt path that led to the Rio Grande. I parked my car and went for a walk. There was no border fence—just the United States on one side of the river, and maybe a hundred feet across, Mexico. It was a searing, inhospitable day, so I veered toward the sparse shade offered by scattered trees. Dry brush crunched under my feet. I came to an area of tree cover and took a seat. The river was still, and the air was stagnant. I thought about my conversation with the surgeon and wondered how many more there were like him, working not just for cartels but at major hospitals across the border for transplant tourists. The disappeared migrants used in these surgeries were as silent as the border river in front of me, the river they were so desperate to cross. I could not comprehend the absurdity that this narrow ribbon of water separated such extremes—hope from despair, dreams from nightmares, life from death.

I wandered further down the river, listening to the crunch under my feet, to the anemic whisper of the breeze. After a few minutes, I came across a tattered sneaker. I looked around, and about twenty feet away, I found its pair, under some bushes. Two feet from the second shoe, I saw a torn pair of trousers, a shirt, a broken pair of glasses, and a large area of dried blood. There was no telling how long the clothes and blood had been there. All borders have blood on their hands, but the U.S.-Mexico border may have the most blood of all. Had I continued walking, it would not have been long before I came upon another remnant of the border's butchery. But I was too tired and too disheartened that day to forge forward in search of more remnants of the border's body count.

That night, I ate fish tacos with Rodriguez and his crew. We talked about sports and cars. It was a distraction for all of us from the darkness we kept buried behind our public faces—theirs born of the blood of war; mine of the blood of slaves.

CHAPTER 5

TECHNOLOGY AND HUMAN TRAFFICKING

Friend and Foe

I have found that, to make a contented slave, it is necessary
to make a thoughtless one. It is necessary to darken
his moral and mental vision, and, as far as possible, to
annihilate the power of reason. He must be able to detect
no inconsistencies in slavery; he must be made to feel that
slavery is right; and he can be brought to that only when
he ceases to be a man.

—Frederick Douglass

AN EXPERIMENT

IN OCTOBER 2012, I placed an online advertisement on the website
Backpage.com that read as follows: "Asian and European girls, young and
ready to please you. Find exactly what you are looking for. Outcalls only.
310-XXX-XXXX." The listed phone number was linked to an unlocked
cell phone that could receive voice messages and texts. The purpose of the
placement was to sample the kinds of responses and the rates of response
the advertisement would receive. I placed the advertisement on three

TABLE 5.1 Responses to Backpage.com Experiment

	TEXTS	VOICE MESSAGES	TOTAL
Week 1	239	192	431
Week 2	206	190	396
Week 3	290	233	523

consecutive Friday afternoons (each advertisement lasted for one week at a cost of $12.00). Table 5.1 summarizes the responses I received.

There were more than 700 similar advertisements on Backpage.com just for the Los Angeles area during the times I posted my false advertisement, and I predicted that I would receive a few dozens texts and calls at most. Needless to say, I was quite surprised when I received several hundred responses each week. More surprisingly, roughly 78 percent of the responses took place within twenty-four hours of my posting the advertisement. These two factors demonstrated to me that there was a high degree of online activity in pursuit of commercial sex in and around the city of Los Angeles. It also demonstrated the power of the Internet as a tool to facilitate commercial sex transactions. Although there is no way to know just how many of the online sex advertisements on Backpage.com relate to sex trafficking victims in particular, it is indisputable that traffickers and pimps exploit the Internet to solicit men to purchase commercial sex of all kinds, including from the victims of forced prostitution. Many of these victims are children. It is highly uncommon to find an online advertisement that specifically indicates that a child is being sold for sex, but key words such as "girl," "young," and "tiny" are strong indicators to online sex consumers that a minor could be for sale.

The content of the responses I received ranged from short texts or voice messages asking for callbacks to more detailed messages expressing a desire for young girls of a particular ethnicity to be available in a specific part of town at a specific time, without holding back details on exactly what the customer expected the girl to perform. These messages were overwhelmingly distasteful and unpleasant, at least to me. I called back a random selection of the consumers who responded to the advertisements. Most conversations were relatively businesslike; others were vulgar. Although I had seen and heard more than my share of male degradation of women and children, it was demoralizing to hear the ways in which these men spoke about females. A palpable disrespect for the female gender pervaded the language of many of these men. Words such as "whore," "bitch," and "slut" were thrown around as common, acceptable ways to refer to women. The expectations the males expressed signified clearly that they perceived the entire process in a transactional and calculating fashion. I even received warnings that the woman would not be paid should she refuse to perform as expected, or appear different (older, different proportions or ethnicity, etc.) from what had been purchased. Many of the males promised to be repeat customers if they were satisfied with the transaction. Some asked for a discount on the first purchase and said they would refer friends if they were pleased. Two of the men with whom I spoke asked me if I accepted bitcoin.[1] I ended up making only half as many callbacks as I had intended because I simply could not stomach the conversations, and to be honest they were also quite repetitive.

When I designed this online experiment, I had intended to use a capture-recapture methodology to estimate the prevalence rate of males over the age of eighteen who were actively online looking to purchase commercial sex in the Los Angeles area. Unfortunately, I was not able to identify specific numbers to 54 percent of the texts and voice messages I received because either the caller ID was blocked or the messages were sent via Skype, which routes most calls through a handful of hub numbers in the region. In addition, the vast regional span of the responses I received made it difficult to calculate a reasonable estimate. In addition to the city of Los Angeles itself, I received responses from Long Beach, Orange County (Irvine, Newport Beach, Lake Forest), the Valley (Burbank, Thousand Oaks, Simi Valley), and even from as far away as Santa Barbara, Carlsbad, and Temecula. Nonetheless, the swiftness and sheer number of responses I received to a single advertisement (that did not even include photographs) persuaded me that even if I did not know the exact prevalence rate, the level of online "shopping" for commercial sex across southern California was far more than I had anticipated. I have no doubt that the same would be largely true in other major metropolitan areas across the United States and around the world.

THE INTERNET AND HUMAN TRAFFICKING

The Internet, social media, and mobile technologies have been used by traffickers to expand the sale of women for sex and forced prostitution and to expand recruitment for labor trafficking victims across the globe. Social media also plays a role in the organ trafficking sector. On the other side of the equation, these same technologies are being used by governments, NGOs, and technology companies to combat sex trafficking and labor trafficking, to prevent labor exploitation in global supply chains, and to prevent human trafficking in disaster and war-torn areas. Limited research has been done on the dual role of technology as both facilitator and prevention/intervention tool of the contemporary human trafficking phenomenon. I have focused my research on understanding the new and developing trends in technology application on both sides of the human trafficking process. Perhaps the most important insight that has emerged from my research is that technology is used by both traffickers and antitraffickers to manipulate one of the most important features relating to slavery—isolation. Human traffickers attempt to isolate their victims, which promotes their exploitation, by confiscating any connectivity tools they may posses, such as mobile phones or email access, and by preventing access to the Internet, landline phones, social networks, or assistance of any kind. This is true whether one is referring to landowners in South Asia who actively isolate debt bondage slaves to advance their exploitation or labor recruiters who confiscate migrants' connectivity tools to coerce them into forced labor at a construction site. Meanwhile, antitrafficking actors are trying to use these same connectivity tools to prevent human trafficking and provide vital connections to migrants, to rural and other vulnerable populations, and to shorten the duration of exploitation of a human trafficking victim.

This chapter explores the dual roles technology plays as both facilitator and preventer/intervener (friend and foe) in cases of sex trafficking and labor trafficking. Much more research needs to be done to maximize the utility of technology and social media tools as forces of empowerment, connection, and intervention against the crime of human trafficking. I hope some of the findings in this chapter will motivate these efforts.

Sex Trafficking

The primary appeal of the Internet for sex traffickers and sex consumers is anonymity. Selling and buying commercial sex can occur in a virtual fashion right up to the point of the physical transaction. If the purchase is of online photos or videos (recorded or streaming), the entire process remains anonymous. For the victim, anonymity comes hand in hand with isolation. Rather than soliciting on the street or in a brothel with physical visibility, the victim can be sold for sex in a virtual manner to consumers anywhere in the world. This isolation assists traffickers and pimps in maintaining control of victims and limiting their opportunities for escape.

My investigations into the intersection of technology and sex trafficking revealed three points of interest: (1) the use by traffickers of online advertisements of victims to solicit purchases of sex, (2) the use by traffickers of social networking sites to recruit victims, and (3) the use by law enforcement of online advertisements to initiate investigations, primarily for those who appear to be underage.

Online Advertisements

Online sex advertisements have exploded with the spread of the Internet. Countless websites around the world sell all forms of sexual content. Innumerable "John's Chat Rooms" provide feedback to male consumers of commercial sex on where and how women and children can be purchased safely. Men on these sites also provide reviews of sex clubs, brothels, and even individual women. The most abhorrent chat rooms are dedicated to pedophiles who give tips on how and where to have sex with children safely, or how to purchase child pornographic images without being traced. Men on these sites even provide reviews of children they have purchased. I assessed forty sites that sell sex on six continents and John's Chat Rooms in the United States. All of these websites and especially the chat rooms are unpleasant, offensive, and inspire a sense of despair for the state of humanity. Imagine, if you will, a dozen or so men bantering back and forth on a Saturday morning about the children they purchased the previous night—what they looked like, how they smelled, how they behaved, how they shared their "love" (such a corruption of the word defies comprehension) with them, and so on. It is difficult not to want to gather these miscreants in an actual room and let loose the dogs of hell. The content of chat rooms that referred to adult females was not much better. They tended to consist of higher levels of outright vulgarity and misogyny. There was no talk of "love" or any other perverted concepts of affection. Crude language and boorish statements about women passed as comedy. Men bragged, touted their rates of purchase, and extolled the virtues of buying sex from certain ethnicities or from specific women. Some men seemed to be in the chat rooms with the purpose of drumming up business for a particular establishment by describing in detail how the women will pleasure the men who buy them. Some men talked about women who were so "doped" that they could do almost anything they wanted to them. Others talked about women who cried or even resisted at the outset, which only seemed to arouse the men further. I wish I could post the statements of these men on highway billboards next to their faces, names, and addresses and let justice run its course.

It is incontrovertible that the Internet is used extensively to sell sex, photos, and videos of women and girls around the world; that it facilitates financial transactions between traffickers and consumers; that it provides anonymity for all parties; that it helps isolate victims of sex trafficking; and that it provides forums for consumers to communicate in a completely uncensored manner to promote the system of male sexual consumption of women and children.[2] Perhaps the most compelling facet of my research into the use of the Internet to facilitate the purchase of commercial sex has been the discovery of how opportunistic this facilitation can be. The Internet appears to be the first port of call for consumers in search of commercial sex during major sporting events, such as the World Cup, the Super Bowl, the Olympics, or the Commonwealth Games. These sporting events naturally bring large numbers of males from around the world into a concentrated area for a short period of time. Aside from sports, food, and beverages, sex is the primary service many of these men are after.

My first exposure to the impact a major sporting event can have on sex trafficking was with the 2010 Commonwealth Games in New Delhi. In *Bonded Labor* I described how local brothels on GB Road and in other areas of New Delhi were receiving upgrades, new AC units, and other embellishments in anticipation of the arrival of thousands of male tourists.[3] The women and children inside the brothels were receiving bovine steroid injections to fatten them up to better cater to Western tastes. Colleagues at local antitrafficking NGOs reported that they noticed a substantial increase in websites selling sex in New Delhi during the time of the Commonwealth Games, and scores of Indian men with small sex cards and flyers roamed outside the stadiums and tourist areas soliciting male customers.

Researchers have begun to focus on the extent to which major national and international sporting events increase sex trafficking and online advertising for commercial sex. Dr. Mark Latonero, at the University of Southern California, looked into these issues at Super Bowl XLV in Dallas in 2011. Prior to the February 6 event, then Texas Attorney General Greg Abbott described the Super Bowl as "one of the biggest human trafficking events in the United States."[4] Latonero's team selected the adult section of the Backpage.com site for Dallas and collected data on more than 5,500 sex ads to measure the frequency of unique posts for one week leading up to the Super Bowl. Their analysis revealed a sharp spike in the number of unique posts each day on February 4 and 5, leading up to the Super Bowl, including more than 300 posts specifically for escort services on Super Bowl Sunday.[5] Less than 100 such posts were seen one week earlier. The researchers analyzed data on the ages of the women and girls being advertised, and more than half the posts that included ages advertised girls between the ages of 18 and 21, with a spike toward younger ages during the Super Bowl.[6] No advertisement specifically offered minors for sale, but many included key words such as "girl" or "very young" or "tiny," or specified an age of eighteen years, which is usually a strong indicator that minors are being sold.

Using the Internet to sell commercial sex, either tied to sporting events or in general, has not been without debate. Indeed, many argue that doing so is a perfectly acceptable mode of conducting business and a protected form of free speech. In the early 2000s, the two primary sites in the United States that provided space for online advertisements for commercial sex were Craigslist.org and Backpage.com. In 2007, Craigslist was the first major website to receive significant criticism for facilitating prostitution via its "adult services" section in cities around the world. In an effort to pacify these concerns, Craigslist began charging a $5 credit card fee for adult advertisements and required a phone number to verify the identify of the individual posting the ad. These requirements were meant to assist police in tracking advertisements that might involve the actual sale of sex where such sales were against the law (as opposed to clubs, massage parlors, etc.).

In March 2009, Illinois Cook County Sheriff Thomas Dart filed a suit against Craigslist, stating that "missing children, runaways, abused women, and women trafficked in from foreign countries are routinely forced to have sex with strangers because they're being pimped on Craigslist."[7] Attorneys for Craigslist used what has now become a powerful defense in the United States, arguing that section 230 of the Communications Decency Act of 1996 protects the company from liability because it specifically states that Internet Service Providers (ISPs) and websites are not liable for content posted by third parties. To assign liability to the ISP would open floodgates of litigation that would cripple the Internet. For example, would YouTube be liable for content posted by one of its users (say, a clip from a feature film) that violates the copyright of the production company that owns the film? The court agreed and the case was dismissed. A firestorm of public pressure ensued, and in what became a triumph of social outrage, Craigslist closed the adult services section of its website in all U.S. cities in September 2010, followed by closure in all cities worldwide in December 2010.

This closure left Backpage.com and Eros.com as the primary websites for online sex advertisements. Unlike Craigslist, Backpage has remained resolute in its right to allow users to post ads for sex services. Backpage charges between $5 and $15 to post these ads and makes approximately $150 million per year from adult advertisements. Backpage further allows the use of bitcoin to make payments, which protects the identity of pimps and traffickers who make the postings. Backpage maintains its rights to facilitate these postings under section 230 of the Communications Decency Act of 1996. A case in the state of Massachusetts filed in 2014 put this defense to the test. *Doe v. Backpage.com* was filed on behalf of two minors who alleged that they were sold for sex through the website more than 1,900 times from the ages of fifteen to seventeen. In May 2015, the court held that Backpage is protected by the Communications Decency Act and could not be held liable for third-party postings. Cases filed around the same time in the states of Washington and Illinois met with the same result. On October 7, 2016, California authorities arrested Backpage CEO, Carl Ferrer, on felony pimping charges. In her suit against Ferrer, Kamala Harris, then Attorney General of California, described Backpage as an "online brothel." Once again citing protection under the Communications Decency Act, the judge dismissed the suit against Ferrer on November 16, 2016. Although the legal scholar in me appreciates the slippery slope argument of assigning liability to ISPs and the need to protect First Amendment rights, the human rights activist in me feels that tools that allow traffickers to exploit women and children in forced prostitution represent a particularly onerous and detestable kind of harm that society must protect against with as much rigor, if not more, than free speech freedoms.

Despite setbacks, activists and lawyers have continued applying pressure on Backpage. Ferrer and other Backpage founders were subpoenaed to testify in front of the Senate Committee on Homeland Security in early 2017. The day before the hearing, Backpage pulled down its adult section, citing an unlawful censorship campaign by the U.S. government. Most commercial sex advertisements on Backpage have since migrated to other sections of the website, such as dating and massage, and some activists have decried the campaign against Backpage, arguing that the online adult section actually helps law enforcement combat sex trafficking. As of May 2017 there is legislation pending in the U.S. Congress that would carve out online sex advertisements as being no longer protected by section 230 of the Communications Decency Act, potentially opening the door for more successful outcomes in litigation against Backpage and similar websites.

Social Media

Social media tools also have become powerful facilitators used by sex traffickers to recruit new victims and to solicit customers to purchase women and children for sex.[8] The traffickers hide in plain sight among the tens of millions of users on these websites, scouring the world from the comfort of their homes for new victims and customers. Melanie, a sex trafficking survivor I met in Seattle, explained how she was recruited on Facebook:

> *This guy Matt friended me. He had the coolest page. It said he was an agent for magazine shoots. We chatted for a while before I met him. He made me feel special, but he never came out and said he wanted me to be a model. He was just a cool guy, and I didn't know many cool guys. My foster parents had two kids of their own and two other foster*

kids. I didn't really fit in. I didn't like school either. I hardly went, you know. I met Matt, and he said he could make me a lot of money. He made it sound like it was so easy, like all you have to do is be lucky enough for someone like him to spot you. He said that's the only difference between the girls in magazines and me. I thought I would be rich and have this awesome life. I felt like I could be free of all the shit in my life. I was so wrong. Matt raped me. He and some guys locked me in a room and pimped me out. They made a ton of money off me. I didn't make a . . . dime. For a while they had a camera in there. People would watch—creeps. After a while, I just went with it. I got more liquor and pot that way. What else was I going to do?

Melanie was one of eighty-three sex trafficking victims I documented around the world who told me they were recruited through social media on Facebook or on numerous online dating websites. Matt's page on Facebook was long gone by the time I met Melanie. It is exceedingly challenging to intervene in this mode of recruitment because all of the initial contact takes place virtually, and the pages are often taken down after the trafficker has recruited a handful of victims. The traffickers then typically set up new pages, under new names, and search for more young girls who are vulnerable, isolated, in abusive families, or otherwise desperate to receive the kind of false attention and affection the traffickers give them. Most of the recruitment tactics are romantic in tone, and they work well. Europe, in particular, has seen a rapid growth in online recruitment of sex trafficking victims, especially from poorer eastern European nations.[9] A young girl named Katya from Moldova described to me how she was recruited through a local dating website (Friendscout24.it) based in Italy:

My family is poor, but not as poor as most people in my country. The situation for life in Moldova is not good. I wanted to go abroad. Most girls in Chisinau go to dating sites to find men in Italy or Germany or Dubai to fall in love with . . . or we look for jobs, but who wants to work if you can marry a rich man? I was chatting with men on Friendscout, and this one man from Italy named Antonio said he was a lawyer and he sent me photos of his home and his BMW. He said since he was a lawyer he could arrange my travel documents. He asked for my address and sent me gifts. He sent me jewelry and a dress. We talked on the phone, and he seemed like a nice man. I was so excited, but I tried not to be too trusting. When I felt safe, I agreed to meet him to see if we could be together. I was so nervous when I arrived in Milan that he will not look like the photos he sent, but he looked exactly like that. I remember seeing him and feeling so happy. That night my dreams were killed. Antonio took me to a club and left me there. They took my mobile phone. The men raped me and gave me drugs. They forced me to take clients for almost one year before the police arrested me. I explained what happened, and the police referred me to this shelter. They said they will investigate Antonio. I tried to find his profile, but it was gone. I called his number, but it did not work. I know he will trick other girls, and that makes me angry. Now I know better than to have dreams. Soon I will be back in Chisinau. I will be grateful if I can find a job and take care of myself. I don't want any man to take care of me.

Stories like Katya's have become increasingly common with the explosion of online dating sites and social media. She was hardly reckless and communicated directly with her supposed suitor for months before agreeing to meet him. However, traffickers are willing to invest a good deal of time to recruit girls through online avenues because—aside from a few gifts and a plane ticket—there is very little expense and risk to them. Raising awareness of these kinds of ruses may have some preventative impact, but it is challenging to thwart human trafficking cases of this manner. There are simply too many young people living in poorer countries with limited opportunities for employment and a burning desire for a better life who are susceptible to false overtures. In regions such as Europe where travel within the EU is open to all citizens, traffickers can recruit from poorer EU countries into richer ones with ease.

Katya's story also is noteworthy in that in many ways it was simply a higher-tech version of stories I had documented several years earlier in Nepal. In *Sex Trafficking*,[10] I describe how false marriage offers are a common recruitment tool for traffickers across South Asia. Vulnerable, disempowered women and girls in rural Nepal are particularly susceptible to marriage offers from wealthy Indians. There were few if any online dating sites when

I documented these cases, so handwritten letters and cell phone calls were the primary tools used to seduce the victims. Since that time, online dating sites in South Asia have spread rapidly. During research in 2010 and 2012, I documented eighteen cases of sex trafficking in South Asia in which online dating sites were used. One victim from Pune, named Dipali, was a teenager who finished secondary school but had not yet started university when she fell for the overtures of Karthik on the website Fropper.com. They went on one date together; on the second date, Karthik raped Dipali and locked her inside an apartment where she was sold for sex for three weeks before she managed to escape. Her captors showed her a mobile-based advertisement they posted of her to recruit customers using photos they took when they drugged her. The customers were mostly middle-class Indian men and university students.

Millions of South Asians in rural areas continue to lack Internet access, so traffickers still write letters and have phone conversations with their intended victims. Awareness campaigns run by NGOs have been somewhat effective at preventing young women from accepting these offers, but the ruses continue with success across much of Asia and the rest of the world, including lower-tech versions of what happened to Katya. The technology tools used by Antonio to seduce Katya are more advanced than letters and phone calls, but they also leave potential digital footprints that can be used by law enforcement to track down the traffickers.

Using Technology to Fight Back

The same technologies used to facilitate all aspects of the business of sex trafficking—from recruitment of victims to solicitation of customers to processing transactions—are being used to combat the business of sex trafficking. While efforts at technology-based interventions have developed more slowly than their criminal counterparts, innovative tools are being crafted that will have a significant impact on combating sex trafficking around the world.

Crowdsourcing, Crowdfunding, and Tagging

Although still spotty in application and reliability, crowdsourcing and tagging have become more prevalent in the past few years as tools to combat various human rights abuses, including sex trafficking.[11] Many technology companies and NGOs have developed crowdsourcing applications that enable users to submit text messages or other content related to potential cases of sex trafficking or human trafficking more broadly. For example, SMS (short message service) lines can be established that allow users to send short messages of potential instances of human trafficking to an NGO. The NGO can then vet the information and act on it if need be, share it with law enforcement, or both. Verifying crowdsourced content and having the capacity to sift through submissions remain challenges that NGOs and application designers are working through, but significant progress has been made in this area. Every year more human trafficking victims are being rescued as a result of crowdsourcing technology.

A related concept to crowdsourcing is crowdfunding. Crowdfunding platforms allow people from around the world to contribute financially to a single project or cause, including efforts to fight human trafficking. Two of the top crowdfunding websites focused on raising resources for projects that fight human trafficking are Endcrowd.org and 6degree.org. On these sites, individuals can make financial contributions to projects that help prevent human trafficking, liberate slaves, or support aftercare services that protect and empower survivors. Some simple initiatives that have had an impact through funding on these websites include the purchase of a van to take children to school in Cambodia so they are not vulnerable to abduction while walking to and from the classroom each day, a jewelry making business in India that helps provide income for sex trafficking survivors, and funds that help trafficked women and children safely return to their home countries. The potential for crowdsourcing and crowdfunding as tools that help in the fight against human trafficking is still nascent, with ample space for new contributions from innovative thinkers and entrepreneurs.

A third technology tool, called tagging, is being used to combat human trafficking by identifying potential cases that require intervention. Users can tag content on websites such as social media sites, online classified sites, online job recruitment sites, or any other similar site that appears suspicious or potentially fraudulent, thereby triggering an investigation by NGOs or local law enforcement. This is the most direct tool to combat the tactics used to recruit sex trafficking victims like Katya and Dipali. The efficiency of the tagging tools varies, and millions of pages need to be assessed, but tagging holds significant potential for anyone with a basic knowledge of key indicators of human trafficking and a mobile phone, tablet, or laptop to contribute as a "Citizen Abolitionist" who can help expand the reach of NGOs and law enforcement by proactively searching for potential trafficking recruitment pages or profiles, simply by scouring certain websites and being on the lookout for indicators of suspicious content. For example, Backpage classifieds that promise "tiny" or "very young" girls are often in the business of selling minors for sex. Online recruitment sites that promise they can help migrants find no-fee or wage-deduction work opportunities abroad could be indicators of labor traffickers trying to recruit new victims. Online dating profiles that actively engage with girls from foreign countries and are trying to entice them to migrate could be a sign of potential sex trafficking. It can be painstaking work, but key words and certain kinds of behavior or key indicators can be tagged for follow-up by experts, potentially leading to the prevention of, or intervention in, human trafficking cases.

"One-Box," Facial Recognition, and the "Deep Web"

Google has been doing innovative work in preventing sex trafficking and child sexual exploitation through the development of an algorithm that provides a "one-box" result of the human trafficking hotlines in several countries based on certain searches, such as "Is my boyfriend a pimp?" or "Am I being controlled by someone?" If an individual initiates a search with phrases such as these, a one-box result is triggered by Google's algorithm that provides human trafficking hotlines for the relevant region based on the IP address of the device being used to conduct the search. The searches that trigger the one-box result of the human trafficking hotlines vary from country to country, and a great deal of engineering went into determining what kinds of searches in which geographies should trigger the result. Google is the first to concede that many victims of human trafficking are not in a position to conduct an online search or even have access to the Internet, however, it is an important tool that could lead to assistance in many cases of human trafficking. As Chris Busselle at Google.org (the philanthropic division of Google.com) told me, "We are putting this information on some of the most valuable real estate on the web," which is a clear indication of how serious the matter is to the company.

Google also has been active in the area of child protection and helping to thwart child sexual exploitation, primarily through a dedicated team of engineers who work to rid the Internet of sexually explicit imagery of children. Much of this work is automated, although some of it is done manually. In some countries, Google places a warning on search results relating to child pornography, such as "You could be prosecuted for viewing this content" or "Do you need help?" It is unlikely that an individual searching for images of child pornography is going to recognize that he needs help, but the pop-up warnings may make the individual think twice about continuing to search for offensive or exploitative images of innocent children.

Facial recognition is another powerful tool being used to help combat sex trafficking and child sexual exploitation. Microsoft has developed a facial recognition technology, called Photo DNA, that serves this purpose. This image-matching technology developed in collaboration with Dartmouth College creates a unique signature for a digital image that can be compared with the signatures of other images to find copies. The technology was donated to the National Center for Missing and Exploited Children (NCMEC) in December 2009 to help the organization find, report, and eliminate some of the worst known images of online child pornography. To date, the technology has assisted with the identification of thousands of offensive images of child sexual exploitation and pornography on the Internet. Law enforcement has also been using Photo DNA to assist with investigations and to limit the emotional damage relating to personal exposure of officers' having to view thousands of images of child pornography to find matches manually. The technology also helps law enforcement identify and rescue victims more efficiently and prosecute those who posted the images because their digital trails can be traced. The technology has been particularly useful in assisting law enforcement coordination across jurisdictions; it can match images of a child who might appear in postings in different cities across time, even when those images may have been altered. Once a match is made, law enforcement can work with counterparts in other jurisdictions to rescue an exploited child much sooner than might otherwise be possible.

One of the most intriguing new tools being used to combat human trafficking is software called Memex, created by the Defense Advanced Research Projects Agency (DARPA). Memex provides advanced Internet search capabilities into the "deep web" and has assisted with several human trafficking investigations in the United States. The deep web is the roughly 90 percent of information on the Internet not indexed by traditional search engines such as Yahoo and Google. The deep web is often filled with temporary pages (such as advertisements for illicit activity relating to drug trafficking, weapons dealing, money laundering, and human trafficking), which are typically removed before major search engines are able to crawl them. The Memex tool can scour the deep web for temporary advertisements used to lure trafficking victims or to sell them for sex and can analyze the data and identify relationships between seemingly unrelated information, thereby creating spatial and temporal patterns that can be used by investigators to track down victims, trace traffickers, and gather evidence for prosecutions. The tool has been so useful that the New York District Attorney's office uses Memex in all its human trafficking prosecutions.

These are just a few examples of the kinds of technology tools being developed and refined by major technology companies and being utilized by law enforcement, prosecutors, NGOs, and everyday citizens to intervene more quickly and efficiently to stop the forced sexual exploitation of women and children and the exploitation of online sexual images of women and children. I am optimistic that the pace of development in antitrafficking technology will continue to accelerate, and that more effective tools will be available each year to combat these offenses. In particular, the sophistication and accessibility of technologies that automate the process of searching for vulnerable individuals through facial recognition and trace patterns of movement or provide digital trails for the prosecution of traffickers and male consumers of commercial sex (especially of children) hold great promise. Traffickers and commercial sex consumers will continue to search for ways to use technology to evade detection, creating a sort of technology "arms war" in the human trafficking space. With sufficient funding and dedication, I fully expect that those on the side of decency will prevail.

LABOR TRAFFICKING

Most of the uses of technology and social media in either promoting or combating labor trafficking are similar to those used with sex trafficking, but a few nuances merit exploration. New developments have provided technology tools in the labor trafficking space that enable connections for victims and at-risk individuals prior to their migration for a work opportunity and upon arrival at the employer's location or the destination country.[12] Isolation is the most powerful force facilitating labor trafficking among migrants, and tools that enable access to fellow migrants, local NGOs, law enforcement, and other resources or avenues of assistance can be vital in preventing labor trafficking or assisting with victim escape. These tools notwithstanding, technology and social media platforms are a popular gateway for recruiting new labor trafficking victims.

Recruitment of Labor Trafficking Victims

The Internet and social media are used extensively to recruit labor trafficking victims. Although social media sites such as Facebook and Twitter are often used to recruit victims, online job recruitment sites that advertise opportunities to work abroad are the primary websites used for this purpose. The number and variety of online job recruitment sites that promise to arrange opportunities for work in developed economies is astounding. Most of the sites focus on recruitment from South Asia, East Asia, and Latin America and offer employment in domestic work, construction, agriculture, shipping, fishing, entertainment, mining, and numerous other sectors that span the global economy.[13] These websites recruit directly into the kinds of slavery cases discussed in chapters 3 (labor trafficking) and 6 (debt bondage). Scores of legitimate work-abroad sites operate in conjunction with licensed recruiters and government agencies to provide foreign employment opportunities for citizens from Nepal, the Philippines, Bangladesh, Indonesia, Sri Lanka, Mexico, India, and many other migrant worker sending nations. These legitimate labor channels are vital for citizens from these countries, and they provide wage-earning opportunities labor migrants cannot find in their home countries. The remittances sent by these workers to their families are crucial for their survival and can help families send children to school or secure medicines when in need. Traffickers feed on the desperation of the poor for sources of remittance income. Although there are millions of legitimate online job recruitment postings, there are also countless postings that are fraudulent. Sometimes entire foreign migrant job posting sites are fraudulent, but more often the fake postings are intermixed with legitimate

ones on fully licensed and regulated websites, making it exceedingly difficult to discriminate legitimate offers from those bound for slavery. It is all
but impossible for the companies operating these websites to verify each of
the tens of thousands (or more) of job postings that may be listed on their
service. One common solution for many of the sites is to include a small box
on the home page that warns about the risks of human trafficking and provides a contact number (in the home country) that can provide assistance.
Unfortunately, this information is unlikely to dissuade desperate individuals
with no alternative other than to migrate for work, and the phone number or
email listed does not help if the migrant cannot access a phone or computer
in the destination country.

Dinesh, a labor trafficking victim from Nepal, tells a story that typifies the
risks of technology as a tool used to recruit labor trafficking victims:

> I am from Jajarkot District. Four years back an NGO brought two
> computers to our village and placed them in the nearby school for
> the children. They taught us how to use the computers to search
> for information. They gave us a list of the websites that we could
> use to search jobs. There were only so many opportunities on these
> sites, so we learned to search in other places also. I found one job
> for construction in Qatar. They promised to make the arrangements
> and said we will earn 2 lakh rupees [$2,000] per month. They had
> pictures of other Nepali men who said how happy they were in
> Qatar. There was one number I rang and I spoke to a recruiter in
> Kathmandu. His name is Arjun. He said the fee for the training and
> other arrangements is 5 lakh rupees [$5,000]. I paid these fees on
> loan because my family did not have so much money. It is not good
> what happened to me. I was in Qatar for more than one year doing
> construction for the football stadiums. The conditions were very
> bad. I saw seven people die from heat and two died from accidents.
> I wanted to leave after the first week, but they took my documents.
> I had no money. I had no place to go. One day the police came to
> the worksite and arrested us. They said we did not have permits.
> They deported us. To this day, I did not receive any wages. I called
> Arjun, but he said it was not his problem. He offered to help me find
> another job, but I told him he must think I am a fool to trust him.

He told me I have to trust someone, otherwise I will never find a job again. He is correct. People from my country know these websites should not be trusted, but they go anyway. We cannot stay in Nepal.

The NGO that set up the computers in Dinesh's village is a well-respected, long-standing organization that has done excellent work throughout rural Nepal. Dinesh's story highlights the perilous nature of introducing connective technologies to impoverished areas. Even with warnings about false recruitment agencies and specific information on which online employment sites could be trusted, there is no way to prevent people from using the Internet to find opportunities for themselves. Furthermore, even with all the warnings about false job offers and excessive fees, people like Dinesh often have no option but to accept the offer and hope for the best because there is no alternate means of survival in their home countries.

I documented dozens of cases just like Dinesh's in several countries that are major sources of migrant workers. The individuals migrated from South and East Asia and Central and Latin America to developed economies where they toiled in several migrant worker occupations, primarily construction, agriculture, domestic work, seafood, and mining. In all cases, the individuals were isolated from potential sources of assistance on arrival in the destination country, their documents were confiscated, mobile phones (if they had one) were confiscated, and they were monitored around the clock and prohibited access to communication tools through which they could potentially contact assistance. Even when presented with the opportunity to leave the worksite, almost all of the victims I documented opted to remain because they were in so much debt due to excessive up-front fees. They all persevered under the hope that they would eventually be paid enough to discharge their debts and begin to send remittances home. This was, after all, the point of their migration. If it were not achieved, they would be forced to return home to far worse circumstances than before—debt, rejection, and stigma. The power of coercion associated with exorbitant debts accrued by the migrant to secure a work opportunity abroad cannot be overstated. The workers cannot return until the debts (however farcical they become) are repaid and some meager amount of income is earned. Lack of local language skills is almost always a primary isolating factor for labor trafficking victims that perpetuates their exploitation.

Despite their potential for harm, social media, mobile technology, and the Internet play invaluable roles in preventing labor trafficking and providing access to information or resources that can prevent labor trafficking and assist with escape from forced labor. These tools are developing rapidly and hold much promise.

Prevention and Escape

The most effective use of technology tools and social media to prevent labor trafficking and assist with the liberation of victims is through applications that connect them to information, family members, local assistance, and social networks before, during, and after migration. Constant connectivity and obviating isolation is crucial. Having access to SMS texts or email can enable prospective migrants to liaise with people who may have migrated safely and found legitimate work opportunities. These same technologies can keep a person connected during travel as well as upon arrival should any issues arise. The provision of advanced contact information for the relevant government authorities, law enforcement teams, local NGOs, or other resources that can potentially intervene are also important aspects of prevention. Unfortunately, vulnerable and desperate migrants rarely contest instructions or create trouble with an employer who demands that they turn over their mobile phones for fear of losing the work opportunity or of being deported with a lifetime of debt they can never discharge. Even when workers manage to retain their mobile phones and wish to pursue assistance to deal with an exploitative work situation, they can run into technology hurdles for which they are unprepared. Pradeep from Sri Lanka explained:

> I kept my mobile phone in a secret place when I arrived in Kuala Lumpur. Immediately they took my documents and locked me inside a barracks. I was lucky that I hid my phone, but how was I to know that the SIM card will not work? The phone was useless. They made us work all day in difficult conditions. I have never been so exhausted in my life. We had only one break for twenty minutes in the day from the work. I ran away during one break to try to get a local SIM card. It was too expensive. I pleaded with the shopkeeper to let me make a call from his phone, but he told me to leave his store. I returned to

the worksite. What else could I do? The boss punished me. He beat me with a wooden board. I had bruises all over my body. They locked me in a small room and did not give me food for three days. I thought they would leave me in that room until I died, but on the third day they dragged me out and told me next time I make trouble my punishment will be worse.

Other labor trafficking victims I documented had similar stories: SIM cards that did not work in the destination country, not having money to purchase a local SIM card, and not having access to the Internet to send an email to ask for help.

Labor trafficking victims such as Pradeep, introduced below, demonstrate that many migrant workers know that communication technology can help them in exploitative situations, but these cases also demonstrate the importance of adequate predeparture training on how to use technology effectively. Even when a labor trafficking victim is able to access the Internet, the victim may not know how to find needed assistance. "Some migrants at the barracks told me about an Internet café not far from our worksite," a construction migrant from Laos named Noi told me, "but I had never seen a computer before. I did not know how to use it." Migrants need to understand the basics of SIM cards, have introductory computer training, and have enough local currency to meet emergency needs.

Despite pitfalls in the application of technology solutions, I documented several cases in which basic access to mobile communications or the Internet provided a crucial connection that prevented labor trafficking or offered an avenue for escape. One such case involved a man named Nok from Cambodia. He was being transported by truck to Thailand where he expected to work in the fishing industry. A friend who had previously migrated to Thailand for fishing work warned him that the recruiters will probably confiscate his mobile phone, so he should hide it at all times. The perils of the Thai fishing sector are well known to migrants in the Mekong subregion, and many have learned that a mobile phone can be the best means of securing assistance. Nok did as he was advised and hid his phone. During his journey from Cambodia to Thailand, his traffickers became increasingly hostile toward the migrants. Fearing the worst, Nok wanted to return home. When he arrived at Samut Sakhon in Thailand, he was told that he had been sold to a ship captain and would have to work off the debt of his transport at sea. Nok did not want to go further.

> *That night, I sent an SMS to my friend. He wrote to me, 'Run from there!' I had no place to go, and I do not speak Thai language. When the guards were not looking, I snuck out of the docks and ran down the street. I found an alley and I hid there. My friend sent me an SMS with information on the Cambodia Embassy in Bangkok. He told me it was a distance of 48 kilometers and which road to take. I walked all the way without stopping. I came to the Embassy and said I needed help. A very kind man wrote down the details, and they arranged for me to take a bus home. I am lucky I kept my phone, otherwise I do not know what would have happened to me.*

Another example in which communication technology helped thwart labor trafficking came from an Indian migrant domestic worker I documented named Anju.

> *When I came to that home in Dubai, I knew I made a mistake. The owners took my documents and my phone. The recruiter said there would be five people in the home, but there were ten! I had to cook and clean for all of them. I could sleep only two or three hours a night on the floor in a very small room. They spoke to me rudely and the Ma'am had no problem slapping me. I was desperate to get out of that home, but I had no way to ring my family. There was always someone watching me. After three months, there was an accident and they went to the hospital. They left the three children and the grandmother in the home. When they fell asleep, I used their phone to ring my father. I told him what happened. He said I must ring the police. Before I left India, the agency told me that the emergency number in Dubai is 999. I rang that number and told the police what happened. They did not understand what I was saying because I could not speak Arabic. I said "Hindi! Hindi!" and eventually I spoke to someone who could speak my language. They sent police to the home. Everyone was shouting. The grandmother said I was stealing from them. They asked for my visa, but I said they took*

everything from me. The police arrested me. They sent me back to
India. They said I would not be allowed in Dubai again.

Access to a telephone gave Anju a crucial connection that helped her escape forced labor. Ensuring access to phones or the Internet is much easier said than done in labor trafficking scenarios, but the more connectivity victims have and the less isolated they are, the more likely they are to avoid or minimize the duration of exploitation. Connectivity is similarly crucial in times of environmental catastrophe or military conflict. These calamities invariably result in the mass displacement of highly vulnerable people, and traffickers are often the first on the scene recruiting new victims. Finding ways of providing connections for displaced people or refugees can help prevent human trafficking or minimize the duration of exploitation. The challenges of ensuring communication access in these cases are significant, and further testing of solutions is sorely needed.

LOOKING FORWARD

Providing technologies and connectivity tools that can help prevent or end sex and labor trafficking violations is perhaps the least developed area of antitrafficking efforts. For labor trafficking, technology companies can collaborate with NGOs on technical assistance and support the development of tools that narrow the information asymmetries between employers and migrants that so often lead to forced labor outcomes. Tools can be developed to integrate migrant communities more cohesively and link them to information and assistance when needed. Formalized channels for regulated, legitimate online recruitment tools can be created and reinforced in migrant communities, and governments can work to attenuate isolation among migrant workers through laws that ensure access to communications, social networks, law enforcement, and other resources. Researchers should be measuring these efforts to identify what works best, from country to country, from region to region.

For sex trafficking, image recognition tools must be enhanced to assist law enforcement with rescues, investigations, and prosecutions. Efforts to rid the Internet of child pornography and shut down websites or social media pages used to recruit sex trafficking victims must receive additional resources and development. Litigation to shut down the sale of commercial sexual services on Backpage and similar websites should be pursued as vigorously as possible until a precedent is achieved that establishes that commercial sexual content is not protected by section 230 of the Communications Decency Act of 1996 or similar laws in other countries. Free speech is fundamental to the fabric of the United States, but the freedom to sell sex online, which results in considerable risks of exploitation of slaves and minors, is a freedom that societies everywhere must agree should not be protected. Put another way, the freedom not to be a sex trafficking victim is a more important freedom to protect than the freedom to sell sex on the Internet.

Two additional areas of future development hold promise in efforts to use technology to combat human trafficking: (1) block chain technology and (2) technology that monitors global supply chains.

Block Chains and Human Trafficking

Block chain technology is one of the primary innovations of the digital currency bitcoin.[14] The block chain is a public ledger of all bitcoin transactions that have ever been executed. Each "block" represents the current part of the block chain, which records each new transaction. Once the transaction is completed, it is added into the block chain permanently and linked in chronological order. The transaction can never be deleted or altered. The entirety of the block chain is available to all users on the bitcoin network at all times.

Applying block chain technology to human rights issues is a new frontier being pioneered by organizations such as BitFury, Bitnation, and the Humanitarian Blockchain. The primary benefit of the technology is the ability to create 100 percent unique, unalterable identities for people who otherwise lack formalized identification documents. The technology also can be used to track movements of people, which can assist both with their protection and with prosecution of human trafficking crimes.

Block chain technology could provide a digital birth certificate registry for the millions of children born each year without formal registration documents, which otherwise renders them invisible and particularly vulnerable to trafficking and exploitation. Online images of child pornography could be linked to the identities of specific children, which would assist in investigations and child liberation and protection. A mobile phone or a similar portable inexpensive tool is required to set up the initial digital identification, so NGOs and governments will need to assist in this process.

The same identification technology can be used for adults. For example, the Bitnation Refugee Emergency Response (BRER) organization provides emergency services and humanitarian aid to refugees by authenticating identities through a Blockchain Emergency ID (BE-ID). The BE-ID can be used by refugees who cannot otherwise obtain official identification documents or may have lost them when fleeing. The technology enables an individual to cryptographically prove his or her existence and family relations, which can be distributed on a public ledger anyone can access to verify the person's identity. This technology could tag forged identity documents used by human traffickers to move individuals from one country to another, either as distress or labor migrants.

Finally, the Humanitarian Blockchain (HB) is dedicated to solving human rights problems using block chain technology. The project focuses on land registration, irregular migration, the inability of billions of people to access formal banking systems, and other identity-based human rights issues. Migration-related vulnerabilities, child protection, and human trafficking all can be addressed using solutions HB is developing.

The promise of block chain–based solutions to enhance protection by providing a verified and authentic identification system for the tens of millions of invisible people in the world has barely begun to scratch the surface. Entrepreneurs, human rights activists, and technology leaders are all exploring solutions to these and other pressing human rights issues. Future editions of this book will undoubtedly require a full chapter on new developments in human rights solutions provided by block chain technology.

Technology to Cleanse Global Supply Chains

Technology is being used more effectively each year to monitor labor abuses, slavery, and child labor in global supply chains. The global economic integration that began in the early 1990s led to several benefits, such as expanding international trade, foreign investment, and acceleration of the transfer of knowledge among countries. Globalization's corresponding ills have resulted in deepening rural poverty, widening the chasm between rich and poor, increasing social instability, and eroding human freedoms.[15] Fallen walls (real and virtual) and the free flow of goods and capital allow multinational corporations to scour the globe in search of cheap or under-regulated labor markets to cut labor costs. From garment manufacturing in Bangladesh to cell phone manufacturing in China, these low-wage laborers at the bottom of global supply chains continue to be exploited in abusive conditions that in the worst cases amount to slavery. Lack of visibility of the bottom of the supply chain, especially two or three levels down the layered subcontracting chain inherent to many informal labor markets, has been a serious challenge for corporations genuinely interested in ensuring ethical and decent conditions for their workers wherever they may be located. Technology is beginning to address this problem.

LexisNexis has developed tools that allow companies to monitor their supply chains more directly and accurately. The Lexis Diligence tool provides an array of information on vendors, suppliers, and even individuals in a single report, including background checks, litigation history, negative news checks, and other risk factors that could be indicators of poor practices. The tool synthesizes data from more than twenty global databases, including public records and news and company filing information, to uncover risks in supply chains. Issues flagged by the Diligence check can receive a deeper investigation through the Lexis IntegrityCheck, which assesses the risks related to specific vendors or labor contractors being used or considered by the company. LexisNexis also produces a global Human Trafficking Index, which automatically searches thousands of news sources around the world and provides a real-time assessment of risks relating to human trafficking from one country to another.

Another application that holds great promise for monitoring and cleansing global supply chains is the Supply Unchained pilot project of GoodWeave and Target Corporation. Supply Unchained creates an online dashboard, coupled with strategic mobile data collection tools, to provide a monitoring and certification methodology that is scalable and can map, analyze, and share detailed supply chain data on a real-time basis. The cornerstones of the project focus on five areas: (1) random, unannounced inspections using customized mobile applications, (2) providing real-time data to companies and service providers based on these inspections, (3) identifying and addressing root causes of supply chain human rights issues, (4) assessing overall trends in violations, and (5) conducting anonymous mobile worker surveys to assess the strengths and weaknesses of the inspection and monitoring procedures. The net result provides corporations with reliable and direct visibility into their supply chains, which in turn facilitates more targeted and immediate responses to address the issues. I asked the president of GoodWeave, Nina Smith, to summarize the project's potential:

> The combination of the mobile data collection system and strategic analysis of supply chain intelligence that Supply Unchained will facilitate is unprecedented. The tool will enable GoodWeave to scale its system to ensure there is no child labor or forced labor anywhere in a supply chain, especially in outsourced production, and to partner more strategically with companies, suppliers, workers and governments to share relevant data to strengthen all of our efforts to protect workers.

In 2015, Humanity United joined with several U.S. government agencies to launch a contest called "Rethink Supply Chains: The Tech Challenge to Fight Labor Trafficking"; the specific goal was to promote new and innovative technology-based solutions to address human trafficking in global supply chains. The winners of the competition were Sustainability Incubator, an advisory firm that helps seafood companies solve human rights challenges, and Trace Register, a traceability software company. The two organizations have collaborated to help companies better understand and address the risks of labor trafficking through a Labor Safe Digital Certificate, which is a digital risk assessment tool that helps seafood suppliers and retailers better screen for risks of forced labor and address high-risk zones within their supply chains. The runner-up, Good World Solutions, has developed LaborLink, a mobile technology that combats isolation and improves visibility of trafficked workers by capturing and analyzing worker feedback through an SMS platform.

Numerous organizations are developing tools to address slavery and child labor in global supply chains, including Verité, the United Nations Global Compact, the International Labour Organisation, and many major consulting firms. The promise of technology-based tools to cleanse global supply chains of slavery and child labor is one of the true bright spots in contemporary antislavery efforts. I expect to see a plethora of ground-breaking solutions in the coming years, but activists must never lose sight of the fact that exploiters will seek to circumvent these new tools. Ongoing monitoring and assessment of these applications will be crucial to their effectiveness.

THE ROLE OF THE MEDIA

One of the most noteworthy changes in the antislavery field since the time of my first research trip in the year 2000 has been a significant increase in the level of media coverage of the issue. Major news outlets such as CNN, the BBC, Al Jazeera, and the *Guardian* have aired hundreds of stories on various aspects of slavery in all corners of the world. Some of these stories are sensational in tone, but by and large these and other news outlets have provided excellent coverage of the issue. In some cases, they have been first to break a story about a new phenomenon taking place in the context of modern slavery.

In addition to news media, dozens of feature films, documentaries, and television shows have explored the many facets of modern slavery. Some of this content is sensational or even misinformed, but for the most part film and television have played important roles in spreading awareness of slavery to the broader public. Most major procedural TV shows in the United States have had one episode on human trafficking, if not several. Some of the best films and documentaries about slavery and related issues include *Not My Life, In This World, The Whistleblower, Dirty Pretty Things, The Selling of Innocents, The Day My God Died, Very Young Girls, I Am Jane Doe, The Price of Sex, Trade in Innocents*, and, of course, the film I wrote based on *Sex Trafficking*, which is titled *Trafficked*.

The CNN Freedom Project is the most important and broad-based news media contribution to raising awareness of slavery in the world today. The Freedom Project began in 2011 as a dedicated initiative by the CNN network to raise awareness of slavery, highlight success stories, and amplify voices of victims and survivors. Through this initiative, CNN has produced hundreds of stories and dozens of documentaries on almost every aspect of slavery across the globe. The Freedom Project was initially meant to be a one-year campaign, but the network felt sufficiently passionate about the cause to continue it on an ongoing basis. The CNN Freedom Project has been the most impactful news network initiative to elevate awareness of slavery and is an exemplary demonstration of the power of responsible and dedicated journalism to effect positive change on human rights issues.

A FATEFUL MEETING

I began this chapter by describing an experiment I ran to assess levels of online activity in the Los Angeles area related to commercial sex. I mentioned that many of the callbacks I made to inquiries I received were quite unpleasant. Only three of these conversations lasted longer than four minutes. The longest, a near thirty-minute conversation, led to a meeting.

His name is Lou, and he is a lawyer. We had a pleasant conversation (inasmuch as conversations about the purchase of women for sex can be), and Lou eventually asked to meet with me to talk in more detail about the purchases he wanted to make. Lou said this was the first time he was thinking about purchasing sex, and he wanted to "feel it out" before proceeding. The first thought I had was that I was being set up by someone who perceived me to be a rival pimp. The second thought I had was that I was being set up by a police officer, which would have been fine with me. The third thought I had was that in either case I would ensure that we met in a public place and, if need be, I could explain who I was and the research I was doing. The final thought I had was that if Lou was who he said he was, then he was either very naïve about asking to meet in person with a potentially dangerous pimp (which defeated the entire purpose of searching for commercial sex online), or he was up to some other sort of game. Either way, a public place would protect us both, so we agreed to meet in the afternoon at a coffee shop in West Los Angeles.

We met two days later, and as it turned out, Lou was exactly who he said he was. He was an intellectual property attorney, in his early forties, recently divorced, father of a six-year-old son, and lonely. He worked long hours, which made it difficult for him to meet new people. I asked Lou why he wanted to meet me.

"I needed to be sure I'm not being set up," he said.

"How many other people have you met with?"

"Just you. You're the only one who didn't sound like a gangster."

I asked Lou why he wasn't going for more upscale escort services, or taking a trip to Nevada to a legalized brothel to obviate risk.

"I don't know," he replied, "I'm not really sure I want to do this."

I told Lou it sounded like he would regret purchasing sex if he ended up doing so.

"You're not really a pimp are you?" he asked.

"No. I'm a researcher."

I told Lou my name, explained my research, and described the experiment I was running on Backpage, as well as the book I was writing. This information made him nervous, and he asked if I was going to write about him in my book.

"I might, but I wouldn't reveal your identity."

Our conversation shifted to life in Los Angeles, the terrible traffic, the lovely weather, the superficial nature of most friendships. Eventually, we returned to the reason we met. I asked Lou why he was contemplating the purchase of sex at this point in his life.

"I think I always wanted to know what it would be like," he said.

"You mean the purchase of another human being?"

"Maybe, you know, just to have it be simple with no strings attached."

"I wouldn't describe the purchase of another human being as 'simple,' or without strings and consequences," I said. "Once you cross that line, I think you will regret it."

"Maybe."

"Let me tell you a little more about what it's going to be like—not for you, but for the young girl you purchase, because in my ad it talked about young girls."

I spent the next several minutes telling Lou about the realities of sex trafficking that I had documented across several years. Lou challenged me on the idea that some prostitutes choose to do the work willingly, and I recounted all the factors that vitiate the voluntary nature of that "choice."

"So are you saying that no one ever chooses to be a prostitute?" Lou asked.

"I can't negate the theoretical possibility," I replied, "but I can tell you this—most cases that seem to be voluntary choices are actually choices driven by duress or a lack of alternatives. For each theoretical case involving an empowered choice based on free will, I am willing to wager there are one hundred other cases of coercion and no true choice at all. So you have to ask yourself whether you are willing to play the odds that you might end up purchasing a slave, a child, or someone who entered prostitution as a child."

"Then maybe the Vegas idea is better," Lou said.

"Actually, prostitution is not legal in Vegas, but in other parts of Nevada, yes. And just because it's legal doesn't mean everyone doing it is there by choice."

"I guess I didn't realize how complicated it is."

"But you're still considering it, aren't you?"

"Maybe. . . ."

"I hope not, but it's up to you."

Lou and I did not speak much longer. My conversation with him remains the only one I have ever had with an educated professional who said he was thinking of purchasing sex for the first time but had not yet done so. I interviewed several white-collar male consumers during my price elasticity research, but they had all purchased sex many times before. Lou was a potentially new male consumer, and I wished I had more time to understand his motivations. He did not appear to be a brute, lacking a moral compass, or a deviant of some kind. He was rational, intelligent, and was evidently intrigued by what the experience would be like to purchase a human being for sex. It is a mind-set that I cannot understand, but it clearly appeals to some people. Understanding these mind-sets and the psychological nuances that drive systems of slavery are just as important to combating them as are other approaches that focus on the structural or systemic drivers (e.g., poverty, corruption) of the phenomenon.

I will never know whether Lou purchased a female for commercial sex, and if so, how many times he did so. I would like to believe that the thoughts I shared might have played some role in dissuading him. He is but one man, but one man can purchase dozens of slaves for sex. Seeking to influence the mind-set of one male consumer at a time may not be the most efficient way to stem the demand for commercial sex, but my meeting with Lou provided a rare moment in which I felt some measure of tangible and direct influence on an individual who might potentially be a new contributor to the problem. I have had thousands of encounters with slaves and scores of encounters with slavers whose mind-sets were ossified, but with Lou I appreciated the importance of making additional efforts to engage with those at the precipice of decisions that could promote servitude and bondage and to try to reason with the more noble aspects of their nature. Doing so might be as much a benefit for me as for them, by reinforcing my fading hopes in the dignified qualities of humanity. It is a lifeline I cling to desperately at this stage of my antislavery work, in the face of what have otherwise been waves of despondency as I question whether my years of effort have accomplished anything of significance. Since the time of my meeting with Lou, I have had other encounters with consumers of commercial sex to see if I could influence them and convince them to influence others. I have tried various techniques, but I am not sure how successful I have been. It is not very efficient work, but it is redemptive, and for a period of time it has helped me to continue to forge forward, and to refrain from looking back at all the frustrations that have accumulated during my journey to understand slavery, and to contribute to its eradication.

CHAPTER 6

DEBT BONDAGE

Beyond South Asia

To deprive a man of his natural liberty and to deny to him
the ordinary amenities of life is worse than starving the
body; it is starvation of the soul.
                                        —Mahatma Gandhi

WHAT IS DEBT BONDAGE?

DEBT BONDAGE, OR bonded labor, is the most extensive form of slavery in the world today. South Asia is without question the home of debt
bondage, with roughly 80 percent of the world's debt bondage slaves living
in the region. In *Bonded Labor*,[1] I explored the myriad industries in which
bonded laborers in South Asia can be found, as well as the reasons debt
bondage remains entrenched in South Asia: immense poverty, the caste system, economic and legal legacies of the British colonial period, corruption,
social apathy, and lack of access to formal credit markets. Following *Bonded
Labor*, I explored the issue more deeply in relation to a specific industry
in *Tainted Carpets: Slavery and Child Labor in India's Hand-Made Carpet
Sector*.[2] This study was the largest single firsthand investigation of slavery

and child labor conducted at the time, and it detailed a shocking prevalence of slavelike exploitation in India's handmade carpet industry. I also traced slave-made carpets from the point of production in India to the point of retail sale at major retailers in the United States. Debt bondage proved to be highly prevalent in this sector, similar to other sectors in India's informal economy. The results of the study show that at least 28 percent of workers in India's carpet sector are in debt bondage and that an alarming 99.9 percent of these individuals belong to minority castes and ethnic groups. Eighty percent of the loans taken out by bonded laborers were to meet essential needs of food, water, and cooking oil. The average size of these loans was $85, a modest sum that ensnared entire families in years of debt bondage.[3]

Many of the same conditions that give rise to bonded labor in South Asia exist in debt bondage cases outside of this region. Although the caste system of South Asia is central to the persistence of bonded labor in these countries, similar class and caste dynamics often operate in debt bondage cases with local populations elsewhere in the world. However, it is vital to note that most of the victims of debt bondage in the Middle East or East Asia are low-caste migrants from South Asia. The forces that have made South Asia home to debt bondage extend beyond the region's borders into informal economic sectors around the world. It is a most regrettable export that brings shame and indignity to the region. Beyond the South Asians exported into debt bondage abroad, the phenomenon typically ensnares other disenfranchised, dispossessed, and minority ethnic communities. As in South Asia, poverty, lack of access to formal credit markets, lack of reasonable alternative sources of income and security, and population displacement are central to debt bondage cases across the globe.

Another vital element to understand about debt bondage beyond South Asia is that the phenomenon is heavily driven by transnational labor migration. Most of the cases of debt bondage I documented outside of South Asia also would be considered labor trafficking, while many such cases in South Asia are also cases either of labor migration or trafficking. These are most often scenarios of seasonal migration from rural villages to urban worksites that might be in another region in the same country. Many cases of debt bondage outside of South Asia do not involve transnational migration, but the majority of the cases I documented did. In every case, the bondage was initiated by up-front fees or other expenses associated with facilitating the migration or the work opportunity in the destination country. This tryst between bondage and migration shows no signs of abating, with rapid increases in labor migration reaching 244 million labor migrants in 2015, which is a 41 percent increase over the 173 million labor migrants in 2000.[4]

The definition of debt bondage under international law is slightly different from the definition under the laws of countries in South Asia, most of which are derived from India's Bonded Labour System (Abolition) Act of 1976. Article 1 of the 1956 UN Supplementary Convention on the Abolition of Slavery, the Slave Trade, and Institutions and Practices Similar to Slavery defines debt bondage as:

> The status or condition arising from a pledge by a debtor of his personal services or of those of a person under his control as security for a debt, if the value of those services as reasonably assessed is not applied towards the liquidation of the debt or the length and nature of those services are not respectively limited and defined.

Under this definition, an exchange of credit for pledged labor becomes debt bondage if the laborer is exploited in such a way that the value of his or her labor unreasonably exceeds the value of the credit.

Under India's Bonded Labour System (Abolition) Act, bonded labor is defined as a system of forced or partly forced labor in which an individual takes an advance in exchange for his or any dependant's pledged labor or service and is confined to a specific geographic area, *or* cannot work for someone else, *or* is not allowed to sell his labor or goods at market value. India's bonded labor definition covers more of the nuanced scenarios in which debt bondage exploitation can take place beyond an unreasonable asymmetry between the value of credit and labor; however, the basic mechanisms of the exploitation are similar. Physical, verbal, and sexual abuses are common in all cases. Creditors almost always manipulate the debts, restrain workers, confiscate identity documents and work permits, and perpetuate systems of wage deductions from overstated debts that leave individuals with little or no actual income for years or more. As in India, attempts in other countries to enact laws or policies to prevent debt bondage are easily circumvented by recruiters, brokers, and employers. In many destination countries, the relevant laws for migrant workers promote debt bondage by legitimizing systems of wage deductions to repay up-front fees that are almost always overstated.

I found a large number of cases of debt bondage among migrant worker communities in numerous sectors around the world, including agriculture, logging, iron smelting, seafood, mining (common and rare earth minerals), garment making, dairy farming, cocoa, palm oil, domestic work, construction, and commercial sex. The most exemplary of these sectors are the last three. Domestic work, construction, and commercial sex encapsulate all of the salient characteristics of debt bondage beyond South Asia.

DEBT BONDAGE AND DOMESTIC WORK

Preying on Those Who Serve

When I was a child, my parents took us to Bombay each summer to visit our extended family. These are the fondest memories of my life, and to this day I feel most at home in India. However, one facet of life in India always left me uncomfortable—servants. In the United States, I had to clean up after myself and do house chores. My parents cooked our meals, did the grocery shopping, and fixed the toilet when it broke. In India, servants do this work. If I started to wash my dishes, my grandmother would tell me to stop. If the toilet broke, the servant was called to fix it. If we needed milk, the servant was sent to the market to buy it. Our servants were darker skinned than we were, and they lived in a separate part of the home with a separate kitchen and bathroom. I could play with the servant's children, but only up to age ten or eleven. After that, it was no longer proper.

I never felt comfortable having another human being serve me, clean up after me, or do my chores. My family has always promoted equality and social justice, especially in India, and our servants were treated with respect and generosity . . . but they were still servants. It was clear to everyone that they were beneath us, not because they were not equal as human beings but because they served us. I understand the arguments that in a country such as India with immense poverty and a severe lack of employment opportunities for the poor, providing shelter and a stable wage to a family in exchange for domestic work when they would almost certainly be in a worse condition otherwise is a reasonable arrangement. The children especially were better off because we made sure to send them to school, an opportunity they would be very unlikely to have in other circumstances. Because many aspects of the arrangement are welfare-enhancing for the servant family, this system is allowed to persist with an air of legitimacy. Nevertheless, when one human being serves another, inequality is inherent to the relationship. This inequality burrows into the consciousness of a society and, despite all best intentions, disassociates the equality of being between those with servants and those who serve. This is the exact mind-set that those who exploit servants in debt bondage or slavelike conditions use to justify their treatment. In Haiti, the *Restavek* (from "reste avec" or "to live with") system[5] of debt bondage for child domestic servitude is driven by caste and poverty dynamics that are nearly identical to the *Kamaliri* system[6] of Nepal. In both cases, upper class/caste homeowners explained to me that the system is a beneficent way of providing room, board, and security for a downtrodden and pitiful low-caste child. "We give them a good life" and "Their alternative would be worse" and "We are doing them a service" were justifications I heard time and again in these and other countries in which I documented the debt bondage exploitation of servants.

Around the world, most upper-middle-class and upper-class households have domestic workers to some degree, a majority of whom are labor migrants. In the United States, the migrant domestic workers are primarily from south of the border, along with smaller numbers from Asia and Africa. Similarly, most upper-middle-class and upper-class households in western European nations have one or more domestic workers who have migrated from eastern Europe, Asia, or Africa.[7] In the United States and western Europe, the typical model is for domestic workers to visit the home of their employers one or more days a week. They tend not to live with those they serve, allowing the arrangement to maintain the semblance of an employer–employee relationship, with the home being the workplace. However, in countries where servants are more likely to live with those they serve, the dynamic can devolve into a more subordinating and potentially exploitative relationship. This is especially the case because the servant is isolated from his or her social networks, and freedom of movement and employment can be completely restricted. They have no place to go and no option to work elsewhere if they are mistreated. Exacerbating the cycle of exploitation, those who mistreat them are rarely, if ever, held accountable.[8] Of all the regions I documented, these dynamics were most prevalent in South Asia, the Middle East, and East Asia.

I uncovered dozens of cases of debt bondage–based domestic servitude in the Middle East and East Asia. Upper-middle-class and upper-class households in China, Japan, Malaysia, Singapore, Brunei, Dubai, Abu Dhabi, Qatar, Saudi Arabia, Oman, and South Korea are commonly served by the impoverished underclass women and girls of India, Bangladesh, Sri Lanka, Nepal, Indonesia, Vietnam, Pakistan, and the Philippines. Interestingly, the construction sectors of these same destination countries are similarly served by the impoverished underclass *men* of the same origin countries. The negative consequences of this en masse traffic of the women and men of these poor Asian nations into bondage and servitude abroad cannot be overstated. Indeed, the origin and destination countries listed here represent the most heavily concentrated flow of debt bondage and forced labor exploited transnational migrant workers in the world.

As upper-middle-class and upper-class homes have increased their share of global wealth in the past few decades, the poor have largely become poorer from a purchasing power parity standpoint. A lack of consistent wage-earning opportunities in their home countries catalyzes immense flows of labor migrants for the purpose of securing remittance income from wealthy nations for their families back home. Table 6.1 shows just how large these flows are.

TABLE 6.1   Remittance Income from Primary Migrant Labor–Sending Nations

COUNTRY	2015 TOTAL REMITTANCES ($B)	AS A PERCENTAGE OF TOTAL GDP
India	68.9	3.4
Philippines	28.8	9.6
Pakistan	19.3	7.0
Bangladesh	15.4	8.7
Vietnam	13.2	6.2
Nepal	7.0	29.2
Sri Lanka	7.0	8.9
World	**581.6**	

Source: Data from World Bank, "Migration and Remittances," September 24, 2015, http://www.worldbank.org/en/topic/migration remittancesdiasporaissues/brief/migration-remittances-data.

Remittances provide crucial sources of income for the poor in Asia, constituting a significant proportion of national GDP in many Asian countries. This is particularly true in Nepal, where remittances account for almost 30 percent of the country's economy; without these remittances, the nation would probably collapse. A bourgeoning industry of recruiters, placement agencies, and brokers provide migrant work opportunities for the poor of Asia, including domestic work. Estimates of the number of migrant domestic workers in the world vary from 50 million to 100 million.[9] The variance is largely due to definitional nuances[10] because of the informal nature of many domestic servant relationships and the difficulty in gathering data because the work takes place inside a residence. The sector is heavily gendered, with 83 percent of domestic workers globally being female.[11] Within the context of migration for domestic work, debt bondage has become a primary tool many recruiters use to ensnare women and girls in conditions of slavery. A young woman named A. Tamang from Nepal told me her story:

> I took the offer from a recruiter who came to our village. She said she can arrange domestic work in Dubai. First, I had to do the training in Kathmandu. The agency charged me ten lakh rupees [$1,000] for the training course and certificate. They also charged for medical clearance, passport and visa, and other fees that I did not understand. I did not have money to pay them, so they told me they will take one-half deduction from my wages in Dubai. The wage they promised was NR 1,400 [$14] per day. After four months I flew to Dubai. A man met me with a sign for the agency and took me from the airport. The air in Dubai made my eyes burn because I was not used to that climate. The agent took me to the home of an Arab family. They took my documents and showed me the work I will do. I worked every day from the morning until midnight. I did the cleaning, cooking, laundry, toilets, and massage. If I made the owners unhappy they shouted at me. Sometimes they hit me. The family was rich, but they were very filthy. Even though I am poor, at least we have a clean home.
>
> After some weeks the agent came to the home and gave me bank papers. I did not understand the writing. He said I had to sign the papers for the loan from the agency for my fees. He said I must repay the bank for these fees from my wages for three years. I did

not understand what was happening. After eight months the family gave me my first wage of seventy dihram [$27] each week. After three years the agency sent me back to Nepal. In that time, I only left the home twice when I was sick and went to hospital. I complained to the agency that I received so little wages in Dubai, but they said they cannot help me.

Although typical, A. Tamang's story is not the most exploitative case of debt bondage in the migrant domestic servant sector that I documented. The worst cases involve sexual exploitation and torture by the "employing" family, severe deprivation of food and sleep, and other abuses. Worse still are cases in which the young women never work as domestic workers but are instead sold into forced prostitution upon arrival in the destination country, as happened with Joyce from the Philippines:

I completed my training at a center near my village to the best of my ability. I was very dedicated and wanted to help my family. I flew with four women to Singapore. When we arrived, a man took us in a van. He did not speak to us. He took us to a small building that had a drawing of two young girls on the front window like a comic. The girls were smiling and I thought this might be a school. I asked if we were going to work in a school but the man did not respond. He took us to the back of the building where we met two other men and a woman named Min. Min gave us tea and told us she was the owner of this club. She said we had to be with clients to pay the fees of our training and then we can work for housecleaning. She said it was not difficult work and we would like it. She said if we stayed with her after our debt we could send more money to our families than in housekeeping.

I told Min I would never do this work. She said I had no choice and it would be better if I did not protest. I felt dizzy and thought I was going to be sick. When I woke up, I was in a bed. I felt pain everywhere. I screamed. I knew what happened to me. Min told me I was going to be okay. She brought me food and tried to console me. I asked her how could she do this to another woman? She said she was trying to help me and I should be grateful.

Min let me speak to my parents once a month to tell them I was
okay. As long as I did not upset her, she treated me with kindness.
She gave us alcohol and pain medicine to help us be with the clients.
I think maybe after six or seven months, she said I could go for house-
cleaning. I wanted to return home, but I needed to earn money for my
family, so I worked in the house of a Singapore family for two years.
When my mother became very ill, I returned home to take care of her.

Joyce and A. Tamang tell stories that are common to the dozens of cases
I have documented of debt bondage servitude in the global domestic worker
industry. In almost every case, the women sign up with a recruitment
agency that organizes their training and migration to a wealthier country,
and also arranges for them to work in a home. Instead of paying the agency
fees up-front for travel and work overseas, the women agree to an advance
by the agency for these expenses, which they are told they can repay over
time through wage deductions. The arrangement becomes debt bondage
when the repayment period far exceeds the actual value of the fees/loan,
when identity documents are confiscated, and when the worker is forced to
toil excessively and under harsh conditions, with little or no pay at the end
of her employment. Contract terms for workers are often switched upon
arrival in the destination country, with lower wages and worse conditions
than were promised prior to their departure. When verbal, physical, and
sexual abuses are added as a means of coercing work, the exploitation wors-
ens. After some period, the worker may be sold to another family or may
be sent home with just a fraction of the wages promised. In all cases, it is
a corrosive journey that leaves the migrant domestic worker, as well as her
family, much worse off than before.

The destructive nature of many migrant domestic worker experiences are
facilitated and exacerbated by the fact that they remain the least protected
category of workers under labor legislation in most countries, particularly
in Asia and the Middle East. Table 6.2 shows just how exposed domestic
workers are in these regions.

The lack of legal protections for domestic workers in the Middle East and
Asia leaves them heavily exposed to abuse and exploitation and serves as
a powerful incentive for agencies and wealthy families to arrange for poor
women to travel to these regions where they can be exploited in domestic

TABLE 6.2 Legal Protections of Domestic Workers in the
Middle East and Asia

PERCENT OF COUNTRIES IN WHICH DOMESTIC WORKERS . . .	MIDDLE EAST	ASIA
Are excluded from labor legislation	99	61
Have no limitation on work hours per week	100	99
Are excluded from paid leave laws	99	97
Are excluded from minimum wage laws	99	88

Source: Data from ILO (2013).

servitude with little or no legal consequence. The countries in these regions should be held accountable for the purposeful and unjustifiable lack of protection of domestic workers. There is no reason equal protection under the law should not be afforded to all domestic workers save to facilitate their servitude, particularly for isolated migrants who are trapped in the jaws of debt bondage.

A Closer Look at Up-Front Fees

Debt bondage in the migrant domestic worker sector is almost always initiated via up-front fees. Despite regulatory efforts in some countries to eliminate these fees, recruiters continue to use them to ensnare servants in debt bondage. Depending on the country of origin, typical fees vary (see table 6.3).

In all the cases, the domestic worker is responsible for the fees associated with her placement with a family by the agency, and also for her passport and visa, police clearance, and securing her birth certificate. In the worst debt bondage cases I documented, the worker was overcharged two or three times the actual costs of these expenses. Additional fees were completely fabricated to inflate the worker's debts, such as a "mobilization fee," an "entrance fee," or "service fees." The worker was responsible for the fees associated with her training and certification to be a domestic worker in the destination country, including room and board during the training, the instructor fees, materials, and so on. To obviate the semblance of charging

TABLE 6.3 Migrant Domestic Worker Up-Front Fees

TYPE	RESPONSIBLE PARTY
Agency placement	Worker
Passport and visa	Worker
Police clearance	Worker
Birth certificate	Worker
Medical check	Worker
Training	Worker
Room and board	
Instructor	
Handbook/materials	
Rent for training tools	
Competency test	
Training Co-fee	
Contract verification	Employer, shifted to worker
Work visa	Employer, shifted to worker
Residence permit	Employer, shifted to worker
Insurance	Employer, shifted to worker
Airfare and taxes	Employer, shifted to worker

exorbitant fees, many agencies advance the fees as a loan from a bank in the destination country, which must then be repaid through deductions from the worker's wages. This mechanism of bank loans for fees is increasingly used by recruitment agencies because they tend to be viewed by governments as private economic arrangements as opposed to up-front fees for employment, which fall outside the parameters of most laws that prohibit the assessment of up-front fees to migrant workers.

Other expenses are supposed to be paid by the employing family, such as contract verification in their country, the work visa, travel expenses, residence permits, and insurance for the domestic worker. In the most exploitative cases, the employing family sends these sums to the agency, and the agency pockets the funds and adds the expenses to the worker's up-front debt. The totality of the fees in the cases I documented depended on the country of origin and typically ranged from $1,500 to $4,000. This is a substantial sum when one considers that the per capita incomes in most of the countries from which the domestic workers migrate might be just a few hundred dollars per year. In the most severe debt bondage cases I documented, the fees assessed to the worker were $5,000 or more, which the worker was never able to work off. To make matters worse, agencies almost always add to the fees even after the worker is placed in a household. They charge bogus fees for permit renewals, new health checks, or placement of the worker in another family in the destination country, even in cases of physical and sexual abuse in the first household. As in traditional South Asian bonded labor, the debts are created and exacerbated by the exploiter to ensnare vulnerable, isolated women in servitude for years on end.

I attempted to speak with personnel at fifteen different domestic worker recruitment agencies across South Asia and East Asia linked to cases of debt bondage that I documented. None of them were willing to speak with me. Unfortunately, at this stage in my research, a simple Internet search of my name revealed exactly the kind of research I do and why I might be interested in speaking with the agencies. In two cases, I tried using a false identity when requesting meetings, but both times when I arrived at the office a security guard asked to see my ID, which of course did not match the name I had given. I tried phone conversations as well, but to no avail. The agencies varied in size and levels of formality, and all of them worked with subcontractors who operated at the village level to recruit domestic workers. I managed to have a few meetings with more legitimate agencies that were not associated with exploitative cases, and they were largely what I expected—full disclosure of recruitment practices, reasonable fee assessments, efforts at monitoring and protection, and a genuine desire to find work for women in need. Some of the most effective efforts by agencies and governments to protect migrant domestic worker populations that I investigated were in the Philippines.

Thousands of women migrate each year from the Philippines to be domestic workers around the world, and the country's recruitment agency sector is highly regulated. Recruitment agencies must first be licensed through the Philippines Overseas Employment Administration, which maintains strict controls and conducts regular audits to help minimize abuses. An official named Mary from the POEA informed me that her administration "is committed to protecting women from the Philippines who travel abroad for work. If women from our country cannot find gainful employment here, we are obligated to ensure they have a safe experience abroad." Mary described some of the efforts the Philippines undertakes to protect migrant workers. First, migrant domestic workers must undergo a mandatory Pre-Departure Education Programme provided by the government. This program includes classes on local languages, culture familiarization, and even stress management. Workers must also undertake a Pre-Departure Orientation Seminar specifically tailored for individuals migrating to Hong Kong or the Middle East because these areas are known to have the highest potential for exploitation. Workers receive information about their contracts, health and safety guidelines, airport procedures, local emergency contacts, and other essential information to help keep them protected. Philippine migrant domestic workers still suffer debt bondage and other abuses, but I documented far fewer cases from the Philippines than from other nations in Asia. I believe the lower number of cases I uncovered is correlated to better regulation and preparation in the home country, and better connections and safety systems in destination countries. Higher education levels and literacy rates among Philippine domestic workers when compared to those from Asian nations also play a crucial role in reduced exploitation levels.[12] The Philippines offers a good model for migrant domestic worker protection and empowerment that other sending countries should adopt.

Meeting a Recruiter

Despite my lack of success in speaking with recruitment agencies linked to the debt bondage cases I documented, I was able to meet with numerous individuals in India, Bangladesh, Indonesia, and Nepal who recruit women into transnational migration for domestic work. These are the men and women who initiate the debt bondage process, operating beyond the scope of regulatory enforcement or oversight. Of all the subcontractors I met, my time with Ashish was the most elucidating.

I met Ashish in the Sindhupalchok district of Nepal, a mountainous region northeast of Kathmandu that stretches all the way to the border with China. Ashish told me he had been working as a recruiter for construction, domestic work, and a few other sectors for more than a decade, covering scores of villages in Sindhupalchok and Dolakha districts. "I am from this area, and I know these people well," Ashish told me. "It is easy for me to speak with them and explain the work opportunities."

Ashish told to me that different agencies focus on different types of jobs and that most of his efforts in the last two years were focused on recruiting domestic workers for the Middle East. "Nepali people are desperate to leave this country," Ashish said. "Even I worked in construction in Abu Dhabi for five years before I returned to Nepal and started this work."

I asked Ashish about his recruitment practices. He explained that he recruited workers for the domestic worker agencies in Kathmandu and received a payment for each woman he sent. He also received an additional fee for each woman who completed her training. "I keep track of all the women I bring to the agencies. I speak to their families, and I encourage them to complete their training responsibly," Ashish told me. "This benefits both of us."

I asked Ashish about agencies that charge excessive fees or engage in fraudulent practices to exploit domestic workers. I was surprised by his answer. "This happens all the time! You must assume this is the case . . . but I do not have anything to do with it."

Ashish explained that corrupt agencies pop up and are shut down regularly. They reopen using a different name, or they just operate illegally and transfer workers they have recruited to licensed agencies for a fee. "The government cannot keep track of the agencies," Ashish said.

I asked Ashish if he would help me arrange conversations with some of the agencies in Kathmandu, but he declined. "If I take you to them, they will not work with me. You understand."

Ashish was willing, however, to allow me to accompany him on some of his recruiting trips to the villages in exchange for a small fee. I spent three days with Ashish hiking through Sindhupalchok district. We visited a total of six villages, two per day. The people were isolated and destitute; many appeared ill and malnourished. Most had been made aware through NGO campaigns of the risks of foreign migration, but as a villager named J. Gopal explained, "See our condition here. We cannot live like this. We must take our chances." J. Gopal had already worked as a migrant laborer in construction in India and Bangladesh, receiving a fraction of his promised wages, but it was enough to keep his family (barely) fed and sheltered. He and the other villagers knew that the outcome of labor migration was likely to be exploitative, but they also hoped they would be lucky enough to earn sufficient income to help their families scrape by on something that might loosely be called a human existence.

I watched Ashish gather the women of the villages, always in the presence of the men, and talk about the opportunities to work abroad as a domestic worker. He described the training and the fees, he talked about what life was like in some of the destination countries such as Oman and Dubai, and he showed photos of the glimmering cities, the glitzy malls, and the elegant homes in which they would work. He played two audio recordings from his smartphone of other Nepalese women who described the process, how happy they were, and how much money they were making. He explained the up-front loan process in vague terms and spoke about wage deductions for the first year, but he promised the deductions would not last any longer if the women worked hard. In his notepad, Ashish wrote down the names, ages, husband's or father's name, and the village name of the women who were interested. He secured a total of forty-seven names during the three days I spent with him.

"Only ten or fifteen of these women will come to Kathmandu and start the training, and of those, only half will complete the training and be placed in a foreign home," Ashish said. I asked why so few who signed up would actually undertake the training, and Ashish said there were many reasons: men may not allow it, they may fall ill or become pregnant, or they may take another offer for work.

During my time with Ashish, I was conflicted about how much I should try to tell the women about the risks of the exploitative debt bondage situations that often occur in relation to the up-front fees he described. I wanted to warn them to keep their documents and a mobile phones in their possession at all times, to know how to contact local authorities should anything happen to them, and that it was okay for them to reject an exploitative situation and return home rather than persist out of a sense of shame or guilt in the hope that things may one day get better. On the other hand, some of these women could end up in good circumstances that would provide vital income for their families, and if I scared them off with too many cautionary tales, I might end up doing more harm than good. It was difficult to find time to talk with the women without Ashish present, but he did take calls on his phone from time to time, and on two occasions he took a nap in the village, which gave me a little time with some of the women he had been recruiting. I tried to temper the dream world Ashish had portrayed and provided a few suggestions for how to keep safe and avoid debt bondage. I can only hope that some of these suggestions proved helpful. More than giving cautionary pointers, I ended up responding to numerous questions the young women had for me. They were more informed about migration and the world in general than their isolated circumstances might lead one to believe. Many of the women had been to Kathmandu for various reasons, although none with whom I spoke had ever left the country. One young woman I met on my last day with Ashish made a lasting impression. Laxmi was bright, curious, and strong-willed. She spoke with remarkable clarity about her circumstances and the life she aspired to achieve:

> I do not want to leave my parents, but what are my options? I will not
> go to India for prostitution, and there is no work in Nepal. If I stay,
> I will have to marry, and then what kind of life will I have? I want
> to earn money so I can take my parents to a better home and we can
> live on our own terms. Most people in Nepal must live on terms they
> do not want. We are no different from anyone else. We want to live
> by our determining. If I must go abroad for domestic work in order
> to have this life, I will do it. But I am not a fool and no one will take
> advantage of me. Please give me your email, Siddharth, and in five
> years I will write to you. I will tell you that I am at university. I will
> be a doctor, so I can help people like us who are always sick. I promise
> you. You will see!

The vigor with which Laxmi described her aspirations was inspiring. She felt like a beacon of hope in a land otherwise interred with the corpses of countless crushed dreams. Most people in her circumstances had resigned themselves to a bleak and brief survival, but Laxmi seemed undimmed by the darkness around her. Her cheer and determination lifted my spirits, and for that I was deeply grateful. I knew the odds were stacked against her, but I also knew it would take more than penury and negative experiences to extinguish her spark.

I gave Laxmi my email address and told her she must contact me any time and I would do whatever I could to help. She asked if I could give her a blessing, but I said that I was not important enough to do so. She insisted, so we settled on a hug and my best wishes that all good things would come to her. It has been seven years since I met Laxmi. I never heard from her, and I never managed to return to her village to see what became of her. I pray, now and again, that Laxmi is at university studying medicine and that she is simply too busy, happy, and thriving to remember me.

A Look at the Domestic Worker Numbers

During the course of my research, I documented 209 individuals exploited in debt bondage conditions in the domestic worker sector in countries outside of South Asia. However, a majority of the victims I documented (~70 percent) originated from South Asia. Here are some of the key findings from these cases:

- 96 percent females
- $71.35 per month ($2.46 per day; $0.18 per hour): average wage[13]
- 21.4 years: average age when first entered debt bondage
- 16 cases of children under the age of eighteen years
- 51 workers from India, 40 from Nepal, 37 from Bangladesh, 22 from the Philippines, 19 from Sri Lanka, 10 from Indonesia, 7 from Laos, and 23 from other countries (Africa and Latin America)
- $2,840: average initial debt
- 98 percent of cases belonged to minority ethnic or caste communities
- 94 percent of cases had passports and work permits confiscated on arrival
- 69 percent of cases had additional fees added after work started
- 63 percent of cases had contract terms changed on arrival
- 21 percent of cases were forced to transfer their up-front fee debts to a loan from a local bank

As awareness of levels of migrant domestic worker abuse continues to grow, many governments, NGOs, and unions are working assiduously to improve protections for these workers. Unfortunately, enforcement and oversight remain inconsistent. The exclusion of domestic workers from most labor laws, especially in Asia and the Middle East, is particularly problematic. Perhaps the most effective organization working to help protect migrant domestic workers is the International Domestic Workers Federation (IDWF). The mission of IDWF is to empower domestic workers, inform them of their rights, promote dignified working conditions, campaign against excessive recruiter fees, and help keep domestic workers in destination countries protected and connected. In addition, IDWF has campaigned assiduously for countries to ratify the ILO Convention on Decent Work for Domestic Workers (No. 189) of 2011. This convention mandates that domestic workers receive protections equivalent to those of other workers, including maximum working hours, minimum wages, overtime compensation, daily and weekly rest periods, social security, and maternity leave. The convention also calls for adequate protection of domestic workers against violence and abuse, and perhaps most important, it calls for the regulation of recruitment agencies and up-front fees specifically to help eliminate debt bondage. To be effective, this regulation will need to work down to the level of local recruiters such as Ashish.

Despite the efforts of IDWF, other NGOs, and new international conventions that focus on protecting migrant domestic workers, millions still fall between the regulatory and oversight cracks of unlicensed agencies, unscrupulous recruiters, and apathy among those who are served (including their governments) to uphold the rights, dignity, and equality of those who serve. This apathy is the soil in which all forms of slavery take root.

DEBT BONDAGE AND CONSTRUCTION

As with domestic servants, severe labor exploitation and debt bondage in the global construction sector is highly linked to labor migration. Overstated fees, unfair wage deductions, and an insufficiency of protections, rights, and connections in destination countries conspire to consign countless migrant construction workers to debt bondage exploitation, or worse. Indeed, every year thousands of migrant construction workers suffer serious injury or perish due to poor safety standards, harsh working conditions, and other abuses. As with domestic work, migrant construction workers in debt bondage are concentrated primarily in Asia and the Middle East. In addition to these regions, I have documented cases in the United States involving migrants from south of the border, in several western European countries involving migrants from eastern and central Europe, and even in Africa involving migrants from the western and northern nations of the continent. Around the world, major cities are being built, developed, or expanded on the backs of cheap, expendable laborers and slaves. Construction is second only to agriculture in terms of global employment numbers, with 180 million construction workers in 2015 toiling on projects worth $8.5 trillion, growing to an estimated 210 million workers by 2020 who will toil on projects worth $10.3 trillion.[14] These immense projects pull millions of poor labor migrants into travel abroad in the hope of securing income opportunities[15] and results in the largest up-front recruiter fees of any migrant worker sector I documented. The fees typically range from $4,000 to $15,000, which represent a lifetime of income (or debt) for most construction migrants. The heaviest flow of migrants in construction work is from India, Nepal, and Bangladesh to Dubai, Abu Dhabi, Qatar, Malaysia, and Singapore. To be sure, the meteoric construction boom in the Middle East across the last two decades has been heavily supported by cheap and exploited migrant labor from South Asia.[16] In many of these countries, informality is the norm with construction work, leading to a lack of protection, safety, and a plethora of exploitative practices.[17] The severe abuses that have come to typify many construction projects in the Middle East in particular have been highlighted in the media, most recently with the 2022 World Cup facilities in Qatar.[18] However, the two countries that provided me with the most interesting case studies of debt bondage in the construction sectors are Singapore and Malaysia. Not only do these neighboring nations have high levels of trafficked construction workers from South Asia, but they also offer very different responses to the issue.

Singapore: Debt Bondage in the Land of Law and Order

Singapore prides itself in being a land of law and order. It is without question a remarkably efficient, affluent, and energetic nation. To achieve these ends, the government can be somewhat autocratic, which unquestionably depresses freedoms for average citizens. Nevertheless, the orderliness and reliability of this remarkable city-state is something to behold. For example, in an effort to contain street congestion, the government levies a tax on the purchase of automobiles that is three or four times the purchase price of the car. This means only the rich can afford a car and most people must take public transportation. Traffic jams in Singapore are highly uncommon because there are simply not enough cars on the road to cause one. This kind of a policy would never work in most countries, however. Here is another example: in food courts at packed malls, finding seating can be a challenge. One simply leaves a tissue or a handkerchief on a table to signal that you have reserved it while you and your friends disperse to purchase your meals. The table will be left alone until you return. Try that anywhere else and, well, forget it. Everyday life in Singapore is a curious experiment in efficiency and order at the expense of personal freedoms. The nation is a well-oiled machine with law and order enforced at every turn, and one would not expect to find substantial issues of slavery within its borders.

Slavery, however, is exactly what I found during my trips to Singapore. The first trip I took was in 2011 on behalf of the U.S. Department of State as an emissary to help raise awareness of human trafficking, especially in government circles. When I first met with government officials in Singapore, they were in a state of understandable denial that human trafficking was any sort of problem in the country. They conceded there could be isolated cases, but they felt the larger problem they faced related to migrants who did not honor the terms of their contracts and tried to game the system. My first task was to conduct research to get a better sense of exactly what was going on in the country vis-à-vis slavery and human trafficking.

I focused on construction sites, shipyards, and the city's red-light area, Gaylong. I documented numerous cases of sex trafficking in Gaylong, particularly at clubs that specialized in minors, and the country's construction and shipyard sectors revealed dozens of cases of trafficked debt bondage slaves from India, Nepal, and Bangladesh. Conducting interviews onsite was challenging; most of the workers were understandably reluctant to be seen speaking to anyone other than their bosses. There was almost always a foreman or other guards at the sites. Although I managed to find a few quiet and unmonitored places for interviews, most of the cases I documented were at shelters with the help of local NGOs. One NGO in particular, Transient Workers Count Too (TWC2), arranged interviews with several former construction workers the organization was assisting.

Each of the migrants I documented took out substantial loans to secure work positions in Singapore. The loans covered a training program and certification course, travel and visas, medical checks, and work contracts in construction upon arrival. The itemization of the expenses was similar to what I had documented in the domestic servant cases. In aggregate, the loans for South Asians in Singapore's construction sector ranged from $6,000 to $10,000. If the worker's family owned land, many recruiters pressured the workers to sell their land to pay some or all of the up-front fees. Most migrants did not have land, so their fees were taken as loans. Upon arrival in Singapore, many of the workers were told that the company that sponsored them did not secure the proper work permits, and they were sent back home penniless, landless, and with a lifetime of debt from the up-front fees. Others were employed as contracted but were told they would have to repay debts from wage deductions that were far in excess of the loans they took. Most of the migrant construction workers were promised wages in Singapore that started at $600 to $800 per month, but the individuals I documented only received a fraction of this sum, if anything at all. As with all debt bondage cases, the deductions were highly skewed against the worker, with excessive and previously undisclosed deductions for room, board, daily transport, new permits and fees, and other expenses. The migrant worker policies of the Singapore government do not help matters. Foreign workers can migrate to Singapore under one of three visas: (1) Employment Pass (192,300 visas in 2016), (2) S Pass (179,700 visas in 2016), or a Work Permit (992,700 total visas with 315,500 visas in construction in 2016).[19] The first type of visa is for professionals such as lawyers and bankers, the second type is for midlevel skilled staff, and the third type is for semiskilled labor such as domestic workers and construction workers (two-year permits, from approved countries only). The Singapore government charges the sponsoring employer of foreign construction workers a levy of $300 to $950 per worker, depending on the kind of work they will perform and their country of origin, and a security bond of $5,000 per worker, which is forfeited if the worker violates any of the provisions of the work permit: they cannot bring family members with them, they must receive approval from the Ministry of Manpower before marrying a Singapore citizen, and they cannot get pregnant or give birth to a child in Singapore, among others. In almost every case of debt bondage I documented in Singapore's construction sector, these expenses were passed on to the worker as part of his wage deductions even though doing so is against the law. After these and other deductions are forced on the migrant workers, they are left with little or no monthly wage. They persevere in the hope of receiving a full wage one day, but in numerous cases the construction companies employing the migrant workers had them arrested for petty offenses around the time they had recouped their expenses. Unable to pay the fines, the workers were deported. A man named Alam from Bangladesh, who was facing deportation after nine months of unpaid work, explained:

> I sold 1.5 bigha of land to pay half the fee of three lakh taka [~$4,300] to come to Singapore and work in construction. This was all the land my family had. The other half I took on loan. When I arrived, I went to a dormitory. More than 300 other workers lived there. It was very crowded, and we were locked inside every night. At four in the morning the company took us in a truck to the city. We worked all day until the night. Then they took us to the dormitory. I was supposed to earn $700 each month, but after nine months I was not paid any wage. The company said I must still repay my loan. They said they deducted $200 from my wage for living in the dorm and $150 for food each month. When I complained, they abused me. Then I was arrested for spitting and fined $400. I did not have money to pay this fine, so they said I will be deported. I am trying to get some of my wages before they send me back to Bangladesh. If I knew they would not pay me, I would not have come here. Now my family has no land and no money. I do not know how we will survive.

Alam's story was typical of the kinds of callous and opportunistic exploitation of impoverished migrant workers I documented in Singapore's construction sector. Data from the Ministry of Manpower in Singapore shows that there are around 1.4 million foreign workers in Singapore, representing roughly 40 percent of the country's workforce.[20] There is no reliable data on the number of irregular migrants in the country, but thousands can be found in construction, shipyard work, and domestic work. To this day, no one knows just how many of these regular and irregular migrant workers are being exploited in debt bondage and slavery.

One particular facet of the situation faced by the migrant workers in Singapore that I was curious to explore relates to housing. Finding accommodations for 1.4 million or more foreign workers in a country of 5.5 million people is no small task. Every one of the foreign construction workers I documented in Singapore told me he lived in numerous dormitories or barracks scattered around the outskirts of the city. I found the largest barracks north of Singapore not far from the Straits of Johor, which separates Singapore from mainland Malaysia. A few barracks were also located on islands in the Straits, just off the coast. I documented several of these barracks, which ranged in size from a few hundred to a few thousand beds. Though cramped and not very clean, they were among the most livable migrant/trafficked worker barracks I have seen. They had kitchen facilities, televisions, and nearby markets. Guards patrolled the areas to maintain order and security. Some of the barracks were locked at night, but most were not. I spoke to several workers at the barracks at night, and most did not have major complaints about the living conditions. They felt constrained and crowded, but otherwise the facilities were not as filthy and unpleasant as others in which they had lived. Rafiq spent three years working in construction in Dubai before coming to Singapore. "The barracks in Dubai were very bad," Rafiq told me. "They were so dirty and the toilets were always broken. The fans were always broken. There was no place to eat except in the dirt. Here the conditions are better."

In Dubai, Rafiq was only paid about 20 percent of his promised wages before he was deported. So far in Singapore he had only received about 30 percent of his promised wages; the remainder, he was told, was going toward repayment of the loan he took to secure the job.

When I visited the worker barracks in Singapore, I also learned that labor recruiters from Malaysia often visit with promises of better work and wages in their country. They claim they can arrange passage to Malaysia by boat across the Straits of Johor. Some workers take the offers, but most do not because they hope they will eventually be paid their full wages in Singapore.

I wanted to spend a few nights in or near the barracks to get a better sense of the living conditions and to document more cases, but the guards did not permit me to do so. Nevertheless, the evidence of debt bondage and labor trafficking that I gathered from Singapore's construction sector, along with the cases I documented at the shipyards and in the red-light area, led me to conclude that the country has a systemic problem with slavery and human trafficking. Once I completed my research, I had to present it in a way that might motivate a change in perception by the government yet not seem so severe that I would be dismissed as a troublemaker rather than an ally hoping to help address the issues.

I held a few meetings with various ministries in the Singapore government to discuss my impressions of debt bondage and labor trafficking in the migrant worker community. I was told by colleagues at the U.S. Mission in Singapore that these meetings played an important role in acceptance by the government that the country had real issues that needed to be addressed. Six months later, the government of Singapore invited me to speak at the launch of the country's first National Plan of Action (NPA) to combat human trafficking, with a focus on construction and domestic work. The NPA included a commitment to draft a law against human trafficking, to improve victim assistance and protection, to tackle excessive up-front fees and unjust wage deductions in the migrant worker community, and to research the prevalence of various forms of human trafficking more diligently. I spoke at the launch of the NPA in March of 2012, and modest progress on the plan has been made in Singapore since.

Singapore's economy is highly dependent on a substantial migrant workforce, and most people in the country look the other way as far as debt bondage and labor exploitation are concerned. The same is true of most of the other nations in the world that receive large numbers of migrant workers; they are either heavily reliant on these workers because they lack the labor base in their countries to meet employment needs, or they have become too dependent on the lower wages and higher profits provided by exploitable foreign workers. I have not returned to Singapore since 2012, but I know that more comprehensive research must be done to document the prevalence rates of debt bondage and labor trafficking in key migrant worker sectors and the up-front fees and wage deductions that lead to much of this exploitation. I suspect not much has changed with regard to these issues in the last few years. It also is possible that additional government focus could lead to unintended negative consequences for migrant workers, such as higher levels of deportation or new policies that could have an adverse impact on migrant worker communities. I hope I am wrong and that this land of law and order will cast a more compassionate eye on the human rights costs of its growth, development, and efficiency. The same can be said for most of the developed world.

Malaysia: More Awareness, More Bondage

Around the time I was working to promote acceptance of human trafficking as a problem in Singapore, neighboring Malaysia already had a high level of awareness of this issue. Paradoxically, this elevated awareness seemed to make the problem worse. Even though Malaysia already had a law criminalizing human trafficking, and even though the government had undertaken numerous efforts to address the offense, my research indicated that the levels of labor trafficking and debt bondage in Malaysia's construction sector were greater than in Singapore. As with Singapore, Malaysia has a robust construction sector, which has been growing 6 percent per year since 1990 and is perceived as the bedrock of the nation's aspirations to become a developed economy.[21] The government estimates that 1.1 million of the country's 2.1 million foreign workers toil in the construction sector, with an additional 1.5 million to 2 million unregistered workers filling out the country's labor market needs.[22] Foreign-born individuals represent an astounding 70 percent of the Malaysian workforce,[23] and South Asians in particular have been taking on heavy debt loads to migrate to Malaysia for construction work for decades,[24] often finding servitude, exploitation, and bondage instead.

I received my first indication that Malaysia was ahead of Singapore (and many other countries) in terms of general awareness of human trafficking before I even arrived in the country. As my plane to Kuala Lumpur entered its final descent, the air hostess came on the intercom system to inform passengers that they should ensure their seatbelts were fastened, tray tables stowed, and seats placed in their upright position. She spoke about landing cards and immigration procedures, and then she said, "Please be advised, Malaysia has strict laws against drug and human trafficking." It was the first time I had heard an announcement of this kind in any of the dozens of countries I had visited.

As I queued for immigration at the airport, I saw several posters on pillars with the picture of a mother and an infant with the tag line, "Human trafficking is a crime" and an instruction to dial "999" with information about any incident of human trafficking. After the plane announcement and the airport posters, I expected to uncover only isolated cases of slavery. The truth was otherwise.

I visited several construction sites in Kuala Lumpur and saw thousands of South Asian workers. I documented several of these workers onsite, at shelters, and in their barracks. The conditions in all cases were worse than in Singapore; impoverished South Asians toiled in severe debt bondage trying to work off the loans they took to secure construction jobs. They lived in subhuman conditions in the barracks, were paid a fraction of their promised wages, and most were ultimately discarded or deported once their usefulness expired. Safety standards lagged what I had seen in Singapore, and numerous workers I met or who were described to me had suffered injuries that ranged from serious gashes to broken bones to death. One worker, Mustafa, temporarily residing at a prisonlike shelter for human trafficking victims, told me the following story:

> I am from Khulna district in Bangladesh. Many recruiters come to our villages. They promise they can arrange work in construction in other countries for very good wages. First, we have to pay a fee of four lakh taka [$5,000] for training and documents. I did not have these funds, so I took a loan. They said my wages will be deducted to repay the loan.
>
> After some months they gave us the documents and the agents arranged travel by ship to Kuala Lumpur. The ship left from Mongla port. More than thirty of us were put inside a container in the bottom of the ship. It was dark, but we were provided torches. We were only allowed out of the container in the late night for maybe one hour for toilet. Otherwise, we had to stay inside the container. It was very hot, and the smell was very bad. We tried to wait for toilet when we are allowed outside, but if we had to use toilet inside we could only use a bucket. Most of us became very sick. I was vomiting. There were two children, and they were crying every day. I thought we were going to die. I think it was maybe nine days to come to Kuala Lumpur.
>
> The boss took us to dormitories. Mine had maybe three hundred men. We slept on mats on the ground. Each morning they took us to the construction site by bus. My work was with cement. If we did not work hard enough, the bosses would beat us. We had to ask permission

to urinate, or they would beat us. They gave us only two meals of rice
and daal each day, then took us back to the dormitory. I did this kind
of work for eight months, and I did not receive any wages. The govern-
ment is going to deport me because I do not have proper papers. They
say I must return by ship.

When I heard Mustafa's story, I could not help but be struck by its similarities to another slave narrative I had read, this one from a more than two
centuries earlier, the story of Olaudah Equiano.

Olaudah Equiano was born in the Benin Empire in present-day Nigeria,
sold to a slave ship at Badagry, and enslaved in the Americas before eventually purchasing his freedom and recounting his life story in the extraordinary book, *The Interesting Narrative of the Life of Olaudah Equiano, 1789.*
Equiano became a pivotal figure in the British abolitionist movement of the
late eighteenth century, and his book is required reading for anyone who
wants to understand the brutal and dehumanizing realities of the Atlantic
slave trade. In his book, Equiano describes in extraordinary language his
first encounter with European slave traders:

The first object which saluted my eyes when I arrived on the coast was
the sea, and a slave ship, which was then riding at anchor, and waiting for
its cargo. These filled me with astonishment, which was soon converted
into terror when I was carried on board. I was immediately handled and
tossed up to see if I were found by some of the crew; and I was now persuaded that I had gotten into a world of bad spirits, and that they were
going to kill me. Their complexions too differing so much from ours,
their long hair, and the language they spoke (which was very different
from any I had ever heard), united to confirm me in this belief. Indeed
such were the horrors of my views and fears at the moment, that, if ten
thousand worlds had been my own I would have freely parted with them
all to have exchanged my condition with that of the meanest slave in my
own country. . . .

At last, when the ship we were in had got in all her cargo, they made
ready with many fearful noises, and we were all put under deck, so that
we could not see how they managed the vessel. But this disappointment
was the least of my sorrow. The stench of the hold while we were on the

coast was so intolerably loathsome, that it was dangerous to remain there for any time, and some of us had been permitted to stay on the deck for the fresh air; but now that the whole ship's cargo were confined together, it became absolutely pestilential. The closeness of the place, and the heat of the climate, added to the number in the ship, which was so crowded that each had scarcely room to turn himself, almost suffocated us. This produced copious perspirations, so that the air soon became unfit for respiration, from a variety of loathsome smells. . . . This wretched situation was again aggravated by the galling of the chains, now become insupportable; and the filth of the necessary tubs, into which the children often fell, and were almost suffocated. The shrieks of the women, and the groans of the dying, rendered the whole a scene of horror almost inconceivable.

Separated by centuries, Equaino and Mustafa tell shockingly similar tales. Both were trafficked by sea into slavery in a far away land. Both were treated as subhumans and crammed like animals in a ship bound for servitude. Although these similarities represent a disheartening measure of how little progress has been made in ridding the world of slavery, there are also some interesting differences between their tales. First, there was no ruse involved in Equaino's ordeal. He was simply bought, trafficked, sold, and enslaved. Because slavery is no longer legal or morally acceptable, Mustafa was tricked with false employment terms that traded on his impoverishment and lack of alternatives. Second, Mustafa's transport was quicker and much less expensive than Equiano's. The time and cost of transportation have dropped by more than 90 percent from the late 1700s to the present day, making it much quicker and cheaper to get slaves from the point of origin to the point of exploitation. Third, Mustafa's duration of servitude was much shorter—less than one year compared to thirteen years for Equaino. This shortened duration of slavery is primarily a function of the greater amount of time and expense required to secure a slave in the past; today slaves are quite easy and cheap to acquire. In the modern context, exploiting a slave for a year or less still provides a robust return on investment, and replacement slaves can be easily procured. Fourth, Equaino had to purchase his freedom, but Mustafa was simply deported due to a lack of proper documentation. Equaino returned home a free man with no debt and was able to contribute to the British abolitionist movement, whereas Mustafa will return home buried in debt and most likely consigned to scraping out a meager existence through low-wage labor or eventually be trafficked and exploited again. Understanding that Equaino's outcome is a one-of-a-kind rarity because most slaves in the eighteenth century died as slaves, a more appropriate comparison would be that of a lifetime of servitude in the Old World compared to a lifetime of repeated episodes of servitude interspersed with periods of grinding poverty today. Although slaves today are still trafficked by sea (though more often through other means), just as they were in the past, they have become much less expensive and much more expendable than in previous centuries. Had Mustafa been able to secure a better alternative to the construction offer, or had the authorities in Malaysia protected and empowered him rather than detained him for deportation, he would have benefited from a vastly enhanced outcome. These two points of intervention—the provision of reasonable alternatives and the sustained empowerment of the survivor regardless of his migration status—are the fundamental areas of deficiency in current responses to slavery in almost every corner of the globe.

I documented numerous cases of debt bondage in Malaysia's construction sector similar to Mustafa's. The persistent theme involved up-front fees taken as loans that ensnared the individuals in debt bondage. Contractors and construction companies illegally charged the workers for the fees associated with their visas, permits, levies, and security bonds, as in Singapore. For its foreign workers, Malaysia provides "Visit Passes" for twelve-month periods of work in four sectors: manufacturing, plantations, agriculture and services, and construction, only from a preapproved list of other Asian nations. Sponsoring employers must fill out a battery of applications, conduct medical checks, produce the relevant training certificates, and pay a levy per worker by sector ($462.50 for construction) and a security bond between $62.50 and $375.00 depending on the worker's country of origin.[25] Approved workers must undergo additional checks and verifications within twenty-four hours of arrival in Malaysia, and once approved, they receive a color-coded ID card that they must wear at all times (gray for construction). The Visit Passes can be extended one year at a time for a fee that was illegally passed on to the foreign workers in most of the debt bondage cases I documented. In short, every conceivable expense is forced onto the workers and deducted from their wages, leaving them with minimal income to show for their backbreaking work as they build the future of Malaysia.

I visited the worker barracks in which the construction migrants lived and found the conditions markedly worse than in Singapore. They were more crowded, filthy, and depressing. I visited six barracks in total, and in each of them the workers were locked inside at night, even on the weekends. The barracks were in varying degrees of disrepair, and the stench of sweat and refuse was overpowering. When I asked the people living in the barracks about the conditions, their answers depressed me further. "At least we have toilets and hot water," a worker from Bangladesh told me. He did not have these luxuries back home.

I could find little that was minimally acceptable about the barracks I visited outside of Kuala Lumpur, even though they provided luxuries such as toilets and hot water, which many of the workers did not have in their home villages. I saw bed bugs in almost every bunk I inspected, along with mold, rusted nails, grime, dust, and other filth and, of course, the heat was stifling. Only the fatigue borne of a fourteen-hour workday spent in backbreaking construction work would allow a man to sleep in these conditions. The barracks were pitiful, and the government-run shelters for victims of human trafficking were not much better.

The government of Malaysia operates a system of shelters for victims of human trafficking as mandated by the country's human trafficking law. In the two shelters I visited, occupants were kept locked inside at all times, although at least the sleeping areas and bathrooms were cleaner than in the barracks. The shelters were drab, depressing, and crowded. They felt more like prisons than homes of freedom and empowerment. A 2010 amendment to Malaysia's Anti-Trafficking in Persons Act of 2007 helped me understand the true intention behind these shelters. The amendment was designed, in my opinion, to make it much easier for Malaysia to wash its hands of almost any victim of human trafficking identified within its borders. Section 26(B)(a) of this amendment created a new offense called "aggravated offense of smuggling of migrants," which was described as follows: "In committing the aforesaid offence, the person intends that the smuggled migrant will be exploited after entry into the receiving country or transit country whether by the person himself or by another person."

In other words, if an individual smuggles someone into Malaysia with the intention of exploiting him or her, this is not human trafficking but aggravated smuggling, even though this act is the textbook definition of human trafficking under international law. A human trafficking victim triggers certain positive obligations of a state to protect and empower the victim, including potential regularization of their migration status, but a victim of aggravated smuggling simply can be held in a shelter until he or she is deported. This is exactly what was happening in the prisonlike government shelters in Malaysia; people who should be clearly identified as victims of human trafficking were being held captive until the state was able to arrange for their deportation. Some smuggled migrants were also in the shelters, for which the appropriate legal response might be deportation, but the conflation of trafficking with smuggling and the deficient nature of the government shelters made the government's intentions clear, Beyond the tragic revictimization of the trafficking victims, this myopic approach to the crime allows traffickers to go almost entirely unpunished. Despite all the awareness, the laws, and the appearances of a robust and reasoned response to human trafficking, Malaysia's handling of slavery offenses appeared to be making matters worse. Before leaving, I decided to share my thoughts with government officials.

The main government complex for Malaysia is in Putrajaya, about 20 kilometers south of Kuala Lumpur. I arranged meetings with the National Anti-Trafficking-in-Persons Secretariat, the Minister of the Interior, the Attorney General, the Malaysian Bar Council, and the Council for Anti-Trafficking-in-Persons (MAPO) to explore the chasm between aspiration and reality vis-à-vis Malaysia's antitrafficking efforts, especially as they related to the system of debt bondage that seemed embedded in its migrant construction worker population. I was received respectfully by everyone I met and was afforded candid conversations. The Minister of the Interior and the Attorney General seemed genuinely concerned about human trafficking, and more important, about the suffering of trafficking victims. The team at MAPO outlined their efforts to tackle all forms of human trafficking and identified a lack of transnational cooperation with prevention and investigations of trafficking offenses as barriers to their efforts. I probed the issue of debt bondage among the country's migrant workforce with every official I met, and I always received reasonable responses. I was assured the government was aware of the problem of excessive wage deductions and would be elevating efforts to prevent the abuses. Most government officials pointed fingers to the governments of origin countries in South Asia and East Asia as not doing more to protect their citizens from being exploited through excessive up-front fees. I explained that the finger-pointing only benefited the exploiters, which received grudging agreement. I also took officials to task over the conflation of smuggling and trafficking in the 2010 amendment to Malaysia's antitrafficking law and the prisonlike conditions at the government shelters I visited, and our perceptions diverged in predictable ways. Officials saw no major problem with the 2010 amendment. They claimed the procedures at the shelters were meant to keep victims safe, and the country was doing everything it could to protect individuals who were identified as victims of human trafficking, forced labor, debt bondage, or child labor. The crux of the issue was the term "identified"—those I identified as victims were clearly falling through the definitional cracks, and the country generally appeared to be looking the other way when it came to debt bondage exploitation of migrants in the name of economic growth, just like Singapore.

Because several government officials in Malaysia pointed fingers at the governments of origin nations for not doing more to protect their migrants and help them avoid the excessive up-front fees that lead to debt bondage, I arranged meetings with consular officials in Malaysia from Bangladesh, India, Pakistan, Nepal, Sri Lanka, Indonesia, Cambodia, Thailand, and the Philippines. They (gently) pointed their fingers back at Malaysia for "maintaining an environment that promotes human trafficking," as the consular official from Sri Lanka explained. The official from Bangladesh told me, "They need the workers, so the construction companies and palm oil companies recruit from my country. These recruiters charge excessive fees and exploit the workers. We try to promote safe migration, but once our citizens are on their soil, there is little we can do to help them. The recruiters make fairy tale promises that any person from the lower economic rungs would be tempted to accept."

Although it is reasonable to critique the governments of these sending countries for not doing more to provide security and economic opportunity for their citizens, I believe destination countries do not really want them to do so because they depend on the exploitable, expendable low-wage workforce these countries can provide. This is the unspoken agreement between developing and developed economies: keep enough of your citizens poor and lacking opportunity so we can recruit them for cheap labor and you will benefit by taxing their remittance income and being relieved of the burden of having to try and find employment for them. Much of the world is being built under the onerous terms of this tacit agreement. Caught in the middle, the vulnerable and downtrodden are recruited and exploited in debt bondage and slavery in a self-perpetuating system that seems increasingly embedded in the logic of the global economy.

Although most of my government interactions left me dissatisfied with their efforts to address the problem of migrant worker exploitation, I had one illuminating conversation with an opposition MP in Malaysia who, under condition of anonymity, told me a very different story from that of the ruling party officials I met. He was an intense, charismatic man who saw his country with very different eyes. He told me at a hotel coffee shop in Kuala Lumpur:

> *The government profits from the human trafficking industry directly. They take kickbacks from the construction companies and the plantation companies from the wages they are supposed to pay the migrant workers, so long as the government looks the other way. Also, the police are corrupt. They allow trafficking in persons to take place. The contractors bribe them, and they do not bring charges if a worker complains his wage is being denied, or that he is living in squalor, or he is forced to repay a fraudulent debt and the boss says he still owes money. The government does not care about the migrants so long as they come here to work and leave without causing problems. The government claims there are no Malaysians to do this work and this is why they must bring in the migrants. The truth is, no one would stand for Malaysians being treated this way, but they do not mind if Bangladeshis or Nepalis are treated like this.*

The opposition MP spoke passionately as he decried a system of rampant corruption and racism that he felt led to the exploitation of millions of South Asians and East Asians trafficked to his country and forced into servitude. "What can be done?" I asked. The opposition MP sighed, "Not many of us are willing to speak out against the government. It is difficult to enact social change when people live in fear of punishment for expressing themselves in

ways that do not appease those in power. You can do this, though. You can
let people know what is happening here. This will help."

I thanked the opposition MP for his courage in speaking with me, and
I promised him I would write about the research I had done in his country
in the hope that this might play some small role in helping his cause.

Before I left Malaysia, I spent some time researching the country's palm
oil sector because it also operates on high levels of human trafficking and
debt bondage.[26] Malaysia exports more palm oil than any other country in
the world (around 45 percent of the world supply), and I documented six-
ty-five cases of labor trafficking, debt bondage, and slavery on four plantations. Every one of these cases followed a model of recruitment and
exploitation similar to what I saw in the country's construction sector. The
men were from the same origin nations, were recruited with lavish promises of high wages and good working conditions, were forced to carry heavy
debt loads for up-front fees, and were routinely exploited in debt bondage
through excessive wage deductions relating to room and board, permits and
fees, and other unjust expenses. They worked excessively long hours, and
because they were hidden deep in plantations, they suffered more physical
abuse, injuries, and illnesses than the construction workers. They were a
captive and largely invisible population of debt bondage slaves, following the
tortured footsteps of the generations of plantation slaves in Malaysia who
came before them. The horrible history of this exploitation was poignantly
described to me by A. Navamykandan.

Navamykandan is head of Malaysia's National Union of Plantation
Workers (NUPW), and he is descended from rubber and palm oil plantation workers who were trafficked to Malaysia by the British East India
Trading Company during the nineteenth century. To say the plight of
these workers is a matter close to his heart would be an understatement.
"The plantation companies make the claim that there are no Malaysians to
do the work," Navamykandan explained, "then they traffic mostly South
Asians to work in the plantations in debt bondage. This has been going
on since the beginning."

Navamykandan described the history of South Asian slaves who were
trafficked to Malaysian plantations since colonial times and how, in his
mind, little save the identity of the traffickers has changed. The NUPW
works diligently to advocate for the rights of Malaysia's plantation workers,

especially decent working conditions, fair wages, and the elimination of excessive recruiter fees, but Navamykandan told me they face substantial challenges from the government. Land grabs and evictions of peasants have been all too common, and there are few if any consequences for plantation companies that traffic South Asians for debt bondage in the palm oil sector. I asked Navamykandan if he felt conditions were better or worse now compared to the time when his ancestors were trafficked to Malaysia by the British. "They are much worse," he said. "People have no value today. That is how I feel about this question."

For many of the same reasons that conditions for someone like Mustafa might be considered worse than for Equiano, conditions for people in Malaysia's palm oil sector today might be considered worse than during the time when Navamykandan's ancestors were first trafficked. The large capital investment and time it took to traffic a worker from South Asia to Malaysia in the nineteenth century would have necessitated a greater investment in the basic "well-being" of the indentured worker to ensure his productivity for as long as possible, whereas workers today take out loans to pay their own way by plane or ship to Malaysia and can be brutally exploited, then deported and replaced at minimal cost by a new slave. Despite the abolition of slavery and all the advancements in human rights in the past two centuries, the plight of many trafficked debt bondage slaves who are exploited in the same plantations as their forefathers have in some ways only worsened. True, the theoretical equality of all human life that is now codified in international law and our collective moral systems is an incalculable improvement over centuries ago, but this theory crumbles against the reality of human beings as expendable cogs in a global economic machine that transforms their bondage into economic growth for the elites whose human rights and welfare unquestionably matter more. One class chews, while the other is chewed. One class serves, while the other is served. The chewed up servants of the world are no better off than they were centuries ago, perhaps even worse off.

A Look at the Construction Worker Numbers

During my research, I documented 445 cases of individuals exploited in debt bondage conditions in the construction sector of countries outside of South Asia. However, a majority of the victims I documented (~80 percent) originated from South Asia. Some of the other key findings from these cases include:

- 100 percent males
- $186.80 per month ($7.18 per day; $0.57 per hour): average wage[27]
- 22.2 years: average age at time debt bondage began
- 21 cases of children under the age of eighteen years
- 127 workers from India, 71 from Bangladesh, 69 from Nepal, 48 from Pakistan, 42 from Sri Lanka, 32 from Indonesia, 11 from Cambodia, and 45 from other countries (Africa, Eastern Europe, and Latin America)
- $4,922: average initial debt
- 97 percent of cases belonged to minority ethnic or caste communities
- 92 percent of cases had passports and work permits confiscated on arrival
- 83 percent of cases had additional fees added after work started
- 68 percent of cases had contract terms changed on arrival
- 26 percent of cases were forced to transfer their up-front fee debts to a loan from a local bank

The extent and pervasiveness of debt bondage in the global construction industry is unparalleled in any other sector I have researched. Add the broader spectrum of labor exploitation that seems inherent to the sector, especially in the Middle East and Asia (harsh working conditions, lack of safety measures, excessive hours, etc.), and much of the world is being built on the backs of human misery. The profits generated through this misery run in the billions of dollars per year. The only sector that would consistently surpass construction on a per slave profit basis is sex trafficking, and debt bondage is highly prevalent in this sector as well.

DEBT BONDAGE AND COMMERCIAL SEX IN THE UNITED STATES

I have documented sex trafficking cases involving debt bondage in dozens of countries around the world, including in the United States. Despite the fact that sex trafficking has garnered extensive attention in the United States only in recent years, the trafficking of women and children to and within the country for forced prostitution goes back at least a few centuries.[28] The cases of debt bondage–based sex slavery I documented in the United States manifest every salient element of the phenomenon, as well as some unique elements that arise due to the relationship between the foster care system and domestic sex trafficking. The U.S. model of debt bondage for transnational commercial sex migrants is similar to that of other countries: credit is taken by the victim to gain passage to the United States or for an alleged work opportunity, and upon arrival the young woman is forced into prostitution to work off her debt. Manipulations of the amount of the advance, deductions for living expenses, and other ploys are used to extend the duration of debt repayment. The promise of one day discharging the debt to pursue the original job offer (say, as a domestic worker) or to remain in prostitution as a means of earning income further ensnares the victim in the hope she will one day achieve a more favorable position.

A young girl named Maria at a shelter near San Diego told me a story that encapsulates the essence of debt bondage in the transnational commercial sex sector. In fact, she reminded me of the first child sex slave I met in Bombay fourteen years earlier—petite, soft-spoken, emptiness in her eyes. She was from a small town in the Tamaulipas state of Mexico, seventeen years old, and had been recruited to leave her home with the promise of a job working as a cleaning lady in office buildings in the United States. This is what she told me:

> I traveled with the recruiter from my home to Ciudad Miguel Aleman. The recruiter left me there in a small house with more than sixty people who wanted to cross the border. Those people were from Mexico, Guatemala, and El Salvador. There were also some men from Nepal. They locked us in the house, and the coyotes told us we had to pay $800 to the cartel or they cannot take us. I did not have the money, so they said I could repay the fee once I was working.
>
> The cartel soldiers came sometimes and took some of the men from the home, and we never saw them again. They threatened to kill us and raped the women. After I think two months, the coyotes took us across the border. It was the middle of the day. They sent us with some other men on the U.S. side. These men took us to a house. Eventually, they took me and two other girls from El Salvador to San Diego.

In San Diego, they locked me inside a house like a brothel and the men in that house raped me for two weeks. I tried to protest, but they raped me until I was unconscious. After that, they forced me to take customers at night. They said I owed them $2,000 and I can repay this at a rate of $10 per customer and then I was free to go. I thought this means I will have to be with two hundred men, but after the first week the pimp gave me an account slip. He deducted $200 that week for my rent, $200 for food, and $100 for clothes. They also deducted for condoms and medicine I needed for pain. My debt had only been reduced by $70. I told the pimp this was not fair, but he said it was the price of coming to America. I cried that night and wanted to kill myself.

I was in that brothel for almost one year before I escaped. Sometimes I had to be with four or five men in a night, sometimes it was twenty. They forced me to do unnatural things. The pimp would beat me if I did not please the customers. I had a broken rib once, but it did not matter how much pain I felt, the pimp forced me to be with customers. When I became pregnant, they made me have an abortion, even though it was against my beliefs.

Every day I prayed someone would help me. No one did, so I had to help myself. Where I am from, we all dream to come to America, but I did not know it was such a bad place.

I have documented dozens of young women just like Maria who traveled to the United States from around the globe: Central and South America, eastern Europe, Africa, and East Asia. Indeed, transnational victims of sex trafficking in the United States hail from dozens of countries, and in a majority of cases organized crime is involved with their recruitment, trafficking, and forced prostitution.[29] I have also documented dozens of American citizens—usually runaway teens or girls who aged out of the foster care system—who were trafficked into forced prostitution across the country. In most cases, both domestic and transnational, these young women were compelled to work off a debt under highly unfavorable terms before being "freed." The hope of potential freedom was used to exploit them until they escaped, or until there was nothing left to exploit. Most of the young women were promised work in hospitality, restaurants, domestic work, or as nannies. Some were told they would work in "entertainment," however, the entertainment was portrayed in far more favorable terms than in reality. For example, the women were told they could decide whether they did or did not want to transact for commercial sex, and if they did so, they could decide with whom, but on arrival they were violently coerced to be with any and all men who purchased them.

Maria's brothel was run by the Sinaloa cartel just outside of San Diego. I highlight her case because she was one of only four sex trafficking victims I met who was given a weekly statement of her debits and credits. Maria told me that this weekly sheet motivated her to persist until she attained her freedom, and that it had the same effect on the other young women in the brothel. Maria kept the first sheet she ever received and showed it to me. She told me the moment she received it she realized it would take her years to repay her debt. Although debt bondage slaves rarely have any sense of the arithmetic of their debt repayments, let alone formal weekly statements, Maria's captors saw fit to provide a detailed statement of their accounts, ostensibly to motivate her to "work" harder or with less resistance. Maria told me that two girls in the house worked off their debts, and in both cases the girls stayed on and kept working under a new arrangement in which they were paid one-third of each transaction, given free room, but had to pay for their food and clothes. I asked if they were allowed to leave the house, and Maria said, "Only on the day they returned to Mexico."

Another sophisticated model of debt bondage in the commercial sex sector in the United States that I documented involves the Russian mafia. The mafia brings Russian women to the United States on various kinds of visas (usually J, Q, or B-2), and most are told they will work in dance clubs. They are assured they will not have to engage in prostitution unless they want to but that doing so will help them work off their debts more quickly. Those debts are usually $10,000 or more, typically the purported cost of arranging documents, travel, and the work opportunity. Upon arrival, the journeys often take a dark turn. Here is what Katya, a young woman from Moscow, told me:

> I heard about agents who arrange work in New York. You can find
> their phone numbers on the Internet. One agent, Rovnik, said he could
> prepare my visa and plane tickets for New York. He said I would live in
> a nice apartment with other girls just like me. He said I could have my
> own bedroom. I knew I would have to dance in clubs, but he said the
> girls can make $1,000 in a night. My father cannot make this amount
> in one month! I came to New York filled with so much hope, but my
> hope was crushed. I lived in Brighton Beach, and I had to dance every

night in a club there. The pimps forced me to do prostitution or they said they would have me deported. The men who came to those clubs were horrible. They only wanted to do cruel acts. The club owner was named Sergey. He said I had to repay him $15,000. They took almost all my tips from dancing and all the money from the clients. I tried to keep count of my debt, but most nights I went unconscious from alcohol. Rovnik kept one promise to me. I had my own bedroom. There was a camera in the bedroom for the Internet. I had to strip in the room and take clients there two nights each week. I know they made money from that camera, but I don't know how much. If I protested, they whipped me like an animal and denied me food. I arrived in New York in December 2010, and I escaped from Sergey in March 2012. For me to stay in this country, they said I must agree to cooperate with the police to investigate Sergey. I can never do this. Who will protect my family? I will return to Russia soon. I was a fool to think I could earn $1,000 every day and live like a princess in America.

Stories like Katya's are common in the Russian sex trafficking circuit. Almost every victim I met accepted an offer to travel to the United States for work in dance clubs, with the promise of a glitzy life and bountiful income after they had discharged their debts. Even though there is increased awareness of these ruses in Russia, young women continue to accept offers in the hope that their fate will be better. To be fair, in every case I documented, the alternative for these young women in Russia was worse, or at least perceived to be worse. Unique to the young women I met from Russia was the vision of romance and the extravagant lifestyle they expected to have in America. "America is where we can find a rich man to give us glamour," another victim named Alisa told me. The story of the beautiful Russian woman who marries an investment banker, shops at Tiffany's, and socializes seven nights a week has been marketed well in Russia.

I found similar models of debt bondage in the commercial sex sector in Chinese and Thai massage parlors, East European apartment brothels, West African street prostitutes, and U.S. domestic victims of sex trafficking at various settings in Las Vegas, Los Angeles, Oakland, Atlanta, Seattle, Boston, San Diego, and McCallen, Texas. Approximately 64 percent (twenty-nine of forty-five cases) of these U.S. domestic sex trafficking victims were recruited into sex trafficking while they were in the foster care system or within six months of aging out. Most of my U.S. domestic sex trafficking research was done after the publication of *Sex Trafficking*, and I can say unequivocally that the foster care system is a major source of domestic sex trafficking victims in the United States. Inadequate protection for U.S. foster care children after they age out is a key driver of sex trafficking, along with abuses and a lack of monitoring and care while they are in the system. Children age out of the foster care system between the ages of eighteen and twenty-one, depending on state law. Many states offer transitional protection for a few years, but to qualify the children must have a steady job or have completed high school, a bar too high for many former foster care children to meet. The laws are in constant flux, and transitional foster care protections often are cut during times of budget constraints. Stephanie, a young woman I met at a halfway house in Riverside, California, told me her story:

> *My mom was a mess. I don't know who my dad is, but I'm sure he's a jerk. I was in three foster homes before I aged out. That was 2012. My caseworker made a transition plan with me. She told me about Assembly Bill 12 and how that could help me 'til I was twenty, but I didn't qualify. I didn't have a job, you know. She didn't really care though. She was doing her job. "Yeah, I told Stephanie about her options." Check.*
>
> *There's places on Facebook where girls like me hook up. I got in with a group. They were cool. We looked out for each other. I met this pimp Sean. I needed the money. I'm not proud of it. Sean said he would take care of me. I guess he did. I had food and a crib. It was bad though. I was with a lot of creeps. I wanted to stop, but Sean didn't let me. He said I owed him. He kept most of the money, but like I said I had food and a crib.*
>
> *It was like that about two years. Sean beat me down pretty bad one night. I knew that man was going to kill me. I was too afraid to run though. Cops saved me I guess. They arrested me. I told the judge what happened. She sent me here. Sean don't know I'm at this home. He texts me all the time though, but I don't respond. I got another couple weeks before I got to leave. I don't know what's next. Not many options for us, you know. I look back and I realize the system don't protect girls like me. They may try, but they don't. They don't want to admit there's girls like me 'cause what does that say about them? I know plenty of girls out of foster care end up with pimps, all messed up on drugs. People don't realize, we're people, too.*

Stephanie was exploited in sex trafficking after she aged out of the foster care system, but a little more than one-third of the U.S. foster care sex trafficking cases I documented involved a minor who was recruited while still in the system. Many foster care homes provide loving and safe environments, but others can be almost as abusive as the homes from which the child is meant to be protected. Traffickers prey on vulnerable and abused foster care children, and debt bondage is often used as a way to ensnare them. Case workers are supposed to provide a safety mechanism to assist with transition and ensure that the children are on a secure path, but most are underpaid, overworked, and crushed with far too many cases for them to monitor each one adequately. The U.S. foster care system is desperately in need of added resources to extend protections for children once they age out. In addition, a significant increase in the number of caseworkers is needed, so they have sufficient time to invest in each case. Beyond the foster care system, sex traffickers in the United States prey on a broad population of vulnerable teens, be they runaways or children from abusive homes.[30] Protections must be enhanced, and law enforcement personnel need more training to identify the indicators that a young woman may be working in prostitution as a result of recruitment and coercion when she was still a child.[31]

Assessing the precise number of sex trafficking cases I have documented that involve debt bondage is more challenging than in other sectors I have researched, such as construction and domestic work. The first few years that I documented these cases I did not include a full set of questions relating to debt bondage. In addition, many of the victims in sex trafficking have very little sense of their initial or subsequent debt levels. Some are given a clear sense, like Maria, but most are just told they have a debt to work off without being given any details because the recruitment channels are more informal than in the construction or domestic worker sectors, which have established and regulated recruiting processes involving predeparture training, work permits, medical checks, and work contracts. Prostitution is not a formal or legal work sector in most of the countries in which I have documented sex trafficking, or if prostitution is legal, coercion, pimping, and the exploitation of minors is not. Nonetheless, I am confident that between 60 and 75 percent of the sex trafficking cases I documented, including in the United States, involved debt bondage. The debts in the cases for which I was able to obtain reliable data ranged from roughly $1,000 to $40,000. These figures represent a significant variance, with the low end being regional sex trafficking victims in Latin America and Asia, and the high end being Nigerians trafficked to Europe. To be sure, most cases of Nigerian sex trafficking victims I described in chapter 2 also would be considered cases of debt bondage, and these victims have the highest levels of debt of any slaves I have encountered. Sex trafficking victims in general who are ensnared in debt bondage have in fact the highest levels of debt of any sector of slavery I have documented. The manner in which they are forced to repay these debts is utterly debasing and should bring shame to each and every man who purchases them, for it is their avid consumption of women and children that makes the immense debts possible, and all the destruction that goes with it.

May 26 and 28, 2016

In *Sex Trafficking*,[32] I describe an anguishing encounter with Sunee, a trafficked sex slave in Los Angeles, whom I last saw on April 26, 2006. She was a Thai girl at a massage parlor near the intersection of Hollywood and Western boulevards. She had been trafficked from her home village of Fang, Thailand, with the promise that she would work as a waitress and send money home to provide life-saving medicine for her father. Upon arrival in Los Angeles, she was told she had to work off a debt of $20,000 through prostitution at a massage parlor; if she did not cooperate, the man who trafficked her from her village, Aran, would make her parents suffer. If she did cooperate, she was told her father would be sent enough money to buy the medicines he needed. Sunee made the only choice a child could—she endured around eight counts per day of rape to save her parents. When I offered to help her leave the massage parlor, she declined. I wrestled with the question of whether to work with a local NGO to rescue her against her will, but I did not take action for fear of the unintended negative consequences against her parents. My choice has always haunted me.

My inability to assist Sunee, a slave being exploited not fifteen miles from my home in Los Angeles, left me in a dark quandary over the purpose of my antislavery efforts. Had I met Sunee some years later, perhaps when I had more powerful relationships with which to assist her, would I have made a different choice? Maybe, maybe not. The theoretical clarity of the right and wrong course of action in slavery cases is almost always clouded by the complexities of real-world consequences. Sunee was desperate to stay in servitude because it was the only way she could save her parents. Who was I to decide otherwise?

About ten years later, I revisited Sunee's massage parlor. I knew she would be long gone, if for no other reason than she would be too old to entice men to purchase a teenager for sex. Nevertheless, I took two trips to her massage parlor on May 26 and May 28, 2016. If I found another slave, perhaps I might be able to redeem the choice I had made with Sunee.

The waiting room of the massage parlor still smelled like lemongrass. The proprietor during Sunee's time, Chuvit, was no longer there. A woman named Malee had taken his place. She showed me a menu of massages and prices, then led me to a back area to pick which girl would massage me. Five young Thai girls in ethnic trousers and white tee shirts stood before me. None were Sunee. I picked the one who looked the youngest, and she led me to a massage room. The rooms had mattresses on the floor with fresh sheets. As before, I was given a pair of loose fitting cotton pants and a shirt to wear. The young girl, Dao, entered and gave me the sixty-minute Thai massage that I had ordered. Unlike Sunee, she did not ask if I wanted to have sex with her. I spoke with Dao during most of the massage to learn more about her. She told me she was from the northern hill tribe region of Thailand, not far from Chiang Rai. She had arrived in Los Angeles with a few other girls from nearby villages two years earlier. She worked at the parlor to send money to her family, which consisted of two younger brothers in school and her mother. I asked if she had paid her own way to Los Angeles, but she said her family took a loan for the flight and travel documents. She thought it was around $5,000, but when she arrived she was told it was $15,000. She had since been working off the debt at the parlor, but she was not sure how much debt remained. She said that Malee showed her a Western Union receipt each month for $500 that she sent to her mother. She also received petty cash for expenses, but no sort of regular wage based on her hours of work. Her overall compensation seemed very low given that she worked around twelve hours a day, six days a week.

I returned to the massage parlor two days later. Malee remembered me and greeted me warmly. If I was going to return often, she told me I should buy a massage package, which would give me a 10 percent discount. I told her I would think about it. I went through the same routine of picking a girl.

Dao was there again, but this time I picked Isra. She gave me the massage, and did not solicit for sex. Her English was not as good as Dao's, but we still managed to have an informative conversation. She too was a hill tribe girl who worked to send money to her family. Isra confirmed that she and the other girls each worked six days a week, around twelve hours a day. She also told me that they all lived in a nearby apartment, which was owned by the massage parlor. They did not go anywhere aside from the apartment and the parlor. Isra was the youngest of three siblings and had been at the parlor for seven months. Like Dao, she had a debt relating to her transport and papers, and like Dao, she was not sure of the overall arithmetic of her remaining debt. She was also told upon arrival that her debt was $15,000, and she received the same Western Union slip each month from Malee showing a transfer to her family of $500, plus some petty cash for her expenses. Isra said she felt proud when she received the slip because she knew she was helping her family.

After my two visits to Sunee's massage parlor without any indication that there were sex slaves inside, I wondered if the parlor still offered these services. Perhaps they had gone more underground (only offering sex at night) or only made offers to "insider" customers who knew how to ask for a different set of girls from which to choose, or perhaps the parlor had been busted some time ago for prostitution and was now under new ownership that restricted the services to massages. I was not able to secure full case histories from Dao and Isra, but all indications were that they were working in exploitative debt bondage conditions for the parlor. They toiled day and night with excessive wage deductions they did not fully understand to help their families survive. The $500 sent by the parlor to their families plus petty cash each month was less than one-fourth of what I estimated their monthly wages should be. They appeared to have no freedom of movement or employment, and as near as I could tell their debt levels far exceeded the actual costs of arranging their transport and work in Los Angeles. As with Sunee, Dao and Isra preferred these debt bondage conditions to freedom because freedom would not help their families achieve a better life.

After these two encounters, I faced a similar dilemma to that of helping Sunee—should I intervene in a scenario that I was certain amounted to bondage and servitude, even if doing so would likely cause material harm to the families of the people I was trying to help? What of the pride Isra felt in being able to provide a better life for her family? I knew that Dao and Isra would likely not qualify as victims of "severe forms of trafficking" under the U.S. Trafficking Victims Protection Act because child sexual exploitation did not appear to be involved in their cases. They would therefore probably not have access to the full protections under the law, including regularized migration status, and in all likelihood they would be deported, which would cause harm to their families. I consulted colleagues at a local antitrafficking NGO about the cases, and they promised to investigate further. This referral was the only step I took. A few weeks later, my colleagues told me they discretely provided their contact information to some of the young women at the parlor, but that no one had contacted them yet. I was agonized once again by my inability to intervene in a case of human trafficking that was right around the corner. Debt bondage and servitude persisted not 15 miles from my home, and I could do very little about it without taking unjustifiable risks. Even if these children were to be "freed" and returned home, they probably would be trafficked again before too long out of their need to support their families.

Freedom is not a one-time event. It is not a box to be ticked or a moment to be congratulated. It is a fragile, precious condition that must be supported and protected for a full human life. The failure to provide true freedom to all classes, genders, and communities in the world remains the great failure of contemporary civilization. No amount of antislavery advocacy, research, rhetoric, or activism will end slavery until we appreciate that its antonym— freedom—must be vigorously preserved through tremendous sacrifice and an unrelenting campaign to exterminate all of its assailants, including poverty, gender and ethnic biases, corruption, greed, or the appalling truth that for most people in the world, servitude often provides more security than does freedom. Freedom for the underclass of humanity remains a shadow, a mythical creature adorned in splendors that mocks, evades, and slips like dust through the fingers of those who dare to grasp at it. Until we truly understand freedom, we cannot abolish slavery. If we cannot abolish slavery, freedom has no meaning.

CHAPTER 7

GLOBAL SUPPLY CHAINS

Blood and the Sea

No civilized society can thrive upon victims, whose
humanity has been permanently mutilated.
—Rabindranath Tagore

A LAND I KNOW WELL

THAILAND IS A country I know all too well. After India and the United
States, it is the nation in which I have conducted more research into slavery than any other in the world. Each trip I have taken to Thailand has
been a fusion of conflicting and frustrating experiences. On the surface,
the country's beauty mesmerizes me. Its pristine beaches, azure seas, and
mist-capped hills are sublime and enthralling. I have been lost for days
hiking in its verdant mountains and found solace gazing at the ocean from
its powder-sand shores. However, beneath this surface I have also unearthed
Thailand's grotesqueries, the beasts beneath the beauty, the right-hand pane
of her *Garden of Earthly Delights*. There is suffering, inhumanity, and misery
in Thailand, and it has consistently worsened across the fifteen-year span
of my research trips to the country. Despite all the attention and resources

deployed to combat slavery in the broader Mekong subregion, the situation in this steamy corner of the world has persistently degraded. Mass graves of trafficked Rohingya migrants uncovered along the Thai-Burmese border in May 2015 put a macabre exclamation point to just how vile conditions have become.

The sex trafficking industry in Thailand is undeniably ruinous and savage, but conditions in the country's seafood sector may be even worse. From a mortality standpoint, it is the most severe face of contemporary slavery I have encountered. The industry chews up human beings without mercy. In doing so, it has become the foremost scourge of slavery in global supply chains. Supply chain research has been a key focus for me during the past several years, and I have investigated slavery and child labor used in producing commodities exported to the West, including seafood, handmade carpets, coffee, tea, electronic component minerals, apparel, dimension stones (marble, limestone, granite), gold, precious gems, palm oil, sporting goods, and more. I targeted my research on seafood in South Asia and East Asia, primarily in the shrimp sector. The presence of slavery in global seafood supply chains is a subset of the broader category of offenses called "illegal, unreported, and unregulated" (IUU) fishing. IUU fishing refers to all open sea or aquaculture fishing that takes place outside the authorization, regulation, or legal frameworks of the relevant states or laws of the sea.[1] No one knows exactly what portion of global IUU fishing activity can be attributed to slavery; however, estimates for the total value of IUU fishing are between $10 billion and $23.5 billion per year,[2] which suggests that billions of dollars' worth of seafood are caught and processed by slaves annually. Most of this activity takes place in East Asia and China, and more than half of global seafood exports from these regions are bound for the United States, the European Union, and Japan.[3] Thailand is the third largest exporter of seafood on the global market, hence abuses in its seafood sector touch the world.

My interest in Thailand's seafood industry was first piqued by Police Lieutenant Colonel Suchai Chindavanich when he described some of the sector's atrocities during an interview in 2005 for *Sex Trafficking*. We spoke at length about human trafficking in the greater Mekong subregion, and toward the end of our conversation he spoke passionately about the brutalities of the Thai seafood industry:

They are mostly Cambodian boys trafficked to the town of Aranya Prathet by bus. From there, a Thai agent takes them to the town of Samut Sakhon, on the coast south of Bangkok. The boys are taken to sea where they are forced to catch the fish twenty hours a day for many months. The ship captains force the boys to take amphetamines so they can work nonstop. Other ships come from the coast and transfer the fish, but the boys are kept on the ship.[4]

When I asked Colonel Chindanavich what happened to the boys at the end of their time at sea, he said many were shot and thrown overboard. I was astounded. Could these kinds of atrocities truly be taking place in full knowledge of major law enforcement authorities and with seemingly little being done about it? I resolved that day to learn more about Thailand's seafood industry. As soul-wrenching as my research into sex trafficking in Thailand was, researching the seafood sector took me to my limits. If I had to do it all over again, I am not sure that I would.

SAMUT SAKHON

My journey began in Samut Sakhon. Hot, debilitating, dreadful. It is the largest of the four main fishing provinces in Thailand, the other three being Ranong, Rayong, and Songkhla. Shrimp is king in Samut Sakhon, but seafood companies there also export several species of tuna (albacore, skipeye, bluejack, yellowfin), squid, crab, and lobster. In addition, many of these companies export pet food and animal feed for livestock to the West; both are made with trash fish or fish by-product. Trash fish are the small, inedible fish caught in fishing nets that are discarded by most fishing fleets around the world, and fish by-product includes the discards from fish processing facilities, such as roe, skin, bones, heads, and entrails. What is rejected elsewhere generates substantial profits in Thailand.

I did not have the resources to tackle the entire seafood industry of Thailand, so I focused on the shrimp and trash fish sectors. I could not visit all four of the main fishing provinces, so I focused on the two largest: Samut Sakhon and Songkhla. At the former, I found workers trafficked mostly from Cambodia, and at the latter I found workers trafficked mostly from

Myanmar. All the workers, even those being paid a reasonable wage (by Thai standards), were suffering under brutal conditions that ground them to the bone without pity.

Conducting research in Thailand's fishing provinces was fraught with challenges. It took a great deal of time to build local trust and to ascertain how to gain entry and conduct research on the fishing docks without attracting negative attention. This was particularly difficult during the last few years of my research when the Thai seafood sector came under heavy international scrutiny for slavery abuses uncovered by several excellent journalistic investigations by the *Guardian*, Reuters, the *New York Times*, the Associated Press, and others. Environmental conditions also created challenges. The sweltering heat and humidity of Thailand perpetually assailed my productivity. As searing as the weather is during Thailand's summer months, conditions on the docks at Samut Sakhon were worse. The heat was oppressive, and the stench of fish suffused the air. Each breath at the docks was a labor, and trying to concentrate while dripping with sweat and attempting to navigate a maelstrom of activity to conduct meaningful research was a serious challenge. Throughout the interviews I conducted, mad dogs growled and scavenged for fish scraps, foremen barked orders, scores of workers made an immense racket as they toiled feverishly to unload thousands of blue barrels of iced trash fish from docked trawlers, and another set of workers loaded the barrels of trash fish into filling trucks for transport to the fish meal processing facilities across the province. Faced with conditions highly antagonistic to efficient research, my first trip to the docks at Samut Sakhon was not very productive. The workers appeared to be locked in a system of backbreaking and monotonous work, and there was little room to conduct interviews. Fatigue and fear weighed heavily on every face. The foremen also kept a sharp eye on anything that seemed amiss.

After a good deal of planning and judicious navigation of hostile conditions, I eventually managed a few productive trips to the docks at Samut Sakhon to document the workers. I first identified a relatively calm corner in which to conduct the interviews with the assistance of a translator, although the noise on the docks still made conversations a challenge. My cover story was that I was a researcher from India trying to understand the fishing economy in the East Asian seafood sector. This story did not garner undue suspicion from the foremen and guards, but they did nonetheless require a hefty fee for each interview that was basically a bribe even though it was posed as compensation for the worker's lost time. The guards did by and large leave me on my own to conduct interviews, but now and again they ambled over to eavesdrop on my conversations. In those moments, I was sure to ask innocuous questions. The informants were always nervous, and many did not wish to complete the interview. Most of the workers I documented at Samut Sakhon were from Cambodia, with a handful from Myanmar and Laos. The Cambodians described their journeys from their homes to Thailand. They all migrated with recruiters who promised work in various sectors, including construction, manufacturing, and seafood. They all crossed into Thailand from four main border cities: Poipet, Battambang, Koh Kong, or Choam. They were all brought straight to the docks, where they were either sent on fishing boats or put to dock work. In either case, they worked around the clock, seven days a week. Many were not allowed to leave the docks and slept there a few hours each night; others went to nearby communal dorms every few nights. They described being paid wages that ranged from $2 to $5 per day, even though Thailand set a minimum wage in 2013 of THB 300 [~$9.25] per day. The working conditions were unsafe, unhygienic, and oppressive. Injury and illness dogged the workers. One Cambodian man showed me his grotesquely blistered fingers and said, "My hands pain so much! But if I do not work, they will bash me." There was little I could do to help the workers because I did not know at that point whom I could trust in Thailand to intervene, or what the consequences of an incomplete or poorly planned intervention would be. In the end, I gathered enough evidence to determine that every one of the workers I documented in full was being exploited in conditions of slavery.

Some of the men I documented on the docks at Samut Sakhon had previously worked on the trawlers that spend months at sea catching the trash fish. They were reluctant to talk about the conditions on the ships. Their faces were broken and fraught with the lingering menace of torture and torment. Leap told me about a safe house not far from the docks. "I stayed at that place a few weeks after I ran from here," Leap whispered to me. "I came back because my sister sent me an SMS and said they were being threatened."

Leap gave me a mobile number for the owners of the safe house. He said many migrants from Cambodia lived there, and most of them had worked in the seafood sector. I rang the number a few times, but there was no answer. I worked through other leads in the Cambodian migrant community, including my translator, and eventually found a possible location for the safe house, which operated in secret. I went to the location and found a non-descript two-story home protected by a cement wall and barbed wire. I rang the buzzer, but no one answered. I noticed a security camera near the top of the entry gate, so I wrote a message on a piece of paper and held it up to the camera: "My name is Siddharth Kara. I am a human rights researcher from the United States. Could I please speak with you?" I added my local phone number to the message. After a few minutes when there was no response, I returned to my hotel.

Two days later, I received a text message from someone who said he lived at the house and asked me to meet him at a nearby bazaar the following day. I arrived at the place and time as instructed, and within a few minutes a small, cheerful fellow introduced himself to me: "I am Anurat." Anurat said he found my name on the Internet and read about the work I do. That was why he was willing to meet. "How can I help you?" Anurat asked.

I told him about the research I was doing and how a man named Leap told me about his safe house. Anurat remembered Leap and said that many men who stay with him eventually leave because of similar threats. I asked Anurat if I could interview the men at his safe house. He agreed. I documented several former seafood workers at Anurat's safe house. Their tales left me stunned. Here is what Prak, a former laborer from Cambodia, told me:

> The recruiter said we can make good wages in Thailand. He said we will earn THB 10,000 [~$320] each month. More than twenty men from two villages went with the recruiter. He took us in a truck to Samut Sakhon. When we arrived, he said he sold us to the ship captains. I did not understand what this meant. The police at the docks said we had to go on the ships or they would arrest us for entering Thailand without documents.
>
> I worked on the first ship for five months. The guards treated us like animals. They shouted at us and beat us. We had to work all the time. We did unloading the fish, cleaning the ship, making the repairs. If we complained, the guards tortured us. They chained us to the deck to burn

in the sun. They threw men overboard to drown. They gave us electric shocks. I saw six men killed on those ships. Some men were so afraid they jumped into the ocean and drowned themselves. My best friend Chan drowned himself. He said, "I will decide how I die, not them."

After five months, the captain sent me to another ship. I was on that ship for seven months, then I was on a third ship for three months. After this time I came back to land for the first time. I worked on the docks unloading the fish and was paid a wage for the first time. After some time the guards said I would go back on a ship. I told them I did not want to go back, but they said I had no choice. I was very anxious those days, so I decided I must escape. I ran away one night and was living on the streets when I learned of this place. Now I am safe.

I have nightmares about the ships. In my dreams I am trying to work, but I cannot move my arms. The guards shout at me. One of them is going to shoot me, but I wake up before he does. For a moment, I cannot tell if it is a dream or real. Then I remember.

Prak asked if we could stop for a while and have something cold to drink. It was clear to me that he suffered from severe PTSD in addition to chronic pain from several broken ribs that had not healed properly and other health ailments resulting from malnutrition and repeated sunstroke. Even though he was only twenty-seven years old, he looked like a worn down carcass, scarcely able to move his bony frame. After a few years in the Thai seafood sector, only the ghost of a human being remained.

Later that day, Anurat introduced me to his wife, Tina. She explained how they opened their first safe house for migrants from her home area in Cambodia a few years earlier. Most of the migrants had been exploited in the fishing and construction industries. This first safe house was raided by the police. Tina told me the migrants were all sold into "slavery" in seafood. Tina and Anurat opened a second safe house beyond the outskirts of Samut Sakhon, and they kept the location a secret for fear of another police raid. At the time of my visit, they housed nineteen Cambodians, two Burmese, and two Laotians, all of whom said they escaped from conditions akin to what Prak described. In addition to interviewing most of the individuals in their safe house, I also spoke with Anurat and Tina at length. They did not have many good things to say about how migrants were treated in the Thai seafood sector.

"The fish are treated better than these men," Anurat told me, "We try to help them return home, but we have very little resources. Many of them are in debt to the recruiters, and if they return home, the recruiters will force them to return until they repay these debts. They will be forced to work until they are dead. That is the system." Tina did not speak to me as much as Anurat, but she uttered one sentence that I will never forget: "People should know where their seafood comes from. . . . It comes from dead bodies at the bottom of the sea."

The broader system of exploitation Anurat described to me was further elucidated and reinforced by the migrants at his safe house. They described how traffickers recruit workers from Myanmar, Cambodia, and Laos and promise them good wages in the fishing sector. They pay bribes to Thai government officials at the border to gain entry and absorb the remainder of the costs of bringing the workers to Thailand. Once they arrive at the docks, they sell the workers to the ship captains for around $600 to $900 each. The ship captains then tell the workers that they each have debts of $1,500 to $2,500, which they must work off on the ships, after which they will receive the wages they were promised. Even if the arithmetic is done correctly, it would take up to nine months to work off the debt at Thailand's minimum wage; however, the arithmetic is never done correctly (deductions for food, board, etc.), and many workers end up toiling for years with scarcely any income to show for it. Much of this time can be spent at sea. The trafficked workers are sold from one ship to the next and eventually are killed, commit suicide, or return to work at the docks, like Prak. The Thai police appear to be an integral part of the system, at least as it was described to me. I did not see any uniformed police officers on the docks at Samut Sakhon, but Anurat told me they are always in plain clothes and they take bribes to protect the docks and ship captains against inspections. Looking back, I suspect some of the men I thought were guards or foremen were actually off-duty or plain clothes police officers. Each ship captain is supposed to ensure that his ship is registered and licensed with the Thai government under the Thai Vessel Act, B.E. 2481 (1938), but Anurat told me that most ships operate with fake licenses. This means that almost no one is monitoring the working conditions on the ships.

The men in Anurat and Tina's safe house described the recruitment and transport stages of their journeys in more detail than I was able to gather at

the docks. Their stories painted a picture of a highly systematized and efficient trafficking network. Than, a reticent, soft-faced man from Myanmar,
described what happened to him:

> We left my village on a Monday. There were eighteen of us with two
> recruiters. They drove us to mountains near the border. From there
> we had to walk. We walked for eight days through the jungle. I was
> very tired. The recruiters did not give us food. We ate what we could
> find in the jungle. Two men fell sick and could not continue, so the
> recruiters left them. If we did not cooperate, they threatened us with
> their guns. One man was shot in the chest because he got in a fight
> with the recruiters. He died. The recruiters made us dig a hole and
> bury him. One day we came to the end of the forest. There was a truck
> waiting. They put us inside the trucks and we were lying on top of each
> other for almost two days when we arrived at Samut Sakhon. There
> were so many people; it was very confusing. I did not know what was
> happening. The recruiter said we had to go on two ships that were at
> the docks. I did not learn until the following day that the ship captain
> paid the recruiter for us. By that time, we were in the sea and there
> was nothing I could do.

I pulled out my map and asked Than to show me the area where they
walked across the border from Myanmar to Thailand. He pointed to the
north, just southwest of Tachilek. Other Burmese men I documented later
in Songkhla had been trafficked along the same route. I knew the area well
because I had spent several days hiking those same migrant routes a few
years earlier. The corridor clearly remained a common route used by traffickers to enter Thailand from Myanmar. It was heavily forested and mountainous and virtually impossible to monitor from a border control standpoint.
In addition to this route, a few of the other Burmese workers I interviewed
had crossed near the refugee camps near Mae Sot, another common route I
documented years earlier that was still being used. The memories of my time
near Mae Sot pain me deeply. It was toward the end of a very bleak period
of research into sex trafficking in the Mekong subregion, one that left me
feeling there was no way to prevent the greedy and barbaric people of the
world from devouring the vulnerable and the powerless. Several years later

in Samut Sakhon I saw the same predation in a completely different sector. Whether for sex or for seafood, the vulnerable peasants of the Mekong subregion were being trafficked along the same routes into Thailand for the same purpose of soul-crushing exploitation.

I conducted interviews across five days on the docks at Samut Sakhon, three days at Anurat's safe house, and three days each at two worker dormitories. After my time in Samut Sakhon, I could not see how the forces of decency and justice would ever prevail in a world that thrived so thoroughly on indecency and injustice. I could not comprehend the galling inhumanity required to exploit another human being to the point of annihilation, only to throw him into the sea like last night's leftovers. The seafood workers I met in Samut Sakhon were being chewed up by a behemoth industry that was fueled by their torment, and to this day far too little is being done to alter this reality. As downcast as I felt in Samut Sakhon, my sense of despair only worsened when I traveled to Songkhla and learned of the plight of the Rohingya.

SONGKHLA AND THE ROHINGYA

Songkhla Province is in the south, on the eastern coast of the narrow strip of Thailand that juts down like a spear toward Malaysia. The top half of this spear is divided vertically with Myanmar, which takes the west-facing land. These two geographic aspects of Songkhla—the proximity to Malaysia and the proximity to a porous border with Myanmar—created a catastrophe for the Rohingya people, a persecuted Muslim minority in Myanmar who fled en masse in search of safety in (predominantly Muslim) Malaysia and Indonesia. Tragically, those few hundred kilometers between the southern tip of Myanmar and the northern border of Malaysia became a feeding ground for traffickers who brutalized the displaced Rohingya in every conceivable manner. Their unconscionable suffering continues to this day.

The main city in Songkhla Province is Hat Yai, which is the primary staging ground for trafficking people from across the Mekong subregion into Malaysia. In *Sex Trafficking*, I share the story of Lisu, a young hill tribe girl from the north, who was driven through Hat Yai on a fake tour bus with numerous other girls and forced into prostitution at a hotel in Malaysia. The sophistication and formalized nature of the network that trafficked Lisu astounded me, and I learned that the same networks continue to operate along the same routes year after year. This fact alone leads one to the inevitable conclusion that the authorities in Thailand have limited interest in truly combating the human trafficking networks in their country.

The docks at Songkhla proved slightly more favorable for conducting interviews than those at Samut Sakhon. They were smaller and not quite as manic, even though the workers still toiled at a feverish pace. As with Samut Sakhon, there were plenty of stray dogs scavenging at the docks, and the entire environment dripped with the pungent scent of near-rotting fish. However, there were some relatively quieter periods at the Songkhla docks shortly after midnight, when work slowed and the guards tended to be less vigilant. I spent a week conducting interviews between midnight and four in the morning at the docks and was able to document more cases than I did in Samut Sakhon.

Most of the workers I documented in Songkhla were from Myanmar, and they crossed into Thailand from the mountainous border just to the north, near Ranong, or from the refugee camps near Mae Sot. Their stories of recruitment, trafficking, and exploitation were carbon copies of what I heard in Samut Sakhon. A worker named Po told me his story:

> The recruiters sold us to the ship captains at the docks. I worked on a trawler for some months, I do not know how many. It was my first job, and it was harder than I imagined. We had to use so much strength to pull the wenches and unload the fish. If we were tired, they tortured us because they knew this pain was worse. One man from my village worked until he died. He collapsed just like that one day. I tried to wake him, but he was no longer in this world. They threw his body into the ocean and shouted at us, "Work! Work!"
>
> Our ship was far in the sea, and I could never see the land. I saw other ships sometimes. I remember one night I could see lights and I thought maybe this is land. I was desperate to get off that ship before I died like my friend, so I thought I can go to the land with a buoy, but I never learned to swim so I was afraid I will drown.
>
> After many months, we came back to land. They let me work at the docks. Oh, did I mention that I did not receive any wage for my work on the trawler? The captain said we would receive a share of the catch,

but when we returned he showed me a book and said I had a debt
from the expenses while I was on the boat and there was no wage left
from the catch. After I worked on a second ship, I received a wage of
THB 3,000 [~$94] for three months work. I broke my wrist here so I
cannot work on the boats any more. I feel lucky, even though my hand
hurts every day. These days I pack ice on the barrels.

I thought nothing could be worse than my life in Myanmar. I was
wrong. I want to go back home, but this is not an option.

Po's tale of blatant and callous exploitation was repeated with appalling similarity by most of the other men I documented in Songkhla. None of them received a written contract for work. They had all been trafficked under the false promise of decent work and good wages in the fishing sector, only to end up as slaves. They all had various injuries—cuts, broken bones, burns—that were not healing properly due to a lack of adequate medical care. Injuries at sea were the most problematic. Several men told me that when a man at sea was injured so severely that he couldn't work he was simply killed. This threat of execution pressured many workers to toil through their broken bones and other injuries, which only compounded their ailments. Another worker I documented, Thet, told me that his ship captain punished his workers if they got injured. "One man broke his finger in the wench. He was screaming. The captain and his men tied him down and gave him electric shocks from the spare battery. The captain said if he was not careful he could harm others, so this would teach him to be more careful. They shocked him until he vomited."

In addition to the docks, I was able to document numerous Burmese seafood workers at migrant dormitories. Several of these workers had been trafficked into Thailand using Tor Ror 38/1 papers. Although no longer in use, these special registration papers were once provided to migrants with permission to stay temporarily in Thailand, and they were especially used with workers from Myanmar. All of the workers I met had their papers confiscated once they arrived at Songkhla. A few of them said the police were the ones who confiscated the documents. Others said the ship captains took them. Even though none of the workers had their papers, they all knew they had been in Thailand far longer than the period they were allowed, and the threat of imprisonment, fines, or deportation back to Myanmar with minimal or no income to show for their time in Thailand kept most of them at the docks, working day after day in the hope of securing more reasonable wages at some point. This was the same method of coercion that was used with the H-2A guest workers I documented in the Central Valley of California. Upon arrival, their documents were also taken, they were exploited in conditions of forced labor, and once they had stayed past the time period permitted in their visas, the threat of deportation with little or no income to take with them was a powerful force of coercion that kept them toiling in servitude in the hope of discharging their debts and being paid a more reasonable wage in the future. Stigma also played a strong role with the Burmese men I documented. "If we go back with no money, the community will say that we were lazy," Thaung told me. "This will bring our family shame. It is not good for us in the community if people feel this way."

I tried to interview ship captains at Samut Sakhon, but the frenetic nature of the docks and the high degree of surveillance and suspicion made it impossible for me to do so. The docks at Songkhla were more amenable, and I managed to conduct a few interviews with ship captains. Most of the ships were docked for a few days while their cargo was unloaded and weighed and new crew were secured for the next run at sea. Some of the same workers were taken again, but attrition at sea required the captains to secure new workers. True to form, traffickers were ready with a fresh set of slaves.

One animated captain, Boom, with a hoarse voice and tattoos covering his arms, invited me aboard his ship for a meal while I asked him questions about how the ships operate. "We have three types of vessel in the waters," Boom explained. "The purse-seiners, the trawlers, and the tour boats." Boom told me that the purse-seiners operate only at night. They use sonar to search for schools of fish, and upon finding them circle them with a net, which is then closed from underneath the fish to capture them. Workers haul the nets on board, unload the fish, and place them on ice in a cargo hold beneath deck. Unlike the purse-seiners, the trawlers operate both day and night. There are two kinds of trawlers, single and double. On the trawlers, the nets are lowered into the water and hauled behind the boat for several hours before being pulled back onboard. The trawlers tend to be larger and go much farther out to sea than the purse-seiners. Most of the workers I documented at Songkhla and Samut Sakhon were exploited on trawlers. Finally, tour boats transport food, supplies, and fuel from land to vessels at sea. They also load the catches from vessels at sea and transport them back to the docks where they can be loaded into trucks and sent to processing facilities. Crews on the purse-seiners tend to be between fifteen and twenty workers, and twin-trawlers can have crews of forty or more.

I asked Boom where the boats did most of the fishing. "Waters in the Gulf [of Thailand] are not good; we go outside Thai waters now, towards Malaysia," he replied.

I asked Boom how he got into this work. He said it was a family business. He hailed from a fishing village just north of Songkhla, and his father bought their first trawler when he was a boy. "I took command of the ship after my father became old," Boom explained. "My son will do the same after me."

I spoke with Boom for most of the evening while picking tentatively at the fried squid he had arranged for us to eat. The squid seemed fresh, but the oil smelled foul like it had been reused too many times. I asked Boom several questions for which I already knew the answer (such as the kinds of boats used in the Thai fishing industry) to keep the conversation light and aligned with my cover story of being a researcher interested in understanding the fishing economy of East Asia. Toward the end of the night I asked Boom about some of the stories I had heard relating to mistreatment of migrant workers. "These stories are not true," Boom told me. "The workers are lazy. They must learn discipline for the safety of the crew. When we are at sea, everyone must work to their capacity or the ship cannot function. My life depends on theirs, and theirs depends on mine. If we do not have discipline, there will be tragedies for everyone."

I pressed Boom further. "I have heard that some migrants are forced to work day and night until they would rather drown themselves in the ocean. Is that what you mean by discipline?"

Boom clicked his knuckles, "Why are you asking this?"

"I told you, I am researching the seafood economy of East Asia."

"What is your purpose?"

"I am writing a report."

"And will you write that Boom mistreats his crew?"

"I don't have any evidence that you do."

"Because I don't."

"What about wages?" I asked. "Do you deduct wages as repayment for recruitment fees?"

"The workers are lazy and want to be paid for doing nothing. That is all you need to know."

"Do you pay recruiters for the workers?"

"How else can I get workers? Do you want me to get them myself?"

"And do you charge these fees to the workers?"

"You are not proper to me. I don't like these questions."

At this point, the conversation was getting tense, so I thanked Boom for his hospitality. As I disembarked, he shouted something in Thai toward the docks. Two guards approached me and escorted me outside. They told me not to return. Fortunately, I had already learned almost everything I needed to at the Songkhla docks, so being prevented from returning was not a serious blow to my research. Still, I would have liked to speak with some of the guards, which I did not venture to do in Samut Sakhon. I suspected I could return to the docks at some point in the future when there were likely to be new guards and ship captains who did not know me. As it turned out, I returned to Songkhla a few years later, but this time it was because I was researching the merciless exploitation of the Rohingya people. Their story is one of the most macabre faces of human trafficking I have encountered.

The Rohingya are an impoverished, stateless people who fled from state-sanctioned persecution in Myanmar straight into the hands of slave traders. They number over one million people and live primarily in the northern cities of Rakhine. They were stripped of their citizenship by the Myanmar government in 1982 based on the flimsy determination that they are refugees from Bangladesh, even though they claim to have been living in Rakhine for centuries. Since 1982, the Rohingya have been one of the largest stateless populations in the world. Like the Karen and other similarly persecuted minorities in Myanmar, the Rohingya have been subjected to oppression, violence, and state-sponsored ethnic cleansing campaigns, and hundreds of thousands have fled the country with little local interest or coverage of their plight.[5] Violence against the Rohingya escalated in 2012, catalyzing a new wave of distress migration into the forests and seas in search of safety in the predominantly Muslim nations of Malaysia and Indonesia. Both routes have proved to be fraught with peril, slavery, and death.

When I began researching the plight of the Rohingya, I heard stories of a shift in the business model of many Thai ship captains—from fishing to human trafficking. International pressure following journalistic exposés of slavery and other abuses in Thailand's fishing industry during 2014 and 2015 led to threats of boycotts by Western seafood importers and a pledge by the Thai government to crack down on the problem. A flurry of government scrutiny of fishing sector conditions resulted in the revocation of 11,700 licenses of fishing vessels in October 2015 for offenses relating to labor abuses and other regulatory infractions. The increased scrutiny by the government displeased many ship captains, who were ordered to pay fines, secure new licenses, or cease operations. At the same time, thousands of Rohingya were fleeing Myanmar by sea, and some Thai ship captains saw a business opportunity. On a per-kilogram basis, a ship full of people can fetch roughly three to four times as much money as a ship full of fish. In addition, a ship can be filled with fleeing refugees in a fraction of the time that it takes to fill it with fish. As a result, many ship captains liaised with human traffickers and began ferrying Rohingya from one country to another, where they were often sold into forced labor or forced prostitution. The new business was called "people transportation," as if it were a ferry service of some kind. However, not everyone who was hauled into the ships made it to land. In the summer of 2016, as many as ten thousand Rohingya remained stranded in floating prisons in the Strait of Malacca and the Andaman Sea because the ships were denied entry by Malaysia, Thailand, and Indonesia. A few hundred Rohingya have been "rescued" and languish in Malaysian and Thai detention centers, but thousands remain incarcerated in these floating prisons, waiting to be ransomed, sold off into slavery, or worse. Survivors in detention centers report being held in cargo holds (like Mustafa and Equiano), with scarcely any room to move, and being tortured, raped, or worse. These maritime trafficking networks continue to expand, with Rohingya victims arriving by ship to Sri Lanka and India in early 2017.

I was unable to document the transport or harboring of Rohingya people at sea. The ship captains, dock workers, and local experts with whom I spoke all repeated the same rumors, but gathering firsthand evidence was impossible. All indications are that the phenomenon will continue due to the worsening economic conditions in the Thai seafood sector, which pressure some ship captains to find other ways to stay in business. The flow of Rohingya refugees from Myanmar has provided these and other exploiters with a prime opportunity to make a great deal of money by trafficking in people rather than catching fish. Efforts by enlightened members of the Myanmar Parliament to pass a bill that would initiate a citizenship verification process for the Rohingya in an attempt to legitimize their presence in the country were soundly defeated in May 2016, and the Rohingya remain highly vulnerable, persecuted, and desperate to flee.

For those Rohingya who fled Myanmar by land, the perils were perhaps even worse than those who fled by sea. On May 1, 2015, thirty-two bodies of Rohingya people were discovered in a mass grave in a remote mountain area of Songkhla Province in Thailand. On May 24, 2015, Malaysian police discovered 139 graves in a series of abandoned camps used by human traffickers on the border with Thailand. Local human rights activists suspect dozens of similar mass graves remain undiscovered in the northern forests of Songkhla, filled with hundreds, if not thousands, of Rohingya corpses. The Rohingya who survived these camps report that they fled from Myanmar with traffickers and were held captive in the forest, either for ransom or until they were sold off to other traffickers, most likely for forced prostitution or forced labor in the Thai fishing sector. Survivors of the forest prisons reported having their teeth pulled out with pliers, women had breasts chopped off and suffered gang rape, and, of course, murder. I was not able to find or document any Rohingya workers at the docks in Songkhla or Samut Sakhon, or in the nearby worker barracks or safe houses; however, I was told by other workers that they had seen many Rohingya at the docks, all of whom were sent on ships to work at sea.

Very little firsthand research has been conducted on the plight of the Rohingya, and no one really knows how many are being slaughtered, held in prisons, or sold as slaves. Even worse, the international response to the crisis has been a failure. No one has any problem calling out the slaughter, torture, and enslavement of the Rohingya, but when it comes time to take the steps necessary to stop the crisis, the international community has been all but inert. In the absence of a more robust response to protect the Rohingya, there is no telling how many will be trafficked, extorted, enslaved, tortured, or killed as a result of their oppression at the hands of the Myanmar government and our collective failure to protect them. They are a stateless, displaced people the world has shunned—a microcosm of the broader functioning of contemporary slavery. If we cannot protect the Rohingya when everyone is staring right at them, there is little hope we can free all of the oppressed, vulnerable, and invisible populations of the world as they toil, suffer, and die in the shadows of the slave economy.

HOW DID IT COME TO THIS?

With seemingly endemic levels of servitude in much of the Thai fishing industry, it is crucial to understand how the sector arrived at this point and whether there is any hope for a systemic remediation of conditions. Thailand has more than 2,600 kilometers of coastline, and the fishing sector has always been important to the nation's economy. Beginning in the 1960s, the country's largely rural, low-technology fishing culture rapidly modernized. The fleet of Thai fishing vessels was upgraded, and along with a lack of regulation this led to significant overfishing and the depletion of fish stocks in the Gulf of Thailand.[6] Catch rates have decreased from roughly 300 kg/hr in the 1960s to a rate around 14 kg/hr in 2015.[7] With this sharp reduction in catch rates, it takes significantly more time to catch the same amount of fish as before, and as with any business, time is money (fuel, labor, etc.). The depletion in fish stocks in the waters near Thailand have been particularly severe, but it follows a similar trend globally, with roughly 85 percent of all commercial fish stocks around the world now being fished up to or beyond their biological limits.[8] In addition, the rise in fuel costs beginning in the 1990s added pressure on the fishing sector to cut costs. These and other pressures led to sharp cuts in wages for seafood workers and a deterioration of working conditions, which dissuaded many Thai laborers from entering the sector. As a result, Thailand's seafood sector began to recruit migrant workers to meet labor needs, which resulted in a cabinet decision by the Royal Thai government in 1993 to grant official permission for migrants to work in the country's fishing sector.[9] Meeting labor shortages with migrants was not enough, and several broader global economic and sector-specific forces continued to push the industry to cut costs further to remain viable. First, the wholesale price of frozen shrimp dropped steadily during a fifteen-year period beginning in the early 1990s.[10] Next, an outbreak of early mortality syndrome (EMS)[11] in 2012 wreaked havoc on the Thai shrimp sector. Indeed, Thailand has yet to recover to its peak of 380,000 tons of shrimp exports in 2011.[12] With exports still down from optimal levels, the industry is losing hundreds of millions of dollars each year. In the face of these pressures, labor costs were the only expense amenable to quick and sustained downward cuts. The Thai fishing sector soon became filled not just with poor migrant workers from across the Mekong subregion but with a significant proportion of migrant workers who are exploited in outright slavery to maintain the industry's economic viability. Determining the proportion of workers who are exploited as slaves requires further research, but one study found that roughly 17 percent of migrant Cambodian workers in Thailand's main fishing provinces were being exploited in conditions of forced labor.[13] I suspect that the real number of slaves, particularly when robust samples from workers at sea are included, is much higher.

Not to be lost in this mix of environmental and global economic forces affecting Thailand's seafood sector is the fact that consumers around the globe have expressed a near-insatiable demand for low-price seafood. Global seafood consumption continues to grow, creating an export market that was worth approximately $150 billion in 2014.[14] The United States is second only to China in total seafood consumption, and American consumers spent approximately $96 billion on fish products (food service and retail) in 2015.[15] To help meet this need, the United States imported around 2.6 million metric tons of edible seafood products in 2015, worth approximately $18.8 billion.[16] Shrimp represented $6.8 billion, or 33 percent, of the total. Thailand, in particular, was responsible for $1.39 billion of the seafood imported into the United States in 2015, around $678 million (49 percent) of which was shrimp.[17] Globally, Thailand is the third largest exporter of seafood products behind only China and Norway, with total seafood exports in 2015 valued at approximately $7.2 billion.[18] In short, billions of dollars are at stake in a highly competitive global seafood market as consumer demand for cheap seafood rises year after year. Price is the primary variable on which retailers compete to attract consumers and capture as much business as possible. This price competition places powerful downward pressure on costs for producers. Conjoined with other global economic and environmental pressures on the Thai seafood industry, severe labor exploitation has become essential to the competitive profile of many Thai seafood exporters. Can anything be done to protect labor in the Thai seafood industry in a way that ensures its economic viability? Answering this question requires a closer look at the Thai seafood supply chain.

THE THAI SEAFOOD SUPPLY CHAIN

The Thai seafood supply chain is part of the complex global seafood supply chain system. These supply chains involve numerous actors, from small-time fishermen to major commercial fishing fleets, with brokers, wholesalers, importers, other middlemen, retailers, and consumers filling out the chain. Seafood products are shipped straight from the fishing fleet to Western markets or are processed through a multitude of stages before reaching the consumer. Seafood bound for the United States may pass through several intermediary countries for additional processing before arriving. It is almost impossible to trace any particular batch of seafood from the point of origin to the point of retail sale, especially given the combination of products from different sources. Persistent issues with mislabeling of products further complicate reliable supply chain tracing. In short, IUU or slave-caught processed seafood can enter global supply chains at any number of points. Very little can be done to prevent this entry without significant expenditures on auditing and monitoring, which may not be economically viable for some producers. Nonetheless, monitoring may be the only way to provide reliable assurances to retailers and consumers that the seafood they are purchasing is untainted.[19]

The numerous commodity supply chains I have documented reside on a spectrum, from simpler ones such as handmade carpets from India to more complex ones such as seafood from Thailand. Supply chains are simpler to document and trace when they have the following elements: (1) discrete products that can be labeled and that are not easily mixed with products from other suppliers, (2) small numbers of exporters and importers in the industry, (3) more vertically integrated companies that encompass the full supply chain from production to the point of retail sale, and (4) more concentrated production bases, both geographically and in the number of production sites. Although fish are discrete products, they are almost always mixed between ships, processors, exporters, and importers, especially smaller seafood items such as shrimp. Each product in the Thai seafood industry (shrimp, tuna, squid, etc.) has a slightly different supply chain. Labor abuses in each product line take place at the fishing or processing stages, and the abuses almost entirely involve migrant labor populations. This is especially true with the trash fish/harvested shrimp (as opposed to wild-caught shrimp) supply chain.

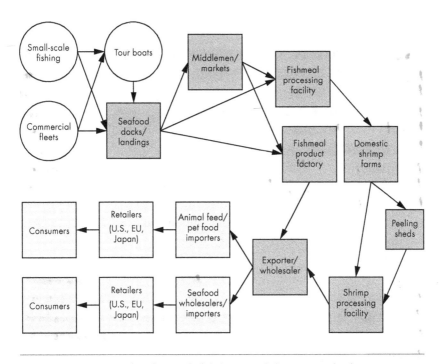

FIGURE 7.1 The Thai trash fish/harvested shrimp supply chain

A basic map of the structure of this supply chain provides clear indications of the optimal points of intervention to stem labor abuses (see figure 7.1). Severe labor abuses primarily occur in three points on the trash fish/harvested shrimp supply chain: (1) ships, (2) docks, and (3) processing facilities. The supply chain begins with the ships at sea catching trash fish. These can be either large, commercial fleets or small-scale fishing operators. The ships either deliver the trash fish directly to the docks or tour boats haul their catch to the docks for them. There are roughly 50,000 vessels officially registered with the Thai Department of Fisheries, and tens of thousands more are not registered or operate with fake licenses. These ships source seafood in the Gulf of Thailand, the Andaman Sea, the Straits of Malacca, and in some cases as far out as the South China Sea. Tracing tainted seafood from vessels that use slave labor is challenging because the ships can trade catches while at sea, and tour boats transport catches to the docks from more than one ship.

Even if a retailer cuts off one particular exporter definitively linked to slave labor, tainted fish may still enter its supply chain through other exporters.

The next step in the chain involves unloading the trash fish at one of the main seafood docks around the country, the main four being in Samut Sakhon, Ranong, Rayong, and Songkhla provinces. At the docks, migrant workers load the trash fish onto trucks to be distributed to seafood processors. These trucks may deliver the trash fish to middlemen first, who transport and sell them to fish meal processing facilities or fish meal product factories, or the trash fish may go straight from the docks to either of these two destinations. The docks are the second area in which forced labor occurs. Unlike ships at sea, these are fixed locations that can be more easily monitored. At present, corruption and a lack of enforcement are the primary barriers to ensuring decent labor standards at many of the seafood docks.

After transport from the docks, the supply chain bifurcates into two paths: (1) trash fish that arrive at the fish meal processing facilities enter the domestic shrimp aquaculture market as shrimp feed, or (2) trash fish that arrive at the fish meal product factories are processed for use as pet food or animal feed abroad.

The Domestic Shrimp Aquaculture Chain

Between eighty and one hundred registered fish meal processors in Thailand generate feed for the domestic shrimp aquaculture industry. It is rumored that significant labor abuses, including forced labor and child labor, occur at these processing facilities. My efforts to document conditions at the processing stage were unsuccessful, as I was turned away at gunpoint at the seven facilities I attempted to investigate. Several telephone messages I left for processors also went unanswered. From the processors, the shrimp feed is sold into Thailand's domestic shrimp farm sector.

Thailand has about 30,000 registered shrimp farms and thousands more unregistered ones, which makes the farming portion of the chain difficult to monitor and regulate. There are three types of shrimp farms in the country: (1) hatcheries for nauplii, or shrimp larvae; (2) nurseries for nauplii to grow into baby shrimp; and (3) growth farms where the baby shrimp mature for a few months to adulthood prior to processing and export. Most of the trash fish–based feed is sent to the growth farms, often through a network of middlemen. Significant labor abuses, including forced labor and child labor, are reported to occur at these growth farms as well. I made efforts to document conditions at ten shrimp growth farms but only succeeded in documenting a handful of cases of forced labor and child labor. I was under almost constant surveillance and could not complete full interviews. Unfortunately, there was no other time or place where I could access the workers.

Once the shrimp mature, they are sent for processing, which includes peeling, beheading, cleaning, and freezing. Some of the peeling takes place in thousands of peeling sheds, primarily located in rural areas in the provinces of Surat Thani and Songkhla. Hundreds of thousands of migrants toil in unregistered and unmonitored mobile peeling sheds where they peel shrimp day and night in forced labor conditions. I documented peeling sheds just like these involving forced labor in Bangladesh,[20] and I was able to document six peeling sheds in Surat Thani. There were a total of 107 workers in these sheds, of which I documented 30. All of them were in forced labor and debt bondage. All were foreign migrants; six were children. The conditions were harsh, unhygienic, cramped, and miserable.

Once processed, the shrimp are sent to exporters who ship them and other seafood products from Thailand to the United States, the European Union, and Japan. The seafood is imported by domestic seafood markets or other importers in these regions, who sell to retailers—restaurants and grocery stores—who in turn sell to consumers. It bears repeating that slavery on the ships that catch the trash fish taints the entire supply chain. This is what Tina meant when she told me that the seafood we eat "comes from dead bodies at the bottom of the sea."

Animal Feed and the Household Pet Food Chain

The second supply chain for trash fish in the Thailand seafood industry involves processing factories that produce household pet food and livestock feed for foreign markets. There are seventy or eighty of these processing factories in Thailand, and many of them are rumored to have forced labor and other abuses in their migrant worker populations. I was not able to verify these rumors, as I was not allowed entry at the eight factories I attempted to investigate, all of which were in Samut Sakhon. All my phone messages also went unanswered, just as they did with the fish meal processors. Following the processing stage, the remainder of the chain is fairly straightforward, involving transport to major exporters, who in most cases are the same as those who export other seafood products, including shrimp, tuna, squid, and crab. The products are imported by the West and used in animal feed (mostly cows and chickens) on livestock farms or sold as household pet food. In the case of animal feed, the entire meat (beef and chicken) supply chain would be tainted by the slave-caught trash fish–based feed that is eaten by the livestock. Household pets would also be eating slave-made pet food by virtue of the same tainted trash fish. The infection of slavery at the bottom of the trash fish supply chain in Thailand permeates several global product lines, from retail seafood to beef and chicken to pet food and beyond, constituting an expansive contamination that touches billions of lives around the world. Add to this the tainted food being produced by trafficked laborers in California's Central Valley, and the global menu of protein, vegetables, fruit, dairy, and more is vulnerable to infection by highly disconcerting levels of slavery.

Rounding Out the Supply Chain

Both of the trash fish product lines (shrimp and feed) typically are consolidated by major exporters in Thailand prior to being shipped abroad, and I made efforts to speak to executives at the country's top seafood exporters: Thai Union Frozen Products (TUF), Kingfisher, CP Foods, Pac Food, Rubicon Resources, and Surapol Food. TUF in particular is a multi-billion-dollar, vertically integrated seafood company that controls roughly half of all seafood exports from Thailand. These exporters sell to some of the largest retailers in the West, including Walmart, Safeway, Darden Restaurants, Albertsons, Sysco, and major fish markets in Boston, Los Angeles, and Seattle. I was not granted in-person meetings by any of the companies, although spokespeople at each company told me that they took the issue of labor exploitation in their supply chains very seriously and refused to conduct business with suppliers who were linked to forced labor or other abuses. Each company expressed a no-tolerance policy for human trafficking. When I described some of the cases I had documented among workers in Samut Sakhon and Songkhla, which would surely touch every major exporter in the country,

I was informed by each company that they would look into the matter expeditiously.

It is all but impossible to trace a single batch of tainted seafood all the way through the supply chain to the point of retail sale, but a basic supply chain mapping exercise reveals that exploitation must be cleaned up at the ship, dock, and processing stages for all products to ensure that supply chains are fully untainted. The docks and processing facilities are fixed locations that can be monitored, if there is a will to do so. Samut Sakhon should be the priority because more than half of the seafood processors in Thailand are based there. However, even if all the docks and processing facilities are cleansed of forced labor, abuses at sea must still be addressed. These sea-based abuses present a unique challenge to cleaning up the seafood sector. The only reasonable solution would be a system of random inspections at sea; however, many of the abuses take place on unregistered ships with no official reporting obligations. A two-step process would be best: (1) an aggressive and sustained Thai government crackdown on unregistered fishing vessels, including random checks at sea and strict prosecution and punishment of any companies or ship captains discovered to be operating without a license, followed by (2) a system of random monitoring of labor conditions at sea on seafood vessels. One need not monitor every vessel, but if the perception in the industry is that there is a reasonable chance of being boarded and scrutinized, conditions on the ships are bound to improve. Random interviews with workers also must be conducted after they return from stints at sea. Additional support services, information channels, and efforts to promote safe and registered migration of workers will help attenuate the abuses that inevitably occur when populations are invisible and are unable to access assistance and information. These efforts should be undertaken in conjunction with local NGOs, which can help assure a human rights approach to the monitoring process. Project Issara is one such organization in Thailand doing promising work in this area, and it provides a model that can be scaled and replicated. Finally, the Thai government, or perhaps the U.S. Coast Guard, must make every effort to track down every vessel at sea that is imprisoning Rohingya migrants. Why this effort has not yet been made is beyond understanding.

Many retailers in the West that purchase seafood in Thailand have become acutely aware of potential issues with their supply chains and have demanded assurances of decent working conditions at all stages. However, as long as abuses persist at sea, there is no way to ensure that tainted fish do not enter the supply chain of any retailer anywhere in the world due to substantial mixing of catches at the docks and processing facilities. Ridding its seafood sector of slavery rests squarely with the Thai government, but much of the Thai seafood industry as currently constructed may not be able to survive economically without relying on severe labor exploitation. Perhaps portions of the sector can be reconstructed and remain economically viable, paying reasonable wages and providing decent working conditions for migrant workers. Until then, every person, farm animal, or household pet in the United States, the European Union, and other primary markets could be biting into slave-produced seafood, beef, or chicken every single day. I cannot say what the chances are, but that there is a chance at all must not be accepted.

LAWS AND CONVENTIONS: NOT NEARLY ENOUGH

Under increasing international pressure, the government of Thailand has made efforts to address severe labor exploitation in its seafood sector, but these efforts appear to be falling short. In April 2014, the Thai Department of Fisheries launched its "Action Plan and Implementation by the Department of Fisheries in Addressing Labour Issues and Promoting Better Working Conditions in the Thai Fisheries Industry." The plan called for greater oversight, regulation, and maintaining labor standards across the industry. One promising step involved the revocation of 11,700 licenses of fishing vessels in October 2015 for offenses relating to labor abuses or other regulatory infractions. Unfortunately, local experts tell me that many of the same ship captains whose licenses were revoked were back in business a few months later, either with new licenses or with fake licenses. Rather than being a one-time event, rigorous monitoring of vessels for regulatory or licensing infractions should be an ongoing practice by the Thai Department of Fisheries.

Thailand also has passed numerous laws meant to maintain decent work standards in the fishing sector, including the Thailand Fisheries Act, B.E. 2490 (1947), the Thailand Act Governing the Right to Fish in Thai Waters,

B.E. 2482 (1939), the Thailand Vessel Act, B.E. 2481 (1938), as well as an abundance of labor laws. However, most of the laws have significant loopholes, lack enforcement, and are outdated. A more promising development is that Thailand signed the ILO's Work in Fishing Convention of 2007 (No. 188) and the ILO Recommendation Concerning Work in the Fishing Sector of 2007 (No. 199). The convention and recommendation are designed to establish global labor standards that apply to all workers in the commercial fishing sector, including minimum wages, minimum age to work, maximum daily hours of work, mandated periods of rest, elimination of up-front fees imposed on workers, elevated safety standards, medical care, comprehensive training, and other policies intended to maintain the dignity and safety of work. Thailand is working with the ILO on implementing these standards, although the country has yet to pass sufficiently robust domestic laws to allow it to do so, let alone adequately enforce the relevant laws that already exist.

At the international level, the UN Food and Agriculture Organization (FAO), Fisheries and Aquaculture Department, is heavily involved in efforts to maintain dignity and decency of work in the seafood industry and overall sustainability of global seafood supplies. The FAO issued a Code of Conduct for Responsible Fishers in 1995, but implementation is inconsistent among most seafood-producing nations, especially those in East Asia. Within Europe, the EU Strategy towards the Eradication of Trafficking in Human Beings (2012–2016) includes language ensuring that supply chains into Europe are not tainted by human trafficking, specifically mentioning the seafood supply chains from East Asia. The UK Modern Slavery Act of 2015 also requires that companies disclose their efforts to ensure that their supply chains are untainted by slavery offenses. Other countries in Europe are contemplating similar legislation, and one can only hope that these laws will be passed and enforced soon.

In the United States, the main law designed to address imports of IUU caught fish is the Lacey Act of 1900. The Lacey Act is intended to stop the import and sale of products that are extracted in violation of the source country's conservation provisions or international law. There have been a few convictions relating to the seafood sector under the Lacey Act, the largest of which involved a case of rock lobsters from South Africa that were illegally caught and smuggled into the United States between 1987 and 2001.

The defendants were sentenced to prison and ordered to pay a fine of $55 million in restitution to the government of South Africa.

The Smoot-Hawley Tariff Act of 1930 in the United States also provides scope for the prohibition of the import of tainted goods; however, the relevant language relating to this prohibition only became practically effective more than eight decades after the law was passed. Section 307 of the act states, "All goods, wares, articles, and merchandise mined, produced, or manufactured wholly or in part in any foreign country by convict labor or forced labor . . . shall not be entitled to entry at any of the ports of the U.S., and the importation thereof is prohibited." The original language of the act included a gaping exception to the import prohibition, namely that the prohibition does not apply to goods for which there is not enough production in the United States to meet domestic demand. This "consumptive demand" exception basically negated the Section 307 prohibition because there is almost never sufficient U.S. production to meet domestic demand for almost any good that ends up being imported, such as rice, seafood, cocoa, steel, rare earth minerals, tea, palm oil, garments, and so on. Across the years, lawmakers attempted unsuccessfully to eliminate this carve out, and, it was finally closed by Congress under Section 910 of the Trade Facilitation and Enforcement Act of 2015 and signed into law by President Obama in February 2016. The act can now be used to ban imports of slavery-tainted seafood products from Thailand, or any other slave-tainted good from any other country, but it remains to be seen just how proactively and rigorously this ban will be enforced.

Numerous other laws, conventions, and treaties offer scope and impetus to eliminate slavery, forced labor, child labor, labor trafficking, and all severe abuses in Thailand's seafood industry; however, as is often the case when it comes to issues of slavery, words on paper will not get the job done. None of the aforementioned laws, conventions, and treaties—or any other human rights instruments, for that matter—seem to have protected the Rohingya from trafficking, slavery, and slaughter. Action requires will, and when those in power lack will, citizens must force it upon them. Consumers must apply pressure demanding that they be served slavery-free seafood, meat, or chicken and that atrocities such as those befalling the Rohingya are tackled swiftly and effectively. Once a sufficient proportion of consumers demand untainted goods, retailers will have no choice but to respond to keep their business. Market economy forces will then work their way down the supply chain, cleaning up much of the global economy. Until that time, global animal protein supply chains are unacceptably tainted, which means everyone is at risk of eating slave-produced meat each and every day. We are what we eat, and if we eat the products of slavery, we are slaves. Let this thought dictate our response.

UNABLE TO RETURN

During the course of my investigations in the Thai seafood sector, I documented 198 cases of slavery in the fish-catching, dock-work, and peeling-shed portions of Thailand's seafood industry. These cases involved both current and former workers. Every one of the individuals I documented was a slave in every sense of the word, and I am confident that a significant proportion of the more than 800,000 migrant workers in Thailand's seafood industry are suffering slavelike exploitation as well. There is a pressing need for more research to document the full scope of these abuses.

Of the 198 cases I was able to document, the key findings include:

- 100 percent males
- 100 percent foreign migrants from Myanmar (101 cases), Cambodia (76 cases), and Laos (21 cases)
- 93 percent involved recruitment by traffickers
- 89 percent did not have a written contract for work
- 80 percent did not have valid documents for residency in Thailand
- 23 percent had proficiency in the Thai language
- 24 cases of children under the age of eighteen
- $68.70 ($2.37 per day; $0.16 per hour): average monthly wage at sea[21]
- $73.85 ($2.74 per day; $0.20 per hour): average monthly wage at docks and sheds[22]
- 21.5 years: average age at time first trafficked
- 8.1 months: average total duration of time at sea for ship workers

There are purported to be higher rates of children and females working in the aquaculture and processing stages of the Thai seafood supply chain beyond those in the hard manual labor stages I documented. Although more investigation is needed, conducting research into the Thai seafood sector is fraught with challenges. It is also severely corroding for the researcher and represents soul-wrenching work on the best of days. In 2016, a major foundation offered me full financial and logistical support to build on my previous research, gathering data to express reliable prevalence rates of slavery and child labor across the Thai seafood industry. I did not accept. It is the first time that I declined an offer to build on previous research, and I have been wracked by a sense of failure every since. My research in Thailand pushed me to my breaking point several times, and it has had a lasting impact on my mind, heart, and health. I simply could not find the fortitude to return. I am confident that I will be able plunge into Thailand's misery again one day, but for the time being, the savagery and ruthlessness I confronted in that country is too much to bear.

REDEMPTION BY THE SEA

Coupled with my experiences at Badagry, my forays into the Thai seafood sector transformed the once alluring and soothing ocean into something dark, painful, and destructive. Human civilization was born next to water, but on balance the seas appeared to me to cause more harm than good to humankind. True, oceans and rivers have provided sustenance from the very beginning and enabled discovery of new lands and trade with new people, but they have also facilitated conflict, subjugation, and slavery. Can the good exist without the evil? Of course not, but the balance is all. In few places have I found greater imbalance than in the global seafood industry. We have been fishermen for millennia, but that pure and ancient ritual has become grotesque in the hands of the global economy. Misery became nourishment; slavery became dinner. I could scarcely bear to look at the ocean after my devastating forays into the Thai seafood sector. The toll was too much. So I fled to a lonely patch of sand on a quiet island, to try to redeem my relationship with the sea.

The patch of sand was on Koh Tao, a remote island in the Gulf of Thailand. I found a small fishing village on the eastern shore and lived in a thatched hut as a guest of a young couple, Rama and Siri. As with most inhabitants of Koh Tao, Rama is a fisherman. He ventured to sea every day at dawn and sold most of his catch to a few of the hostels on the island. The rest he kept for his family. He fished in a wooden boat, the ancient way, with a pole and patience.

I fished with Rama for five days. We sat in silence much of the time, listening to the water, watching the hue of the ocean transform as the sun passed from east to west—azure, cobalt, and gray. My thoughts wandered to the torture chambers further at sea. To wash them away, I plunged into the deep. It was serene, cleansing, meditative. I thought how peaceful it would be to stay.

Rama and I caught mostly grouper and snapper. The experience was not entirely idyllic; the searing sun burnt my skin no matter how much protective lotion I applied. We returned to shore each day by afternoon, and Rama went off to sell his catch. Siri kept the fish she wanted, and I helped her clean and cook them for dinner: lemon, salt, and an open flame. Rama brought back a few beers for us each evening from the nearby market, and we all three ate on the beach at twilight. Darkness falls quickly on the islands. The sky bears shades of sapphire, crimson, steel, and black. Night takes hold without restraint. All is silent, save the placid waves that caress the mind to sleep.

My time on Koh Tao brought me some measure of tranquility, and helped heal a sea that had become scarred with too much pain. It also brought me closer to accepting the undeniable truth of slavery—we consume their suffering. Their suffering sustains us.

May God forgive us.

CHAPTER 8

A FRAMEWORK TO ERADICATE SLAVERY

Therefore, we declare on each and every one of our creeds that modern slavery, in terms of human trafficking, forced labor and prostitution, and organ trafficking, is a crime against humanity. Its victims are from all walks of life, but are most frequently among the poorest and most vulnerable of our brothers and sisters. On behalf of all of them, our communities of faith are called to reject, without exception, any systematic deprivation of individual freedom for the purposes of personal or commercial exploitation; in their name, we make this declaration.

—Pope Francis

IN EVERY CORNER of the world, slaves are exploited, dishonored, and degraded for profit. They are forced to endure conditions of indignity, misery, and oppression. Greed and prejudice have breathed life into the institution of slavery since the dawn of human civilization, and although it was proclaimed abolished centuries ago, it persists because of the following central thesis:

The immensity and pervasiveness of slavery in the modern era is driven by the ability of exploiters to generate substantial profits at almost no real risk through the callous exploitation of a global subclass of humanity whose degradation is tacitly accepted by every participant in the economic system that consumes their suffering.

Slavery is a relic of history that disgraces us all. As long as there is even one slave in the world, the legitimacy of contemporary civilization is threatened. I believe the moral test of our time is whether we will undertake every effort required, for as long as it takes, to rid the world of slavery permanently. Slaves permeate the global economy, and their torment touches our lives every day, from the food we eat to the clothes we wear to the technology that makes our lives possible. For our existence to be valid, we must eradicate slavery. Many brilliant activists are working at this task every day. I offer the following thoughts in the hope that they might prove useful in these efforts.

RECAPITULATION OF THE TWENTY FORCES THAT PROMOTE SLAVERY TODAY

In chapter 1, I listed twenty forces that promote slavery centered on a "Five P" framework of prevention, protection, prosecution, partnership, and progress. Those forces are:

Prevention

1. Failure to provide reasonable alternatives to the most destitute and vulnerable populations.
2. Failure to provide access to formal credit markets.
3. Failure to protect displaced people in a postcrisis context.
4. General acceptance of the subjugation of low-class/caste groups and minority communities.
5. Failure to provide connectivity and information tools to foreign migrants.
6. Imposition of up-front fees for labor migrants.

Protection

7. Penchant to see survivors as offenders.
8. Failure to provide long-term empowerment of survivors and break the cycle of slavery.

9. Failure to protect survivors of slavery, as well as their families, from former exploiters pursuant to being witnesses in a prosecution.

Prosecution

10. Failure to prioritize slavery cases, except for the easy ones.
11. Laws that do not adequately penalize the economic nature of the crime.
12. Corruption and the failure to implement or enforce laws where they exist.
13. Inadequate training of law enforcement, prosecutors, and judges to recognize the offense and prosecute it effectively.
14. Failure to effectively penalize the demand side of sex trafficking.
15. Failure to introduce sufficient cost and risk to corporations to motivate cleansing of global supply chains.

Partnership

16. Lack of transnational cooperation with investigations and prosecutions.
17. Insufficient resources and coordination among antislavery NGOs and shelters.
18. Inadequate coordination between sending and destination countries of labor migrants.

Progress

19. Insufficient research and data gathering on all aspects of slavery.
20. Lack of sustained and adequate resources to promote progress in anti-slavery efforts.

If these twenty forces are effectively tackled by a fully resourced and sustained campaign across all levels of government, industry, civil society, and citizenry, I am confident that slavery will become an offense of the past. The remainder of this chapter focuses on the logic of the ten initiatives I believe will provide a comprehensive strategy to address the twenty forces listed here.

TEN INITIATIVES TO ERADICATE SLAVERY

The following ten initiatives must be undertaken without interruption for as long as it takes to eradicate slavery. There are no vital considerations relating to sequencing the initiatives, although legal and policy reforms would optimally take place prior to the others. Some of the efforts I describe are already being pursued in various forms, but they are typically resource constrained and not designed or executed effectively.

Elevated Scaling and Effectiveness of Global Antipoverty Programs

This is the most resource intensive and important of the prevention initiatives I am proposing. Extreme poverty, a lack of sufficient credit resources and alternative income opportunities, and the inability of the poor to educate their children (especially girls) are among the most powerful forces that render individuals vulnerable to slavery, child labor, and other forms of exploitation. A comprehensive and fully resourced set of antipoverty initiatives that target these forces will go a long way toward the long-term attenuation of some of the most fundamental vulnerabilities faced by the poor around the world. Many of these issues are already the focus of international and national initiatives, but corruption, a lack of funding, inadequate execution, mismanagement, and numerous other barriers render these efforts much less effective than they should be. Almost every slave I met lacked a stable source of income and security and a reasonable alternative to the condition of servitude. The following efforts can assist in inverting this reality.

Microcredit Expansion

The absence of reliable and sufficient credit sources pushes many poor people to take loans from unscrupulous lenders and traffickers, which often result in debt bondage. Microcredit has been a powerful tool for poverty alleviation as well as for prevention of debt bondage. The concept was born in South Asia through the genius of the Nobel Peace Prize winner Mohammed Yunus of Bangladesh. In 1976 he founded the Grameen Bank ("Village Bank"), which provides small loans to the poor (mostly women) toward small business ventures. The system includes programs on savings and self-help groups, business training, and a low cost of borrowing that have helped lift millions of people out of poverty. Since its inception, microcredit has expanded to dozens of countries; however, these institutions are limited by access to capital and the need to be self-sustaining businesses. These loans have to "perform," which in turn requires that a high percentage of the loans must go toward income-generating activities (IGAs), so they can be repaid to the lender, who can then repay its own costs of capital and fund operations. Unfortunately, the credit needs of the poorest of the poor often do not generate income. Those needs may be for basic consumption, medicine, or life rituals. From the data I gathered in *Bonded Labor*, upward of 80 percent of the credit needs of the bonded laborers I documented in South Asia were unrelated to income-generating opportunities.[1] Microcredit or other alternative credit sources must be designed to meet the spectrum of credit needs of the poorest of the poor, especially for non-IGAs. In addition, far more capital must be made available to microcredit lenders to expand their reach to as many of the poor as possible and to blend their lending portfolios to increase the ratio of lending that does not have to go toward IGAs. More formalized regulation and record keeping of microcredit lenders is also required to ensure that different lenders do not give loans to the same borrower, and to ensure that pressure or bullying tactics are never used to coerce repayment. Expanding and redesigning microcredit in this way will take time, but doing so would go a long way toward addressing the inadequate levels of credit available to the poor.

Global Economy Integration

In every corner of the world, the poor must be integrated more directly and equitably into the global economy. This is the optimal way to ensure that they have reasonable alternatives to the offer of servitude, and to promote the overall income reliability and human development of rural and impoverished people everywhere. Immense global economic forces and trade barriers disenfranchise the poor in developing nations and keep them from participating fully and equitably in the global economy. Initiatives based on tying the products of rural labor directly to Western consumers represent a prime opportunity to link the poor with global markets and provide them with diversified and sustained sources of income. Many NGOs and even small enterprises are focused on everything from fair trade initiatives to investing in the production and distribution of rural products straight to Western (or nearby urban) markets. These efforts must be expanded through elevated funding by governments and foundations. Governments should create and expand initiatives designed to integrate the poor into markets, without exploitative intermediaries. This means linking laborers and craftspeople directly to consumers and returning a fair level of profit participation to the workers. The world is rife with exploitative subcontractors and intermediaries who often exploit the individuals at the bottom of the supply chain. They are the recruiters/traffickers, loan providers, wage underpayers, and other exploitative actors that allow the producer to claim "It's the subcontractor who is misbehaving, not me," even though the producer may sanction the exploitation. The more directly workers can be linked to the point of retail sale, or to executives running the retail companies selling their products through supply chain transparency initiatives (such as the Supply Unchained project of GoodWeave), the less likely the workers are to be exploited. Unregulated and unmonitored labor intermediaries block the light of scrutiny and darken the underbelly of the global economy, which allows slavery and human trafficking to thrive. It is high time they were removed from the equation.

Achievement of Universal Primary School Education for the Poor, Especially Girls

One of the most powerful tools to prevent slavery is ensuring that children, especially girls, are educated through the age of eighteen. Attendance rates for children in school have improved across the last two decades, but completion rates for girls continue to lag boys significantly, which increases their vulnerability to various forms of exploitation.[2] Many government education programs around the world aim to achieve complete primary education for boys and girls, but most fall far from the mark because they are not tied to programs that provide sufficient income or stability for the family to replace the lost (albeit meager) wages a child laborer might be paid, or to programs that help alter the perception that girls are not worthy of an education and are better suited to be homemakers and laborers. The thirty or forty cents a day secured through child labor could mean the difference between family survival and oblivion. Children often report that they would prefer to work to help their families, and that going to school cannot benefit them. Child labor is bad enough, but it is often the first step toward worse forms of exploitation. This is especially true for girls, who are much less likely than boys to receive a primary education in many parts of the world, and instead might be trafficked for forced prostitution or be forced to marry at a very young age, perpetuating the cycle of poverty. Some of the best results in demonstrating how the education of girls can create a new cultural norm of valuing females as economic contributors to their families and preventing trafficking and early marriage has been achieved in Nepal by the American Himalayan Foundation and its STOP Girl Trafficking program. Girls in villages prone to sex trafficking and early marriage are provided with full tuition to school and even scholarships to college, and their families are provided with additional support to ease the strain of "losing" a child earner. Almost all of the girls in the STOP program graduate and have helped lift their families out of poverty. It is a small example of what is possible when sufficient resources and expertise are deployed in a comprehensive strategy to support families and to ensure that children are educated. This type of program should be scaled globally because there is no greater preventative tool to slavery than education.

Rapid-Response Teams Focused on Prevention and Protection in Crisis Zones

Human traffickers are almost always the first responders to crisis zones around the world. Whether an environmental catastrophe or a military conflict or a sudden economic collapse, whenever crisis strikes, women, children, the poor, and outcastes are disproportionately affected, exploited, and recruited by traffickers. Faced with destitution, starvation, or worse, desperate people flee en masse to find security. The mass migration in 2015 and 2016 of millions of despairing families from North Africa and the Middle East into central and western Europe is a searing example of this phenomenon. The same phenomenon took place with the Rohingya of Myanmar in 2015. Almost every major crisis or catastrophe follows a similar pattern of distress migration and exploitation. To stem this pattern, rapid-response teams that immediately travel to crisis zones with a focus on alleviating economic and medical needs, child protection, and guidance on safe migration options will provide crucial relief to vulnerable people. Block chain technology that can help secure identities and document the movement of people is invaluable. The more resourced and sustained these efforts are, the more effective they will be.

Awareness and Education Campaigns

Slavery operates on the tacit or explicit acceptance by mainstream societies and their governments that the servile exploitation of certain subordinated communities and ethnic groups, as well as those of the female gender, is not only acceptable but in some cases is deemed a preferable outcome. Awareness campaigns for the public, as well as educational programs for law enforcement, judiciary, and government officials, focused on promoting the equality of minority castes and ethnicities around the world must be deployed to motivate the necessary change in social consciousness. Creative media personnel can devise the most effective ways to disseminate these messages, but some of the campaigns could include the following messages. First, the realities of the oppressive and dehumanizing nature of slavery, as well as its extent around the world, must be conveyed accurately. Second, consumers must be made aware that they purchase products produced by slaves and child laborers every day. Third, education and sensitization efforts devised for law enforcement, judiciary, and government officials must focus on disseminating accurate (not anecdotal) knowledge of how and why slavery operates, how to identify it, and that the rights and voices of the subclasses are just as valid as those of their exploiters. Fourth, the general impression among exploiters that slavery and child labor are acceptable because the alternatives for the enslaved individuals are worse must be dispelled.

To be most effective, media, entertainment, and sports celebrities can be recruited to support these campaigns. They could spearhead programs such as a "No More Slavery Day" that stresses the equality of all communities, genders, and ethnic groups. The ability of these individuals to sway public opinion will prove crucial to the overall efficacy of the messages. The film industry also can invest in a series of public relations messages or even short-form and long-form documentaries and feature films highlighting slavery and the need to eradicate it. These efforts will be particularly important in South Asia where "untouchables" are still treated as subhumans by mainstream society. On the day that a critical mass of people reject the oppression of minority castes and those of the female gender, and the exploitation of these communities as slaves, everything else that is necessary to abolish slavery will follow.

A "Technology Trust" Focused on Creating Innovative Solutions to the Current Barriers in Antislavery Efforts

Technology solutions will provide the edge in combating slavery at every step. Technology has been used with alarming success by sex and labor traffickers to recruit victims and to conduct business, but the potential to use these tools to fight back against traffickers represents the largest untapped opportunity in contemporary efforts to eradicate slavery. Many major technology companies are already investing in the development of antitrafficking applications, although they have only begun to scratch the surface. To reach their potential, I propose the creation of a Technology Trust that would be composed of leading executives, coders, and engineers from major tech companies who will work in collaboration with subject-matter experts to develop an array of mechanisms that will prove crucial in eradicating slavery. Some of the tools that have already proved useful were discussed in chapter 5, but with greater input from slavery experts and greater coordination between technology companies, the potential is limitless. Needless to say, this trust would need to bring with it a substantial commitment of resources to get the job done. I am confident that the abolition of slavery will be achieved through technology-based solutions, and a Technology Trust provides the best chance for achieving this goal.

Redesign of the Process and Governance of Labor Migration

The global economy requires labor migration to thrive. Remittances sent by migrant workers also provide a vital source of income for poor families. However, the current process and governance of labor migration feeds directly into labor trafficking and debt bondage. Numerous changes must be made to prevent these abuses among migrant worker populations. The two most important changes are (1) the elimination of up-front fees for foreign worker placement and (2) improved coordination between sending and receiving countries to protect migrant worker populations.

Up-front fees are the primary tool through which traffickers coerce migrant workers into forced labor and debt bondage. Poor migrants should not be saddled with fees that represent ten or twenty years of their per capita income to secure a work opportunity abroad. Both the worker and the employer benefit when labor migration is pursued equitably. There are certainly costs associated with basic training, medical checks, travel documents, and travel; however, in all cases these should be paid solely by the employer without any burden on the migrant for repayment. Strict laws and monitoring are required to enforce this policy change throughout all global labor migration channels.

To maximize the protection of migrant workers, sending and receiving countries must coordinate in a more transparent and honest way to prevent labor trafficking. At present, there appears to be a tacit agreement between many sending and receiving nations that the labor needs of the latter will be met with the low-wage, expendable migrants from the former, and to that end many labor laws and regulations meant to protect migrants remain largely unenforced. Indeed, laws are even passed that help facilitate the exploitation of vulnerable migrant workers. Taxes and fees on labor migrants provide a robust source of income for sending governments, and receiving governments similarly benefit from levies and bonds paid by companies for each migrant they employ. Receiving governments also benefit by keeping their industries more profitable through the exploitation of low-wage, expendable migrants. The net result of these implicit agreements is the pitiless exploitation of millions of migrant workers, which must be jettisoned in favor of fully transparent and regulated agreements between sending and receiving countries to enforce all labor laws as well as a host of protective mechanisms to ensure migrants are not exploited, and that when they are, they have full access to rights, protections, recompense, and justice, as opposed to immediate detention and deportation. Some of these cooperative ventures would include (1) enhanced predeparture training and cultural preparation for migrants relating to their destination countries, (2) arrival registration and orientation with government officials in the destination country, including a full review of rights and contacts available to them,

(3) the provision of a working cell phone with a local SIM card that cannot be confiscated by the employer, (4) rigorous labor inspections and offsite interviews to ensure that all laws are being upheld and wages paid, and (5) the elimination of all "tied-visa" programs that prevent workers from switching employers in their destination countries. These and other alterations in the process and governance of labor migration, as well as the protection of labor migrants and the elimination of all up-front fees, will help eliminate slavery in the global migrant workforce.

Legal Reform

In addition to the first initiative, this initiative is perhaps the most ambitious and complex, yet it is crucial to the eradication of slavery. Numerous legal reforms are required to create a system that can optimally protect survivors and prosecute traffickers and slavers. The four most important reforms are described next.

Minimum Standards for Effective Survivor-Witness Protection

Inadequate and misconceived protection of survivor-witnesses results in retrafficking and makes it exceedingly difficult to prosecute traffickers and slavers. Trafficking survivors often are subject to prosecution, deportation, or worse. Some countries make an effort to protect and empower survivors, but the quality of these efforts varies significantly around the world. Protection and empowerment systems must be standardized to include, at a minimum, (1) ninety-day reflection periods; (2) full residency, work, legal, health, and psychological support and rights for the survivor; (3) safe, respectful, and hygienic shelters; (4) access to rights and protections divorced from cooperation with a prosecution; (5) fully funded protection for the survivor and his or her family members in the case of cooperation with a prosecution; and (6) elevated standards in all areas for minors that prioritize the best interests of the child.[3] These and other measures will ensure that survivors are treated with a human rights approach first, and they will ensure that the survivor-witness is in the most secure position from which to participate in a prosecution. Without the survivor-witness, it is exceedingly challenging to bring successful prosecutions against traffickers, and without successful prosecutions, the crimes go unpunished and are free to thrive.

Sharp Increase in the Economic Penalties for Slavery Offenses

Laws that do not include severe economic penalties for the crime of slavery are laws that do not effectively punish the offense. Slavery is fundamentally an economic crime driven by the ability to generate substantial profits in a nearly risk-free system of human exploitation. Most laws against slavery stipulate prison terms, while economic penalties often are nonexistent, modest, or unstipulated. The absence of robust economic penalties means that even if an offender is prosecuted and even if he is convicted, the economic fines may be far less than the profits generated from slavery, which means slavery is still good business. The relatively low-cost and risk-free nature of slavery must be inverted to a high-cost, high-risk offense. Increases in economic penalties, along with efforts outlined in initiative ten, provide the best chance to achieve this goal. I provide a detailed exploration of this argument in my law journal article, "Designing More Effective Laws Against Human Trafficking";[4] the remainder of this section provides a summary of this argument.

The first step in the design of economic penalties for slavery offenses is to understand the *real* economic penalty currently associated with the offense. The second step is to assess the total economic profits currently associated with the offense. The third step is to determine the level at which the real economic penalty should be set to severely diminish, if not eliminate, the economic profits associated with the offense. These three steps must be executed for each kind of slavery crime because each form presents different economic profiles and one penalty cannot effectively punish them all. One could theoretically apply the most severe penalty to all slavery cases, but doing so may run afoul of the legal principle of proportionality.[5]

The following example is based on the penalties in Thailand's Anti-Trafficking in Persons Act of 2008, which were made more severe in a 2015 amendment to include a maximum of life in prison and a fine of 400,000 baht ($11,430) for the most severe offenses. This increase in penalties was partly in response to the downgrade of Thailand to Tier 3 in the U.S. Trafficking in Person's Report the previous year.

STEP 1

A simple formula for calculating the real economic penalty for an offense is:

> Real economic penalty = probability of being prosecuted × probability of being convicted × maximum financial penalty in the law.

Simple formulas for the probabilities of being prosecuted and convicted are:

> Probability of being prosecuted = number of prosecuted criminal offenses in a year / total number of criminal offenses in a year.

> Probability of being convicted = number of convictions for an offense in a year / number of prosecutions of that offense in a year.[6]

I calculated the average probability of being prosecuted for the offense of sex trafficking in Thailand from 2010 through 2015 as being approximately 0.2 percent, and the probability of being convicted once prosecuted as being 18.86 percent.[7] Multiplying these numbers results in a real economic penalty of approximately $4 ($11,430 × 0.2 percent × 18.86 percent). This $4 real economic penalty is reflected in the phrase "no real risk" in the essential thesis I offered as driving slavery in the modern era. In essence, the current real economic penalty for the crime of sex trafficking in Thailand is meaningless, and thus it produces no incentive for offenders to obey the law.

STEP 2

The tables in appendix B provide a sense of the profits associated with various forms of slavery around the world. These values range from a few hundred dollars per year per agricultural bonded laborer in South Asia to $75,000 or more per year for a sex trafficking victim in the United States or western Europe. However, slaves are not exploited for just one year. Table 1.4 in chapter 1 provides the weighted average durations of enslavement by type

from the cases I documented. To calculate the total economic profits associated with the crime of slavery, we can use the concept of exploitation
value (EV), which I introduced in *Sex Trafficking*. Chapter 1 provides the
summary data on exploitation value by type. The details and full explanation of the EV calculation can be found in table A.5, which shows a range
from $2,545 for bonded labor to $68,117 for sex trafficking. These values
are global weighted averages derived from highly conservative calculations
of the total economic value of a slave to an exploiter by type of servitude
across the aggregate duration of enslavement. Regional values vary significantly, with sex trafficking in the United States having an EV more than
double the global weighted average, and sex trafficking in Thailand having
an EV less than half the global weighted average. Individuals also may be
exploited in more than one type of slavery and across several industries
and regions during the course of their exploitation, so it can be argued that
at a minimum a blended average of the global EV numbers derived from
the cases I documented would capture the total exploitation value to the
exploiter of slavery in general. I would still argue for specific sex-trafficking
penalties given the immense profits generated by this crime. To decrease
the exploitation value of a slave, a significant increase in the economic costs
of operating the business must be created, and this can be most effectively
accomplished by elevating the real economic penalty of committing the
crime to a profit-compromising level. The level to which this penalty should
be increased is discussed in step 3.

STEP 3

To elevate the economic costs of exploiting slaves to a profit-compromising level requires that one maximize the formula discussed in step 1: real
economic penalty = probability of being prosecuted × probability of being
convicted × maximum financial penalty in the law. At present, that value
is around $4 in our example of Thailand, whereas the weighted average
exploitation value in Thailand of sex trafficking is $29,345 and $3,460 for
labor trafficking in the country's seafood sector. The precise level of economic penalty that should be stipulated in the law is open to debate, but the
concept is clear: the greater the real economic penalty of slavery, the lower
the profitability, desirability, and viability of the crime.

One benchmark for more economically meaningful penalties could be drug laws. The Thailand Narcotic Act, B.E. 2522 (1979) stipulates a maximum penalty of fifteen years in prison and a fine of 1,500,000 baht ($42,850) for trafficking in a Category 5 drug such as marijuana. This financial penalty is almost four times more severe than the recently increased fine for human trafficking. In other countries, the fines for drug trafficking can be ten or twenty times those for human trafficking. Given the moral repugnance of the crime of human trafficking, as well as its substantial economic benefits, one could argue that the economic penalty for enslaving another human being should be several times greater than that of trafficking in marijuana. Having said this, simply substituting 1,500,000 baht for 400,000 baht as the penalty for human trafficking would result in a real penalty that is virtually meaningless due to the anemic levels of prosecution and conviction of the crime. Hence, in addition to elevating the economic penalty, the probabilities of prosecution and conviction must be increased.

To demonstrate the point, assume for the sake of argument that the penalty in the law for each offense of sex trafficking is 3,000,000 baht ($85,714), that the prosecution probability of the crime of human trafficking is 33 percent (one in three sex trafficking offenses is prosecuted in a given year), and that the probability of conviction is 67 percent (two in three prosecutions result in a conviction or settlement). Then the real economic penalty would be $85,714 × 33 percent × 67 percent = $18,951. This is roughly two-thirds the EV of sex trafficking and certainly a more deterrent number when sex traffickers start making calculations about the risk–reward profile of the offense. It is also a far more profit-compromising number than a real penalty of $4. Most important, a value like this would make sex trafficking a far less economically appealing crime, particularly if the offender is brought to justice and convicted well in advance of the expected average duration of exploitation. One could apply this penalty equally across the spectrum of slavery offenses, or apply slightly more proportional penalties for less profitable forms of slavery, such as in agriculture or seafood.

More broadly, consider for a moment if one were to impose penalties such as these on corporate executives relating to slavery in their supply chains. Companies would probably be deterred from allowing slavery to occur in their production bases. Add prison time to the mix, and the tacit or apathetic acceptance of slavery in global supply chains would probably come to an end.

With these and other legal and regulatory reforms in place, the environment would be optimal to ensure that the system of slavery would no longer be a risk worth taking for any exploiter or commercial entity in the world.

Setting aside theoretical arguments, the point of this exercise is to demonstrate the importance of creating a judicial and law enforcement regime that elevates the deterrent and retributive value of the real economic penalty of slavery. Criminals, like all people, are rational economic agents, and when a high-profit, low-risk business opportunity presents itself, they will pursue it and fight to maintain it until that reality is forcibly and irrevocably altered. Whatever paper penalty is stipulated in the law, and whatever prosecution and conviction probabilities are ultimately achieved, the outcome must transform slavery into a highly toxic, costly, and risky business venture. Amending laws is one thing, but achieving enormously elevated prosecution and conviction levels is quite another. The tenth and final initiative discussed in this chapter is intended to help achieve these increased probabilities.

Severe Penalties for Consumers of Commercial Sex

The third legal reform I propose is the most controversial, but I believe it provides the most effective way to dismantle the business of sex trafficking in the near term. In Sex Trafficking, I presented an initial argument that male demand to purchase commercial sex is highly elastic.[8] This hypothesis was corroborated by a small sample size of four male consumers in a brothel in India, whose demand curve demonstrated an elasticity of demand of 1.9 (highly elastic). I have since completed a survey of sixty male consumers of commercial sex in India, Denmark, Mexico, and the United States. Although there is variation between countries, the aggregate demand curve of all sixty male consumers is 1.82. When the retail price of a commercial sex act doubles, demand among these sixty consumers drops by 76 percent. This result reinforces the hypothesis in Sex Trafficking and affirms that demand-side interventions have the most potential to reduce sex trafficking in the near term.

The results of this research led me to think about another set of tactics to attack sex trafficking. Male demand to purchase cheap sex very well could be sensitive to deterrence-focused interventions in addition to those predicated on creating upward shocks in retail prices. Put another way, if demand fluctuates significantly based on price, it can very well fluctuate significantly based on efforts to deter the purchase more directly. Interventions focused on deterring the purchase of commercial sex can best be tested in systems in which the purchase is criminalized. One can then assess policies such as severe economic penalties, prison time, naming and shaming, or placement on a sex offender list, among others. These policies are being tested in small pockets around the world, with some of the most interesting work being done by Demand Abolition, based in Boston. I believe that consumer-deterrent laws and policies coupled with demand-side efforts to elevate cost and risk to the trafficker provide the best chance of having a major impact on the business of sex trafficking.

Laws or Strategic Litigation That Establish Strict Liability for Owners/Employers Relating to All Actions of Labor Subcontractors

A large proportion of the slavery and child labor offenses in the world take place at the hands of labor subcontractors operating in the shadows of global supply chains. Liability for these abuses rarely extends to the owners/employers/producers/corporations availing themselves of the cheap, expendable labor forces that exist primarily in unregulated and underregulated labor markets. To be fair, many of these companies have little or no visibility regarding what is occurring at the bottom of their supply chains, and they rely on assurances from local contractors that labor laws are being upheld. Because of the plausible deniability and the lack of liability at the corporate or producer levels, and because there is little benefit in trying to track down and punish a lowly labor subcontractor, the system of servile labor exploitation persists in the shadowy underbelly of the global economy. To remedy this lacuna in the principle of vicarious liability, laws should be passed that establish strict liability for owners and employers relating to all actions of their labor subcontractors, no matter how many levels of subcontracting down the chain the abuses take place. In common law jurisdictions, strategic litigation can be pursued to establish a legal precedent that extends strict liability to the corporate level. Once this liability is established, and once it is enforced with stiff penalties, there will surely be a significant shift in the amount of attention devoted by the top of the supply chain to what is taking place at the bottom.

Policy Reforms

Three immediate policy reforms should be undertaken in every country in the world to assist in the fight against slavery. The first reform is to ensure that any foreign migrant arrested or detained on suspicion of any offense should be presumed to be a potential victim of human trafficking. This possibility must be investigated first, and only if law enforcement, in conjunction with local NGOs, determines that the individual is not a victim of human trafficking should offenses against local laws be pursued. This policy reform alone will enhance protective measures for survivors of human trafficking and promote more effective prosecutions against traffickers. As matters stand, most human trafficking victims are seen as offenders first and as victims second. They are hauled up on charges, then detained and deported, and they most often return home all the more vulnerable to exploitation. The slavers and traffickers who exploited them not only go unpunished but do not even have to absorb the cost and risk associated with returning their victims to their home countries. Investigating the possibility of slavery offenses first under a presumption of exploitation is the optimal way to protect the human rights of vulnerable migrants while pursuing a more effective system for punishment of potential offenders.

A second policy reform is for countries to provide tax and tariff incentives for companies that credibly demonstrate that their supply chains are consistently untainted by slavery and child labor. These incentives need to be sufficient to motivate companies to expend the resources required to cleanse their supply chains, even though the ethical imperative for doing so should be sufficient. The most reliable way for companies to provide unassailable assurances that their supply chains are untainted is through independent, third-party certification regimes that have sufficient expertise and experience with forced labor inspections.

A third policy reform is for countries to provide most favored nations trading status to other countries that enact and enforce laws that meet the criteria of the core ILO labor conventions, including numbers 29, 87, 98, 100, 105, 111, 138, 182, and P029. OECD nations could begin the process with a commitment to achieve this goal, which would then flow through to many other countries to ensure favorable trading status, which would result in a systemic cleanup of the global economy.

A Mandatory United Nations Fund for Slavery

The United Nations already has a Voluntary Trust Fund for victims of human trafficking; however, the voluntary nature means member states can decide how much, if anything, to contribute each year to the fund. Many nations invest in antislavery efforts individually, but the fact that the UN's trust fund has received only a few million dollars in donations from a handful of member states since its inception in 2010 is a sad testament to the global commitment to eradicating slavery.

Therefore, I propose a United Nations Fund for Slavery that would be resourced with *mandatory* contributions of 0.01 percent of the GDP of every member state each year. That is the equivalent of just one penny on every $100 of national income. If you could support a fund that would significantly enhance efforts to end slavery, wouldn't you part with one penny on every $100 of your income? These donations would amount to $4 billion per year, which I believe is more than enough to get the job done. To put the amount in perspective, the United States spends this same amount on defense every four days, so the United States alone has sufficient resources to allocate $4 billion each year in the fight against slavery. The funds would be directed toward tackling each of the forces that promotes slavery today, with a particular focus on protection and empowerment initiatives (including the antipoverty initiatives previously described), capacity support for antitrafficking NGOs and survivor shelters, prosecutions of traffickers, and much-needed research and measurement of all aspects of slavery. The fund would be overseen by a core group of slavery experts with equal representation from each region of the world. In short, a lack of resources is the single greatest hurdle in efforts to eradicate slavery, and this fund could solve that problem permanently.

International Slavery Courts

A system of international slavery courts (ISCs) should be created to prosecute slavery cases around the world. Laws against slavery are *jus cogens* in international law, and any victim in any nation would have standing to bring a claim to one of the ISCs. The independent, objective, transnational standing of the courts would abrogate numerous issues of corruption, case prioritization, jurisdiction, definitional variations, and other hurdles that prevent cases from being effectively prosecuted.

A Transnational Slavery Intervention Force

This final initiative is designed to create constant pressure on slavers and traffickers, support investigations and prosecutions, and liberate slaves around the world through the creation of an elite, fully trained, and fully resourced transnational slavery intervention force. This force will substantially increase the probability that criminals who exploit slaves will be prosecuted and convicted of their crimes. By liberating slaves, this force will reduce the average duration of enslavement of victims, and when coupled with elevated economic penalties and higher probabilities of being prosecuted and convicted, this will help to invert the high-profit, low-risk nature of slavery and render the crime uneconomic.

To achieve these goals, the intervention force would specifically be tasked with the following:

- Investigating any and all areas where there is a suspicion of slavery
- Identifying and liberating all victims and liaising with local NGOs to empower and protect them
- Tracking down and detaining traffickers and slavers and gathering evidence required to prosecute and convict them in the international slavery courts
- Conducting random wage and labor condition inspections throughout the informal and low-wage sectors of the global economy
- Focusing on inspections of, or support the inspections of, global supply chains
- Providing, or arranging to provide, protection for freed slaves during a trial against their exploiters

The force can be funded and operated by the United Nations, with permission from all member states to operate in any jurisdiction. In conjunction with guidance from subject matter experts, this intervention force can very well function as the tip of the spear in global antislavery efforts.

These ten initiatives, undertaken to the fullest degree possible, will alleviate many of the forces that promote slavery and other forms of labor exploitation around the world and destroy the economic logic of the business of slavery in the modern era. These initiatives will protect survivors, punish offenders, measure results, promote technological solutions, and clean up global supply chains. The road to a slave-free world is long, but it can be achieved. Dignity and fairness for all people will help end the millennia of misery and degradation of the most downtrodden sectors of humanity. Ensuring that all people are protected by law and enjoy full freedom and dignity will result in a proud legacy for the generation that achieves these long-overdue imperatives. In so doing, I have no doubt that the archaic system of slavery will be buried in history, once and for all.

A FAREWELL

At the end of *Bonded Labor*, I shared the story of a remarkable child, Anand. He was born a *dalit* and a slave in Bihar, India. When Anand was ten years old, his father was beaten to death by the slave owner's men for protesting when the owner sold Anand's mother and sister to traffickers. Bereft of his family, Anand lived in the slave owner's home as a domestic servant, crying himself to sleep each night. Eventually he ran away in search of his parents. A kind citizen found him hiding in an alley and helped him to a shelter for boys, which is where I met him. Anand was small for his age and very sickly, but he had an extraordinary spirit that touched me profoundly. Even though he had suffered bitterly in his short time on this earth, there was a sparkle of innocence in his eyes that refused to be dimmed. His smile was so radiant and forgiving—I felt it alone could heal the world.

Anand did not fully understand what had happened to his parents, and he spoke of them with an undeniable intention to find them one day. I remember fondly when he took me to play with a horse and an elephant that he had fashioned from clay, galloping off together to a far away land where he was joyfully reunited with his family.

Across the years, I followed Anand's progress through the head of his shelter, Rajesh, and sent support for his education. He excelled in his studies and wished to be a lawyer one day, so he could protect the rights of children.

Four years after I met Anand, I was in Sikkim documenting child trafficking in the Lepcha community. I was in the remote mountain village of Lachen when my phone rang. It was Rajesh. Anand had taken very ill, and though he fought bravely, he succumbed a few days later. He was fifteen.

Anand's demise struck me deeply. Many children die tragically every day, but Anand held a special place in my heart because he helped give me hope during a very dark period of my research, hope that the nobility of humanity was destined to defeat the prejudice and greed that was responsible for the enslavement of children like him. When I learned that he had been coldly snatched from the earth after a brief life stricken by degradation and suffering, I lost my hope. I lost my way. I lost any faith in the purpose of my efforts. I wanted to pay my respects to Anand, so I paused my research to make a trip to Gurudongmar Lake.

At an altitude of 17,100 feet, Gurudongmar is one of the highest lakes in the world, just a few kilometers south of the border with Tibet. It is a sacred place, named after Guru Padmasambhava, also known as Guru Dongmar, who is said to have blessed the lake when he arrived there in the eighth century, rendering its icy waters healing and redemptive. I set off from Lachen at dawn for the six-hour journey to the lake.

The dirt mountain road from Lachen to Gurudongmar winds through scenery that beguiles the eyes. Initially, the road traverses exquisite fields of rhododendrons, pink and crimson and amaranthine. The last outpost of humanity is at the alpine village of Thangu, just above 13,000 feet. Beyond Thangu, the landscape is barren and solitary. Jagged ridges, ethereal skies, and the odd languid yak accompany the crawling journey through the high-desert plateau to the lake.

At the end of the path at the roof of the world, the lake reveals itself in sudden and arresting splendor. The cerulean waters ebb serenely beneath the uninhibited winds jetting downward from the Himalayan peaks. Snow-capped and majestic, Kanchenjunga guards the lake like a titan.

It was spring, and only a few patches of ice remained on the surface of the lake. I passed a string of Tibetan prayer flags as I walked toward the western edge of the water. Hovering low, the sun cast a thin, spectral light across the landscape. At the far side of Gurudongmar, I removed my shoes and outer clothing and knelt in the glacial waters. My legs went numb. I cupped the waters into my hands and pressed the water against my face, my arms, my chest, spreading the numbness across my body. I immersed, and from the deep came whispers that would take lifetimes to understand.

I emerged tentatively, shuddering and faint. My heart thumped wearily, struggling to press life back into my body. I peered beyond the lake, toward the sublime peaks, and felt as if I had passed into another world where the boundless expanse of time and space had collapsed into a single moment. I thought of Anand, and I prayed for him. I thought of Sita, and I prayed for her. I thought of them all, the many slaves I met who had since crossed through the thin membrane between life and death. They were one and the same, known only by oppression, torment, and suffering. I prayed for them with a broken heart because I finally understood that for most slaves in the world, freedom embraces them only in death.

What, then, was my purpose? The question had mocked me from the beginning, but no longer could I ignore its unrelenting call.

I meditated for an answer at the banks of Gurudongmar, in the frost and solitude, searching for a reason to continue. But there was no *reason*, none at all. Reason had long ago abandoned me. The moment I embarked on my first research trip, I passed beyond my own point of no return. I had bound my spirit to this task. I had taken an implicit oath, drunk from the well of my erasure, and committed to wherever this journey might take me, as sorrowful and incomplete as it may be. It was not for me to see the day in which Anand would be equally human and dignified and free. I chose this merciless path knowing I was at best a speck who deigned to contribute, meriting neither reassurance nor result.

Alone by the waters of Gurudongmar I said farewell, not to Anand, but to myself. I folded my hands and bowed my head—to the lake, to the mountains, to the only journey before me.

A torrent of wind swept wildly across the plateau and swirled upward to the peaks, like the first exhalation at the dawn of time.

I rose to my feet, and looked south.

There were slaves processing tea near Darjeeling. I would go to them next.

GLOBAL SLAVERY METRICS

SLAVERY ESTIMATES

Table A.1 provides my estimates of the number of slaves in the world at the end of 2016. I have divided slavery into three categories: bonded labor/debt bondage, human trafficking, and other forced labor. Other forced labor captures those cases of slavery for which the person is not trafficked or bonded by debt into the servitude, and which meet the definition of forced labor established under ILO Convention No. 29. One person can theoretically meet criteria for all three of these conditions, so my hierarchy of categorization is (1) human trafficking, (2) debt bondage, and (3) other forced labor. When deciding between human trafficking and debt bondage for migrants, I categorized the case as being debt bondage if there was a formal debt agreement relating to up-front training, fees, or arranging the work opportunity abroad prior to the migrant's departure, and that they were specifically informed that the debt would be repaid through wage deductions. If the debts were imposed on the migrant after arrival in the destination country as a way to pressure the person into forced labor, I categorize the case as human trafficking. The lines between these two categories are particularly blurry, and I used my best judgment with categorization based on the available facts.

TABLE A.1 Number of Slaves in the World, 2016

	MEAN (MILLIONS OF SLAVES)	PERCENT OF TOTAL (%)
Bonded Labor/Debt Bondage	19.1	61.2
Human Trafficking		
Sex Trafficking	1.8	5.8
Labor Trafficking	3.0	9.6
Total Human Trafficking	4.8	15.4
Other Forced Labor	7.3	23.4
Total	**31.2**	**100.0**

The data in table A.1 present the mean of a range for each category of slavery based on an extrapolation model I built and have been refining for several years.

The mean estimate of total number of slaves in the world is 31.2 million: 19.1 million debt bondage slaves, 4.8 million trafficked slaves, and 7.3 million other forced laborers. The data used to calculate these estimates are based on two sources: (1) ongoing direct data sampling that I began conducting in 2004, and (2) the aggregation of as much reliable secondhand data on slavery estimates as possible (weighted downward by virtue of being secondhand). These data sources were fed into a highly conservative model that uses certain assumptions to calculate total global slavery numbers by type. As compared to my previous estimates in *Sex Trafficking* and *Bonded Labor*, the level of debt bondage in the world has remained relatively static, whereas my estimate of the number of human trafficking victims has increased by approximately 60 percent (+1.8 million), with a 15 percent decrease in the number of other forced laborers (−1.0 million). These changes are largely due to recategorization as well as an organic growth rate in the human trafficking category unleashed by several mass migration events from 2012 to 2016.

SLAVERY ECONOMICS

Tables A.2, A.3, and A.4 provide my updated calculations on slavery economics and profits for the year 2016. Slave labor generated revenues of $206.6
billion in 2016, with total profits of $124.1 billion accruing to the exploiters
of these slaves: $20.0 billion from bonded labor, $70.9 billion from trafficked
slaves (of which $62.3 billion is from trafficked sex slaves), and $33.3 billion
from other forced labor.[1] Worldwide, the average slave generated $3,978 in
net profits for his or her exploiter during 2016, at an average net profit margin of 60 percent. Debt bondage slaves are the least profitable, at $1,056 per
year per slave, and trafficked sex slaves are by far the most profitable, at
$36,064 per year per slave. Just over 50 percent of all slavery profits are gen-
erated by sex trafficking victims, even though they represent only 5.8 percent
of the total number of slaves in the world.

Given the immense profitability of sex trafficking, it is important to take
a closer look at the specific economics of this form of slavery, which are
detailed in table A.3. Revenues for sex trafficking vary significantly in terms
of dollar values by region, with a low of $21,742 per victim in South Asia and
a high of $132,805 in western Europe. The total revenues generated by sex
trafficking in 2016 were $92.2 billion, and total profits were $62.3 billion at
a 67.6 percent global weighted average profit margin (or a global weighted
average of $36,064) per victim. Contemporary sex trafficking is the most
profitable form of slavery the world has ever seen.

Table A.4 summarizes key economic metrics on slavery, in particular the
return on investment (ROI) and the exploitation value (EV) of a slave. The
first column of this table is carried over from table A.1, and the second column is carried over from table A.2. The weighted average acquisition costs
for each category of slavery are based on data from the 5,439 cases I have
documented. The acquisition costs range from $295 for debt bondage slaves
to $2,220 for trafficked sex slaves. The weighted average acquisition price
of today's 31.2 million slaves is $550. This compares to a global weighted
average acquisition price of approximately $4,900 to $5,500 in 2016 dollars
for a slave roughly two hundred years ago in 1810. This value was calculated through a sampling of acquisition prices of slaves around the world
in 1810, which on average ranged from approximately $7,000 to $10,500 in
2016 dollars (depending on age, gender, health, time of year, geography, skill,

TABLE A.2 Summary of Global Slavery Profits, 2016 (in 2016 U.S. dollars)[1]

	WEIGHTED AVERAGE ANNUAL REVENUES PER SLAVE ($)	IMPLIED ANNUAL REVENUES FROM SLAVE LABOR ($B)[2]	WEIGHTED AVERAGE NET PROFIT MARGIN (%)[3]	WEIGHTED AVERAGE ANNUAL PROFITS PER SLAVE ($)	IMPLIED ANNUAL PROFITS FROM SLAVE LABOR ($B)	PERCENT OF TOTAL (%)
Bonded Labor/Debt Bondage	2,112	39.9	50.0	1,056	20.0	16.1
Human Trafficking						
Sex Trafficking	53,335	92.2	67.6	36,064	62.3	50.2
Labor Trafficking	5,374	16.0	53.5	2,875	8.5	6.9
Total Human Trafficking		108.2			70.9	57.1
Other Forced Labor	8,090	58.5	56.9	4,603	33.3	26.8
Total		206.6			124.1	100.0%
	per slave 6,621			*per slave* 3,978		
			Global Slavery Net Profit Margin (%) 60			

[1] 2016 US dollar valuation is based on average of relevant CPI and GDP deflator adjustments from the dates of slave's acquisition(s).
[2] Based on average of starting and ending number of slaves during 2016.
[3] For bonded labor, some forms of forced labor, and where the sale of commercial sex is legal, this is a pretax profit margin, although it includes an assumption of minimal tax payments or bribes paid to avoid full tax rates.

TABLE A.3 Global Sex Trafficking Metrics, 2016

	ESTIMATED SEX TRAFFICKING VICTIMS	WEIGHTED AVERAGE RETAIL PRICE PER SEX ACT[1]	AVERAGE ANNUAL REVENUES PER SEX SLAVE	REVENUES FROM SEX TRAFFICKING ($B)[2]	WEIGHTED AVERAGE PROFIT MARGIN PER SEX SLAVE	AVERAGE ANNUAL PROFITS PER SEX SLAVE	PROFITS FROM SEX TRAFFICKING ($B)
South Asia	465,000	$5.40	$21,742	9.9	69.0%	$15,002	6.8
East Asia and Pacific	425,000	$5.85	$24,928	10.4	68.5%	$17,075	7.1
Western Europe	180,000	$38.40	$132,805	23.4	67.0%	$88,979	15.7
Central and Eastern Europe	170,000	$19.50	$68,133	11.4	68.0%	$46,330	7.7
Latin America	165,000	$12.15	$48,114	7.8	69.5%	$33,439	5.4
Africa	160,000	$5.50	$21,978	3.4	70.0%	$15,385	2.4
Middle East	140,000	$28.10	$109,759	15.1	67.5%	$74,087	10.2
North America	95,000	$35.35	$116,524	10.8	64.5%	$75,158	7.0
Total	**1,800,000**		*Weighted Average Revenue*	**$92.2**		*Weighted Average Profit*	**$62.3**
			$53,335			**$36,064**	

[1] Average price of a sex act in each region is derived from sampling various venues of exploitation, including brothel, club, street, hotel, massage parlor, and home/apartment.
[2] Based on average of starting and ending number of sex trafficking victims during 2016.

and other factors) for African slaves in or trafficked to/within the Americas, to $900 to $3,500 in 2016 dollars for slaves in or trafficked to/within South Asia, Africa, East Asia, and the Middle East (prices determined by similar factors as in the Americas). In addition to these average ranges for the prices of slaves sold in 1810, it is important to note that some slaves were sold for much less—in some cases for less than the price of a cup of tea—and others were born into slavery, which renders their acquisition costs close to nil.[2] Even though the weighted average cost of a slave has decreased substantially across time, some slaves are purchased today for several thousand dollars, and some slaves were purchased 200 years ago for a few dollars. The ban on European slave trading from Africa to the Americas is one of many reasons for a sharp increase (up to 100 percent) in the market value of a slave in the Americas between 1810 and 1860. Prices in Africa, the Middle East, and Asia did not increase as sharply, primarily because slave trading continued within and to/from many of these regions through the 1800s and into the early 1900s (especially in Asia).

Perhaps the most important metric in table A.4 is the exploitation value (EV) of each slave category. Without knowing this value, it is impossible to understand just how profitable contemporary slavery is; in turn, it is challenging to design effective laws against those who seek to engage in human enslavement. The weighted average net EVs by category of slavery range from $2,545 for debt bondage slaves to a startling $68,177 for trafficked sex slaves. When a slave exploiter acquires a debt bondage slave for a global weighted average of $295, he can expect to enjoy net profits from the exploitation of that slave of $2,545 before the individual escapes, is freed, or perishes. These global debt bondage numbers provide a percentage total ROI of 863 percent, or 170 percent per year for the average duration of enslavement (~5.1 years). Trafficked sex slaves have the highest percentage ROI of 3,071 percent, or 1,004 percent per year for the average duration of enslavement (~3.1 years). The annual ROI for other forced labor is 347 percent, and the global weighted average annual ROI for all forms of slavery is 383 percent for the average duration of enslavement (~4.5 years). This aggregate data is based on a global weighted average acquisition cost of a slave of $550, after which the exploiter can expect to enjoy net profits generated through the exploitation of that slave of $9,367, before that slave escapes, is freed, or perishes. This net cash return per slave demonstrates the powerful demand-side forces to acquire and exploit slaves of all kinds.

TABLE A.4 Key Slavery Metrics, 2016 (in 2016 U.S. dollars)[1]

	MILLIONS OF SLAVES	WEIGHTED AVERAGE ANNUAL PROFITS PER SLAVE ($)	WEIGHTED AVERAGE ACQUISITION COST PER SLAVE ($)	OPERATING EXPLOITATION VALUE ($)	NET EXPLOITATION VALUE ($)	IMPLIED TOTAL ROI (%)	IMPLIED ANNUALIZED ROI (%)
Bonded Labor/Debt Bondage	19.1	1,056	295	2,840	2,545	863	170
Human Trafficking							
Sex Trafficking	1.8	36,064	2,220	70,397	68,177	3,071	1,004
Labor Trafficking	3.0	2,875	670	6,495	5,825	869	232
Other Forced Labor	7.3	4,603	755	9,928	9,173	1,215	347
Total / Weighted Average	31.2	3,978	550	9,916	9,367	1,704	383

[1] 2016 US dollar valuation is based on the average of relevant CPI and GDP deflator adjustments from the dates of slave's acquisition(s).

TABLE A.5 Exploitation Value (EV) of a Slave, 2016[1]

	BONDED LABOR/ DEBT BONDAGE	SEX TRAFFICKING	LABOR TRAFFICKING	OTHER FORCED LABOR	GLOBAL SLAVERY, WEIGHTED AVERAGE
Revenues	176	4,445	448	674	552
Total Operating Costs	88	1,439	208	291	220
Recurring Contribution	88	3,005	240	384	332
Average Total Duration of Exploitation (months)	61	37	45	42	53
Operating EV	2,840	70,397	6,495	9,928	9,916
Average Acquisition Cost	295	2,220	670	755	550
Net EV	2,545	68,177	5,825	9,173	9,367
Implied Total ROI (%)	*863*	*3071*	*869*	*1215*	*1704*
Implied Annualized ROI (%)	*170*	*1004*	*232*	*347*	*383*

[1] Dollar values in 2016 U.S. dollars.

Table A.5 includes summary calculations of the EVs of each of the primary forms of slavery in the world today, including a global weighted average for all those forms combined. The EV is calculated by deducting operating costs from revenues, which provides a monthly recurring contribution. This figure is multiplied by the aggregate average number of months of enslavement to generate an operating EV. Deducting the weighted average acquisition cost of each type of slave from operating EV provides the net EV of the slave.[3]

SELECT SLAVERY ECONOMICS

TABLE B.1 Sex Trafficking: Brothel (India)

General Assumptions

20 slaves per *Malik*
Average 10 sex acts per day
1 of 5 customers buys 1 alcoholic drink
1 of 5 customers buys 1 condom
1 slave per month requires bail
50% "tip" per 30 sex acts
1 slave retrafficked every 4 months
2016 U.S. dollars

Unit Assumptions

Revenues	Unit Prices ($)	
Sale of sex	5.60	
Alcohol	2.00	
Condoms	0.20	
Retrafficking	2,000	

Variable Costs		
Food, beverage, drugs	4.00	per slave per day
Police *hafta* (bribe)	2.00	per slave per day
Rent	21.00	per day
Clothing, makeup, grooming	2.00	per slave per day
Bouncer / guard (2)	14.00	per day
Gharwali	15.00	per day
Cost of alcohol, condoms	1.00	per unit
Bail	130.00	per month
Medical	0.50	per slave per day
"Tip"	2.80	per slave per 30 sex acts
Retrafficking	800.00	per slave per retrafficking
Utilities and miscellaneous	1.50	per slave per day

Fixed Costs	
Up-front hafta for new brothel	3,000
Average acquisition cost of slave	800

Monthly Profit and Loss

Revenues	
	33,600
	2,400
	240
	500
Total Monthly Revenues	**36,740**

Operating Expenses	
	2,400
	1,200
	630
	1,200
	840
	450
	1,200
	130
	300
	560
	200
	900
Total Operating Expenses	**10,010**

Gross Profit	**26,730**
% gross margin	*72.8%*

Depreciation	
Up-front hafta	*25*
Acquisition cost of slaves	*400*
Total Depreciation	**425**

Net Profit	**26,305**
% net profit	*71.6%*

Annual Revenues	**440,880**

Annual Net Profit	**315,655**
per slave	*15,783*

TABLE B.2 Sex Trafficking: Brothel (Thailand)

General Assumptions

20 slaves per brothel
Average 12 sex acts per day
1 of 5 customers buys 1 alcoholic drink
1 of 5 customers buys 1 condom
50% "tip" per 30 sex acts
1 slave retrafficked every 4 months
2016 U.S. dollars

Unit Assumptions

Revenues	Unit Prices ($)		
Sale of sex	5.95		
Alcohol	2.25		
Condoms	0.25		
Retrafficking	800.00		

Variable Costs			
Food, beverage, drugs	5.00	per slave per day	
Police bribe	3.00	per slave per day	
Rent	20.00	per day	
Clothing, makeup, grooming	3.50	per slave per day	
Bouncer / guard (2)	22.00	per day	
Madam / cashier	20.00	per day	
Cost of alcohol, condom	1.33	per unit	
Bail	150.00	per month	
Medical	1.00	per slave per day	
"Tip"	3.00	per slave per 30 sex acts	
Retrafficking	500.00	per slave per retrafficking	
Utilities and miscellaneous	2.00	per slave per day	

Fixed Costs		
Up-front bribe for new brothel	3,000	
Average acquisition cost of slave	900	

Monthly Profit and Loss

Revenues	
	42,840
	3,240
	360
	200
Total Monthly Revenues	**46,640**

Operating Expenses	
	3,000
	1,800
	600
	2,100
	1,320
	600
	1,915
	150
	600
	720
	125
	1,200
Total Operating Expenses	**14,130**

Gross Profit	**32,510**
% gross margin	*69.7%*

Depreciation	
Up-front bribe	*25*
Acquisition cost of slaves	*500*
Total Depreciation	**525**

Net Profit	**31,985**
% net profit	*68.6%*

Annual Revenues	**559,680**

Annual Net Profit	**383,818**
per slave	*19,191*

TABLE B.3 Sex Trafficking: Brothel (United States)

General Assumptions

10 slaves per brothel
Average 8 sex acts per day
1 of 5 customers buys 1 alcoholic drink
1 of 5 customers buys 1 condom
1 of 10 customers buys 1 cigar or snack
50% "tip" per 20 sex acts
1 slave retrafficked every 6 months

Unit Assumptions

Revenues	Unit Prices ($)	
Sale of sex	37.00	
Alcohol	7.50	
Condoms	2.50	
Cigars, snacks, other	14.00	
Retrafficking	3,000	

Variable Costs		
Food, beverage, drugs	18.00	per slave per day
Allocated rent	60.00	per day
Clothing, makeup, grooming	6.00	per slave per day
Bouncer / guard (2)	150.00	per day
Cashier	100.00	per day
Cost of alcohol, condom, snack	9.00	per unit
Medical	5.00	per slave per day
"Tip"	18.50	per slave per 20 sex acts
Retrafficking	2,000	per slave per retrafficking
Utilities and miscellaneous	8.00	per slave per day

Fixed Costs		
Average acquisition cost of slave	4,000	

Monthly Profit and Loss

Revenues	
	88,800
	3,600
	1,200
	3,360
	500
Total Monthly Revenues	**97,460**

Operating Expenses	
	5,400
	1,800
	1,800
	9,000
	3,000
	4,320
	1,500
	2,220
	333
	2,400
Total Operating Expenses	**31,773**

Gross Profit	**65,687**
% gross margin	*67.4%*

Depreciation	
Acquisition cost of slaves	*1,248*
Total Depreciation	**1,248**

Net Profit	**64,438**
% net profit	*66.1%*

Annual Revenues	**1,169,520**

Annual Net Profit	**773,259**
per slave	*77,326*

TABLE B.4 Sex Trafficking: Nigerian Street Prostitution (Western Europe)

General Assumptions

8 slaves per madam
Average 10 sex acts per day
10% revenue participation by slave
1 slave sold to new madam per year
2016 U.S. dollars

Unit Assumptions

Revenues	Unit Prices ($)	
Sale of sex	24.00	
Retrafficking	1,000	

Variable Costs		
Food, beverage, drugs	18.00	per slave per day
Apartment rent	60.00	per day
Bribe/organized crime payoff	1,500	per month
Clothing, makeup, grooming	7.50	per slave per day
Guard	150.00	per day
Revenue participation	2.40	per transaction
Medical	4.00	per slave per day
Retrafficking	250.00	per slave per retrafficking
Utilities and miscellaneous	6.00	per slave per day

Fixed Costs	
Average acquisition cost of slave	5,000

Monthly Profit and Loss

Revenues	
	57,600
	83
Total Monthly Revenues	**57,683**

Operating Expenses	
	4,320
	1,800
	1,500
	1,800
	4,500
	5,760
	960
	21
	1,440
Total Operating Expenses	**22,101**

Gross Profit	35,583
% gross margin	*61.7%*

Depreciation	
Acquisition cost of slaves	*1,001*
Total Depreciation	**1,001**

Net Profit	34,581
% net profit	*60.0%*

Annual Revenues	692,200

Annual Net Profit	414,978
per slave	*51,872*

TABLE B.5 Bonded Labor: Brick-Making in India

General Assumptions

50 bonded laborers per brick kiln
Loans advanced to 40 laborers out of 50
Wages paid only to laborers receiving loans
550,000 bricks made each month
90% of bricks sold during season (10% lack of demand)
Weighted average brick unit sale price: Rs. 2.2
Bricks made 8 months of the year
Extra capacity sold during rainy season
20% price premium for bricks sold during rainy season
Transportation costs paid by buyer
2016 U.S. dollars

Unit Assumptions

Revenues	Unit Prices ($)	
Bricks	0.04	
Wage deduction	0.63	

Variable Costs

Weighted average wage[1]	1.25	per laborer per day
Foreman/manager/*kamdar* (×4)	9.00	per day
Accountant	14.00	per day
Government royalty[2]	750.00	per month
Fuel (coal, oil, diesel)	4,167	per month
Jamadar commission	0.33	per 1000 bricks
Utilities, repairs, and miscellaneous	0.30	per laborer per day

Fixed Costs

Kiln construction	22,500
Tools, molds, pump, other equipment	3,000
Aggregate loan advance	250

Monthly Profit and Loss

Revenues	
	18,150
	713
Total Monthly Revenues	**18,863**

Operating Expenses	
	1,425
	1,080
	420
	750
	4,167
	183
	450
Total Operating Expenses	**8,475**

Gross Profit	10,387
% gross margin	*55.1%*

Depreciation	
Kiln construction	94
Tools, molds, and other equipment	50
Loan advance	128
Total Depreciation	**272**

Taxes/tax bribe[3]	1,452

Net Profit	8,663
% net profit	*45.9%*

Annual Revenues	**170,260**
Annual Net Profit[4]	**95,064**
% net profit	*55.8%*
per bonded laborer	*1,901*

[1] This is a weighted average based on piece-rate wages and day wages paid to the various labor types at the kiln.
[2] The precise royalty depends on the state in India in which the kiln is located. Some are fixed sums for the year, others are fixed sums plus variable amounts per 1,000 bricks made. In variable scenarios, the brick kiln owners can pay bribes to reduce the royalty, and they often "cook" the books to show a lower number of bricks produced and sold. The weighted average of kilns across northern India for which I secured data is around $9,000.
[3] Almost all kiln owners offer bribes to local officials to avoid paying full taxes. These rates vary, but the figure tends to be around 8% of operating revenues (excludes laborer debt repayment) or less.
[4] Assumes remaining bricks produced but not sold during the season are sold during the off-season at a 20% price premium; only associated costs are government royalty, tax bribe, depreciation, and one foremen and accountant.

TABLE B.6 Debt Bondage: Domestic Work (South Asia to Middle East)

General Assumptions[1]

10 domestic workers placed per month
Fee paid by receiving family: $4,000[2]
Recruiter fee: $100 per worker
2016 U.S. dollars

Unit Assumptions

Revenues	Unit Prices ($)	
Fee paid by receiving family	4,000	
Variable Costs		
Predeparture expenses	500	per worker
Travel and documents	1,150	per worker
Licensing fees	1,500	per year
Recruiter fees	100	per worker
Infrastructure	900	per month
Marketing	300	per month
Insurance	300	per month
Personnel	600	per month

Monthly Profit and Loss

Revenues	
	40,000
Total Monthly Revenues	**40,000**
Operating Expenses	
	5,000
	11,500
	125
	1,000
	900
	300
	300
	600
Total Operating Expenses	**19,725**
Gross profit	**20,276**
% gross margin	*50.7%*
Taxes/tax bribe[3]	5,069
Net Profit	**15,207**
% net profit	*38.0%*
Annual Revenues	**480,000**
Annual Net Profit	**182,484**
per debt bondage worker	*1,521*

[1] This profit and loss statement is modeled from the standpoint of the domestic worker placement agency in South Asia, the primary economic beneficiary of debt bondage exploitation. The employing family also would benefit economically through the underpayment or nonpayment of wages; other intermediaries and destination country agencies can benefit from the exploitation as well.
[2] Some families will pay this amount in full up front, then deduct payment from worker wages; others will pay a portion of the fee up front then deduct the corresponding amount from worker wages.
[3] Assume 25% tax rate on the business.

TABLE B.7 Labor Trafficking: Agriculture (Mexico to California)[1]

General Assumptions

> 20 workers managed by FLC
> 1 new worker acquired each month by FLC
> 1 worker transferred each month by FLC
> Wage deductions for food, board, medical, repairs
> Each worker takes one trip per month to city @ $40
> FLC is not vertically integrated to recruitment stage in Mexico
> 2016 U.S. dollars

Unit Assumptions

Revenues	Unit Prices ($)	
Employer fees	150	per worker
Wage deduction	36	per worker per day
Transport fees	40	per worker
Transfer fees	250	per worker

Variable Costs		
Worker accommodation rent and utilities	3,000	per month
Food and beverage	300	per worker per month
Mexico recruiter fees	500	per new worker
Repairs	400	per month
Equipment and fuel	2,000	per month
Licensing and regulation fees	1,200	per year

Monthly Profit and Loss

Revenues	
	3,000
	18,720
	800
	250
Total Monthly Revenues	**22,770**

Operating Expenses	
	3,000
	6,000
	500
	400
	2,000
	100
Total Operating Expenses	**12,000**
Gross Profit	**10,770**
% gross margin	*47.3%*
Taxes[2]	2,693
Net Profit	**8,078**
% net profit	*35.5%*
Annual Revenues	**273,240**
Annual Net Profit	**96,930**
per labor trafficking victim	*4,847*

[1] This profit and loss statement is modeled from the standpoint of a nonintegrated FLC in California; a different model would be used for a vertically integrated FLC that includes recruitment and border crossing agents in Mexico, as well as modest economic benefits for the nonintegrated recruiters and *coyotes* contracted by the nonintegrated FLC.
[2] Assume aggregate tax rate of 25% for the FLC.

TABLE B.8 Labor Trafficking: Trash Fish (Myanmar to Thailand)

General Assumptions

20 trafficked workers per trawler
Ship spends 12 months at sea
Trash fish wholesale price: $0.12 per kg
Catch rate: 14 kg per hour
Trawler operates 22 hours per day
4 workers perish/killed each year (no wage paid)
10 new workers acquired each year
Wages paid at 20% rate
2016 U.S. dollars

Unit Assumptions

Revenues	Unit Prices ($)	
Sale of trash fish	0.12	per kg
Variable Costs		
Crew wages	70	per worker per month
Guards (×3)	500	per guard per month
Food	1,800	per month
Fuel	4,000	per month
Repairs	300	per month
Bribes	2,000	per year
New worker acquisition[1]	7,000	per year
Fixed Costs		
Vessel and equipment	200,000	

Monthly Profit and Loss

Revenues	
	13,306
Total Monthly Revenues	**13,306**
Operating Expenses	
	1,120
	1,500
	1,800
	4,000
	300
	167
	583
Total Operating Expenses	**9,470**
Gross Profit	**3,836**
% gross margin	*28.8%*
Depreciation	
Vessel and equipment	833
Total Depreciation	**833**
Net Profit	**3,002**
% net profit	*22.6%*
Annual Revenues	**159,667**
Annual Net Profit	**36,027**
per labor trafficking victim	*1,801*

[1] Half of the crew is assumed to refresh annually, so acquisition cost is expensed and not depreciated.

General Assumptions

26 forced laborers, 3 groups for each size of carpet
Wages paid at 33% rate
Carpets made and sold:
  10: 2′ × 5′ (small)
  3: 5′ × 8′ (medium)
  0.5: 12′ × 15′ (large)
Wholesale rate: $10 per square foot
Cost of thread: $0.45 per square foot
5% of thread lost each month
2016 U.S. dollars

Unit Assumptions			Monthly Profit and Loss	
Revenues	**Unit Prices ($)**		**Revenues**	
Carpets (small)	100			1,000
Carpets (medium)	400			1,200
Carpets (large)	1,800			900
			Total Monthly Revenues	**3,100**
Variable Costs			**Operating Expenses**	
Wages	0.43	per worker per day		290
Thread	0.45	per square foot		198
Guard	10.00	per day		300
Repair and miscellaneous	0.15	per worker per day		117
			Total Operating Expenses	**905**
Fixed Costs			**Gross Profit**	**2,196**
Looms	1,250		*% gross margin*	*70.8%*
Tools and other equipment	350			
			Depreciation	
			Looms	10
			Tools and other equipment	10
			Total Depreciation	**20**
			Taxes/tax bribe[1]	155
			Net Profit	**2,020**
			% net profit	*65.2%*
			Annual Revenues	**37,200**
			Annual Net Profit	**24,245**
			per forced laborer	*932*

[1] Almost all carpet loom owners offer bribes to local officials to avoid paying full taxes. These rates vary, but the figure tends to be around 5% of operating revenues.

General Assumptions

20 acre coffee plantation

30 forced laborers

Wages paid at 33%

2 harvests per year (3 month season, 3 month off-season)

$30 per acre fertilizer and pesticide

1,000 lb yield per acre

Wholesale spot price $1.40 per lb (grade AA)

90% of each harvest sold

2016 U.S. dollars

Unit Assumptions				Harvest Profit and Loss	
Revenues	**Unit Prices ($)**			**Revenues**	
Coffee beans	1.40	per lb			25,200
				Total Monthly Revenues	**25,200**
Variable Costs				**Operating Expenses**	
Wages	0.66	per worker per day			515
Water and irrigation	50.00	per acre per harvest			2,000
Food and beverage	0.30	per worker per day			1,620
Guards (×2)	3.00	per day			1,080
Accountant	5.00	per day			900
Fertilizer and pesticide	30.00	per acre per harvest			1,200
Off-season planting and maintenance	500.00	per harvest			500
Utilities, repairs, and miscellaneous	0.20	per worker per day			1,440
				Total Operating Expenses	**9,255**
Fixed Costs					
Tools and equipment	3,000			**Gross Profit**	**15,945**
				% gross margin	*63.3%*
				Depreciation	
				Tools and equipment	50
				Total Depreciation	**50**
				Net Profit	**15,895**
				% net profit	*63.1%*
				Annual Revenues	**50,400**
				Annual Net Profit	**31,790**
				per forced laborer	*1,060*

SAMPLE RESEARCH QUESTIONNAIRE

I USED THIS questionnaire to document slaves in Thailand's seafood sector. I adapt the questionnaire for different industries and countries, but in all cases I interrogate all potential manifestations of slavery. The interview typically opens with a brief explanation of who I am and why I wish to speak with the individual. I then undertake a consent process in which I explain the kinds of questions I will be asking, assure the individual that he or she can stop speaking at any time and that there is no penalty for doing so, and explain that the individual can choose not to answer any question. For minors, I secure verbal assent because children cannot consent to human subject research. In addition, if I am in a shelter and there is a responsible adult in charge of the child, I ask that person for consent. If the child is being exploited and there is no responsible or trustworthy adult available, I secure verbal assent only from the child. With children, questions are adapted to be as innocuous as possible, and I take special care to pause often and assess whether the child appears uncomfortable. Children often feel pressured to continue answering questions even if they do not feel comfortable doing so. Rather than go down a list of questions, I engage in a semistructured conversation in which I intermix casual discussion with the questions. At no point do I document confidential information. I assigned a number, time, date, and location to each interview, as well as a pseudonym.

KEY INFORMANT QUESTIONNAIRE

Thank you for talking with me. My name is Siddharth Kara, and I'm a researcher. This is my translator _____. We are working together to talk to people who work in the seafood industry in Thailand. I will be recording our conversation and taking notes while we talk. Is that okay?

Go through the CONSENT or ASSENT PROCESS. Document verbal consent/assent.

If the participant agrees to take part, continue with the interview.

Location of Interview: (City name and location of worksite by street name or intersection or other geographic landmark.)

————————

Total number of workers in the site:

Let's start by talking a little about your background.

Background and Nature of Work

1   What is your date of birth?
2   Gender?
3   Ethnic group or community?
4   Where were you born?
5   Where did you live before you came to Thailand?
6   Are you a citizen in your home country? A refugee? Unregistered?
7   Where does the rest of your family live?
8   What are the ages of the other members of your immediate family (spouse, siblings, parents, children)?
9   Can you read and write?
10   What level of education did you complete?
11   How long have you been at this workplace?
12   Do you have migration papers to work in Thailand? If so, please describe.

13   Please describe the work you do here.

14   Do you own your dwelling or any land? If so, please describe.

15   If you do not own your own dwelling or land, what is your tenancy arrangement?

16   What languages do you speak?

17   How long have you been working in the seafood sector in Thailand?

18   What other work have you done in the past?

19   Do you have a written agreement for this job?

20   If yes, did you understand the agreement when you signed it? Were all the terms explained to you?

21   How much do you get paid for the work you are doing (piece rate, weekly, monthly)?

22   Who pays you?

23   How often are you paid?

24   Do you receive the full wage you are promised?

25   If not, how much do you receive?

26   For how long have you not been receiving the full wage?

27   Is your payment ever delayed?

28   If payment is delayed, how often and by how long?

29   Have you been at other work places in Thailand? If so, please describe. [*NB: query potential previous instances of slavery*]

30   Have you migrated to Thailand for work previously? If so, please describe. [*NB: query potential previous instances of slavery*]

31   Have you ever migrated to another country for work previously? If so, please describe. [*NB: query potential previous instances of slavery*]

32   *Document the working conditions at the worksite in detail, especially elements that are hazardous and can cause ill health or injury.*

Section A: Forced Labor under ILO Convention No. 29—Involuntariness

1   Are you able to leave the worksite freely, or must you ask permission? [*NB: observe presence of locks/restraints or guards that prevent the worker from leaving*]

2   Are you locked in the worksite and not allowed to leave?

3   In the place where you sleep, are you locked inside at night and not allowed to leave?

4   Are you free to pursue work with other employers if you want to? What would happen if you tried to leave this job?

5   Have you ever left this worksite since arriving? If so, how many times?

6   Are you able to communicate with friends or family freely? If so, how do you do so?

7   Are you free to go to the toilet when you wish, or must you ask permission?

8   Where do you go to the toilet? Do you feel it is private? Sanitary?

9   Where do you bathe? Do you feel it is private? Sanitary?

10   How many hours do you normally work each day?

11   How many days a week do you normally work?

12   Who decides how long you will work?

13   Are you paid extra if you work longer than eight hours in a day?

14   Do you feel pressure to work more than eight hours a day? If so, why? What happens if you do not?

15   Have you ever had an illness or an injury while working here? If so, please describe.

16   If you get sick or injured, do you feel pressure to keep working?

17   If you get sick or injured, are you given medical care?

18   Are you allowed days off for a holiday or rest?

19   Is there equipment here that keeps you safe while you are working?

20   Do you have any untreated health problems? If so, please describe.

21   How often do you eat a meal? Do you feel you have enough food to eat? Please describe the meals you eat.

22   How many hours do you sleep each night? Are you prevented from getting as much sleep as you would like?

23   *Ask about any other conditions the worker would like to share that may indicate involuntariness.*

Section B: Forced Labor under ILO Convention No. 29—Coercion

1   Have you ever been threatened or punished through physical, verbal, or sexual abuse if you (1) stop working, (2) do not work as much as you are told, (3) object to your working conditions, (4) object to your wage payments, or (5) for any other reason? If so, please describe.

2   Have you ever received threats against your family members for any of these same reasons? If so, please describe.

3   Have you ever seen others receiving threats or punishments that dissuaded you from taking issue with any of these same reasons? If so, please describe.

4   Have you ever been denied food or sleep for any reason? If so, please describe.

5   Does your employer keep your identity documents, or do you have them?

6   Can you get your identity documents if you ask for them?

7   Do you sleep in a different place from where you work?

8   How often does the supervisor check on you?
     [*NB: observe and describe surveillance of the workers*]

9   Would you rather leave this job but feel you must stay and keep working because you have no other alternative?

10   *Ask about any other conditions the worker would like to share that may indicate coercion.*

Section C: Debt Bondage

1   Have you ever borrowed money or taken a wage advance or any other kind of advance from your employer or the person who found you this job?

2   What was the reason?

3   How much money did you borrow?

4   How many times have you borrowed?

5   How much for each of these other instances?

6   What were the reasons for each of these other instances?

7   Is part of your wage deducted in any amount to repay your debt?
     [*NB: probe various types of deductions such as for food, lodging, supplies, errors, injuries; do family members have to work for the debt as well; is interest charged on debt and if so how much; does the informant work more than ten hours each day but is only paid an eight-hour wage, etc.*]

8   Do you still have a debt you are working off?

9   Do you know how much it is?

10   Is there a written agreement for the debt?

11   Is any accounting provided to you for your debits and credits?

12   Do you feel you cannot leave this job because of the debt?

13   What would happen if you tried to leave before repaying the debt?

Section D: Human Trafficking

1   Did you accept this job from someone who recruited you?

2   Who was this person? Where was he or she from?

3   Did you know this person?

4   When you agreed to take the job, did you have to travel to get here?

5   How far did you travel?

6   How did you travel? Please describe in detail.

7   Who paid for the travel arrangements?

8   Did the recruiter make any promises to you about (1) working conditions, (2) wages, (3) living arrangements, (4) type of work, or (5) amount of work, that were not true? If so, please describe.

9   If the recruiter made any false promises, did you have the option of declining the work and returning home? If not, why?

10   Did the recruiter charge any up-front fees for arranging this job? If so, how much?

11   Did the recruiter explain what the fees were for?

12   Did the recruiter give you a receipt or statement of the expenses?

13   Does the recruiter deduct money from your wages? If so, how much?

14   What were the circumstances that led you to accept the job offer from the recruiter? Please describe.

15   Are you still in touch with the recruiter?

16   Did you bring any other members of your family to work with you, or elsewhere in Thailand? Please describe.

17   *Ask about any other conditions of coercion that were used by the recruiter to place the worker in the job.*

Section E: Child Labor (For any Interviewee under eighteen years of age)

1   Do you attend school? If not, why not?

2   Have you ever attended school in the past?

3 Are you at the worksite with a parent or guardian?
4 If you are unaccompanied, would you like to return home?
5 If yes, are you prevented from doing so? Why?
6 If you do not wish to return home, why not?

Section F: Thank you

Thank you very much for talking with me today.
Do you know of anyone else who might like to speak with me?

CATEGORIZATION GUIDELINES

After securing answers to the questions, I apply the following categorization guidelines to establish one or more of the manifestations of slavery, human trafficking, forced labor, or child labor.

1. Forced Labor under ILO Convention No. 29

Any individual who meets the criteria of both involuntariness *and* coercion under ILO Convention No. 29 as follows:

- Involuntariness: restrictions on freedom of movement in at least two of the first three questions, *and* restrictions on freedom of employment in question four, *plus* clear indications of involuntariness in an additional eleven of the remaining questions.
- Coercion: threats or punishments in at least three of the five cases in questions one, two, or three, *plus* clear indications of coercive conditions in at least four of the remaining questions.

2. Debt Bondage

Any individual who has taken an economic advance of any kind, *and* is subject to severely exploitative deductions in wages to repay the advance (severity of deductions determined under question seven), *and* who is unable to leave the job prior to repayment of the debt without facing severe exit costs.

3. Human Trafficking

Any individual who is recruited by a third party into a job under false promises, *and* in which the individual works in conditions of Forced Labor under ILO Convention No. 29 or Debt Bondage, *and* who migrated more than one day's journey to the worksite, *and* for which there was no option to exit the job opportunity upon learning of the exploitative conditions.

4. Child Labor

Any individual under eighteen years of age who works at least eight hours a day, five days a week, *and* does not attend school.

NOTES

1. MODERN SLAVERY: AN OVERVIEW

1. The names of all slaves in this book are pseudonyms. In some cases where discussing precise geographic locations might risk the safety of the interviewee, I have provided an alternate setting. In cases where providing the names or locations of specific organizations or activists helping the slaves might risk their safety, I have refrained from providing these details.
2. Throughout this book, when I share a slave narrative, that narrative was typically spoken to me as part of a conversation in which I asked questions to guide the interview and gather data. I have edited the narratives as minimally as possible to aid with readability.
3. All U.S. dollar values are converted at the exchange rate at the time the case was documented.
4. *Aadhaar* is a twelve-digit unique identification number provided to each citizen of India under a program managed by the Unique Identification Authority of India (UIDAI). The *Aadhaar* is issued upon registration of biometric and demographic data of the recipient. Commenced in 2009, it is deemed to be the largest national identification number project in the world.
5. A *sarpanch* is the head of a village's statutory institution of local self-government in India, called a *panchayat*. The *sarpanch* is typically elected by members of the village.
6. For thorough explorations of the history and evolution of slavery, see Meltzer (1993), Patterson (1982), Thomas (1999), Klein (1993), and Lewis (1992).
7. Kara (2012), chapter 1.
8. Article 1, League of Nations Slavery Convention, 1926.

9. Patterson (1982).

10. Article 2(1), International Labour Organisation (ILO) Forced Labour Convention (No. 29), 1930. Three exceptions to the definitions are (1) compulsory military service, (2) prison labor, and (3) certain forms of compulsory labor in cases of emergency or war (Article 2(2)).

11. ILO (2012).

12. Ibid.

13. Forced marriage is defined as a marriage in which one or both parties are betrothed without consent or against his/her will. Article 16 of the United Nations Universal Declaration of Human Rights (1948) states that "marriage shall be entered into only with the free and full consent of the intending spouses." The Appeals Chamber of the Special Court for Sierra Leone was the first international criminal tribunal to recognize forced marriage as a distinct crime (*Prosecutor v. Brima, Kamara and Kanu*, 2008).

14. The United Nations Convention on the Elimination of All Forms of Discrimination Against Women (CEDAW), 1979, calls on states to ensure that the betrothal and marriage of children has no legal standing, and its treaty-monitoring committee recommends a minimum marriageable age of eighteen years. Also, the UN Convention on Consent to Marriage, Minimum Age for Marriage and Registration of Marriages (1964) similarly emphasizes consent, a minimum age for marriage, and the registration of all marriages by a competent authority.

15. Defined as any child (under eighteen years of age) associated with an armed force or armed group who is, or who has been, recruited or used by an armed force or armed group in any capacity—including but not limited to children, boys and girls—used as fighters, cooks, porters, spies, or for sexual purposes (Paris Principles on the Involvement of Children in Armed Conflict, 2007).

16. Article 3, United Nations Protocol to Prevent, Suppress and Punish Trafficking in Persons Especially Women and Children, supplementing the United Nations Convention Against Transnational Organized Crime (2000).

17. Article 3(c) of the Palermo Protocol states that "the recruitment, transportation, transfer, harbouring or receipt of a child for the purpose of exploitation shall be considered 'trafficking in persons' even if this does not involve any of the means set forth in subparagraph (a) of this article;" and Article 3(d) defines a "child" as any person under eighteen years of age.

    The ILO's International Programme on the Elimination of Child Labour (ILO-IPEC) provides further guidance on the definition of "exploitation" as it relates to child trafficking:

    > (a) all forms of slavery or practices similar to slavery, debt bondage and serfdom and forced or compulsory labour, including forced or compulsory recruitment of children for use in armed conflict (ILO Convention No. 182, Art. 3(a));
    >
    > (b) the use, procuring or offering of a child for prostitution, for the production of pornography or for pornographic performances (ILO Convention No. 182, Art. 3(b));

(c) the use, procuring or offering of a child for illicit activities, in particular for the production and trafficking of drugs as defined in the relevant international treaties (ILO Convention No. 182, Art. 3(c));

(d) work which, by its nature or the circumstances in which it is carried out, is likely to harm the health, safety or morals of children (ILO Convention No. 182, Art. 3(d) and Convention No. 138, Art 3);

(e) work done by children below the minimum age for admission to employment (ILO Convention No. 138, Art. 2 & 7).

18. Defined in Article 3(a) of the UN Protocol Against the Smuggling of Migrants by Land, Sea and Air (2000) as "the procurement, in order to obtain, directly or indirectly, a financial or other material benefit, of the illegal entry of a person into a state party of which the person is not a national."

19. Kara (2012), chapter 1.

20. See Kumar (1965) for an investigation of the links between caste and debt bondage and the role caste has played in the broader evolution of labor relations in India.

21. For a thorough discussion on medieval European feudalism, see Stephenson (1952); for feudal India under the Mughal Empire, see Habib (1963); for the economic and social structure of Tokugawa Japan, see Smith (1959); for more detail on peonage in the American South, see Pete (1990).

22. Article 1(a), United Nations Supplementary Convention on the Abolition of Slavery, the Slave Trade, and Institutions and Practices Similar to Slavery, 1956.

23. Article 2, India Bonded Labour System (Abolition) Act, 1976.

24. Kara (2012), chapter 1.

25. For examples of those who argue debt bondage may not be slavery, see Shultz (1964), Cherney and Srinivasan (1988), Sitglitz (1989), and Genicot (2002).

26. "Other forced labor" captures those cases of slavery for which the person is not trafficked or bonded into the servitude but who meets the definition of forced labor established under ILO Forced Labour Convention (No. 29).

27. ILO (2005).

28. ILO (2012).

29. Capture-recapture (CR) is a methodology originally used to count and track animal populations. The methodology was later used to estimate the size of hidden or difficult-to-reach human populations, such as homeless people. Four assumptions must be met to generate reliable CR estimates: (1) the population under observation is closed, (2) each of the two captures are independent, (3) all members of the population have the same probability of being captured, and (4) the capture date of each member is accurate.

30. "Findings," The Global Slavery Index, accessed May 5, 2017, http://www.globalslavery index.org/findings/.

31. Ibid.

32. Ibid.

33. ILO (2005).
34. ILO (2012).
35. Kara (2009), chapter 1 and appendix A.
36. Hochschild (2005).
37. Ibid.
38. U.S. dollar valuation for 2016 is based on averages of CPI and GDP deflator adjustments. The GDF deflator was also used because, unlike CPI, it extends beyond consumer goods and services and provides a broader base of comparison for the sale of human beings.
39. Fogel (1989).
40. ROI measures the benefit to an investor resulting from an investment in an asset of some kind. The standard formula is (gain from investment − cost of investment)/cost of investment.
41. In a university setting, an Institutional Review Board (IRB) is an academic committee that reviews and approves research involving human subjects with the purpose of ensuring that the research is conducted in accordance with legal, institutional, and ethical guidelines.
42. See Acemgolu and Wolitzky (2011) for an economic model demonstrating that enhanced alternative economic opportunities reduce the level of coercion in labor arrangements.
43. Kara (2009), chapter 1.
44. Ibid., chapter 1 and appendix A.
45. Kara (2009), chapter 8; Kara (2012), chapter 8.
46. Kara (2011).

2. SEX TRAFFICKING: THE CASE OF NIGERIA

1. Kara (2009), chapter 6.
2. For an interesting exploration of the relationship between corruption and human trafficking in Nigeria, see Agbu (2003).
3. For a thorough account of the history of the Benin Empire, see Malaquais (1998).
4. For more on the Cult of Ayelala and traditional Yoruba beliefs, see Awolalu (1996) and Awolalu (1968).
5. Okonofua (2004).
6. Ibid.
7. For more information, see Ajibade (2013) and Alaba (2004).
8. Section 214 of the Nigerian Criminal Code.
9. Nnadi (2013).
10. For thorough summaries of Nigeria's recent political and economic histories, see Sowunmi (2015) and Campbell (2013).

11. For incisive examinations of the evolution and relations between Muslims and Christians in Nigeria, see Boer (2003) and Falola (1998).

12. For more information on West Africa and the trans-Atlantic slave trade, see Ajayi and Uya (2010) and Green (2014).

13. See Kara (2009), chapter 1 and appendixes A and B.

3. LABOR TRAFFICKING:
SLAVERY AT YOUR DINING TABLE

1. Statistics mentioned in this paragraph are from the California Department of Food and Agriculture (2016).

2. The H-2A temporary agricultural program allows employers to bring nonimmigrant foreign workers to the United States to perform agricultural labor or services of a temporary or seasonal nature. For seasonal or temporary nonagricultural work, the H-2B visa can be used.

3. For instance, the U.S. Department of State issued 134,368 H-2A visas in 2016, up from 55,384 just five years prior (see https://travel.state.gov/content/dam/visas/Statistics /Graphs/H%20VisasWorldwide.pdf, retrieved May 2, 2017); however, not every visa that is issued translates into a migrant working in the United States during that fiscal year, and there are also a small number of petitions for extensions of visas granted in the previous year that are not publicly reported.

4. Definition provided at California Department of Industrial Relations website, "Rules and Regulations for FLCs," http://www.dir.ca.gov/dlse/Rules_and_Regulations_for _FLCs.htm, retrieved September 10, 2016.

5. Data available at BLS, "Occupational Employment and Wages," http://www.bls.gov /oes/current/oes131074.htm, retrieved May 2, 2017.

6. See "Migrant and Seasonal Agricultural Worker Protection Act (MSPA) Ineligible Farm Labor Contractors," http://www.dol.gov/whd/regs/statutes/mspa_debar.htm for the current list, retrieved November 1, 2016.

7. Kara (2012), chapter 5.

8. To learn more about the history of labor in California's agricultural sector, see McWilliams (2000), Daniel (1982), Vaught (2002), and Griego (1981).

9. As quoted in Calavita (2010).

10. Average hourly wage for workers I documented were calculated as monthly wage, divided by average work days per month of 26, divided by average of 12.5 hours of work per day.

11. Data on the average hourly wage for U.S. agriculture workers is from the BLS website, "National Occupational Employment and Wage Estimates," https://www.bls.gov/oes /current/oes_nat.htm#45-0000, retrieved May 2, 2017.

4. ORGAN TRAFFICKING: SOLD FOR PARTS

1. Human trafficking for organ removal refers to the practice of trafficking in people for the purpose of removing their organs, whereas organ trafficking more precisely refers to the illicit traffic in organs separate from the body. These two terms have become interchangeable in common usage because the illicit traffic in organs separate from the body would invariably be preceded by the act of trafficking in a person for the purpose of removing his or her organs.
2. There is limited data on payments for kidneys in India; one study of 305 kidney sellers in the state of Tamil Nadu found that the sellers were paid about one-half to two-thirds of what they were promised, which is higher than the data I collected in North India. See Goyal et al. (2002).
3. See "Kidney Racket at Top Delhi Hospital," from the BBC, http://www.bbc.com/news/world-asia-india-36452439, retrieved June 14, 2016.
4. Kara (2012), chapter 4.
5. Grameen Bank is a microfinance bank founded in Bangladesh. It began informally in 1976 under the leadership of Professor Muhammad Yunus, who launched a project to study how to design a credit delivery system to the rural poor. In 1983, Grameen Bank was authorized by national legislation as an independent bank. In 2006, the bank and Muhammad Yunus were jointly awarded the Nobel Peace Prize.
6. BRAC is the largest NGO in the world in terms of employees (over 100,000) and focuses on poverty alleviation in Bangladesh. It was founded by Sir Fazle Hasan Abed in 1972.
7. Nathan et al. (2003).
8. Data are from the U.S. Department of Health and Human Services' Organ Procurement and Transplant website, https://optn.transplant.hrsa.gov/data/, retrieved May 4, 2017.
9. Gortmaker et al. (1998). Research has shown that families who spend more time speaking with an OPO or other donor organ official prior to brain death of their loved one are up to five times more likely to approve donation; see Siminoff et al. (1995).
10. The "Guiding Principles on Human Cell, Tissue and Organ Transplantation," by the World Health Organization (1991), can be downloaded at http://www.who.int/transplantation/Guiding_PrinciplesTransplantation_WHA63.22en.pdf.
11. World Medical Association, "Statement on Human Organ and Tissue Donation and Transplantation," Fifty-Second WMA General Assembly, Edinburgh, October 2000.
12. The "Declaration of Istanbul on Organ Trafficking and Transplant Tourism" (2009) is available at http://www.declarationofistanbul.org/component/content/article/118-uncategorised/83-links.
13. Radcliffe-Richards et al. (1998).
14. Zargooshi (2001) and Scheper-Hughes (2003).
15. Goyal et al. (2002).
16. Zargooshi (2001a, 2001b).
17. Ibid.
18. Mironov et al. (2003) and Murphy and Atala (2014).

5. TECHNOLOGY AND HUMAN TRAFFICKING: FRIEND AND FOE

1. Bitcoin is a decentralized virtual currency.
2. See Latonero (2012) and Dixon (2013) for further discussion of these points.
3. Kara (2012), chapter 5.
4. As quoted in Latonero (2011).
5. Ibid.
6. Ibid.
7. The Associated Press, "Illinois Sheriff Sues Craigslist," *New York Times*, March 5, 2009, http://www.nytimes.com/2009/03/06/us/06brfs-SHERIFFSUESC_BRF.html.
8. Vanderschaaf (2013).
9. Athanassia (2007).
10. Kara (2009), chapter 2.
11. Heinzelman (2013).
12. Chawki and Wahab (2005).
13. Verité (2010).
14. Bitcoin, a decentralized virtual currency, was released as open source software in 2009. Transactions take place between users directly, without an intermediary, and are verified by network nodes and recorded in a publicly distributed ledger called the block chain.
15. Stiglitz (2003); Frieden (2006).

6. DEBT BONDAGE: BEYOND SOUTH ASIA

1. Kara (2012).
2. Kara (2014). This study is available at https://fxb.harvard.edu/tainted-carpets-report/.
3. Ibid.
4. United Nations Department of Economic and Social Affairs (2015).
5. For a poignant biography from a former *Restavek* slave, see Cadet (1998).
6. Kara (2012), chapter 2.
7. For a thorough examination of migration and domestic work in Europe, see Lutz (2008).
8. Chuang (2010).
9. ILO (2013).
10. ILO Domestic Workers Convention (No. 189), Article 1, provides the following definitions:

    (a) the term "domestic work" means work performed in or for a household or households;

    (b) the term "domestic worker" means any person engaged in domestic work within an employment relationship;

    (c) a person who performs domestic work only occasionally or sporadically and not on an occupational basis is not a domestic worker.

11. ILO (2013).

12. Sayres (2007).

13. Daily wage is calculated on an average of 29 days worked per month; hourly wage is calculated on an average of 14 hours worked per day in the cases documented.

14. Construction Intelligence Center (2016).

15. ILO (2007).

16. Buckley (2012).

17. Wells (2007).

18. "Revealed: Qatar's World Cup Slaves," *Guardian*, https://www.theguardian.com/world /2013/sep/25/revealed-qatars-world-cup-slaves; "Qatar 2022: Forced Labor at World Cup Stadium," BBC, http://www.bbc.com/news/world-middle-east-35931031; and "US Adds Pressure on Qatar to Move on Labor Reform,"(*Huffington Post*, http://www .huffingtonpost.com/james-dorsey/us-adds-to-pressure-on-qa_b_10854364.html.

19. Data are from "Foreign Workforce Numbers" available on the Singapore Ministry of Manpower website at http://www.mom.gov.sg/documents-and-publications/foreign -workforce-numbers, retrieved May 4, 2017.

20. Ibid.

21. Khan (2014).

22. Data from Malaysia Ministry of Human Resources, 2017; and from a data request by the author to the Malaysia Department of Statistics in August 2016.

23. Narayanan and Lai (2005).

24. Abdul-Rashid (2001).

25. Data are from the Ministry of Home Affairs, Immigration Department, available at http://www.imi.gov.my/index.php/en/foreign-worker.html, retrieved October 2, 2016.

26. Humanity United (2013).

27. Daily wage is calculated on an average of 26 days worked per month; hourly wage is calculated on an average of 12.5 hours worked per day in the cases documented.

28. Raymond and Hughes (2001); Bromfield (2016).

29. O'Neill (2000).

30. For more information on domestic sex trafficking of minors in the United States, see Kotrla (2010), Estes and Weiner (2001), Walts (2011), and Deshpande and Nour (2013).

31. Clawson et al. (2006).

32. Kara (2009), chapter 7.

7. GLOBAL SUPPLY CHAINS: BLOOD AND THE SEA

1. For more information on IUU fishing, see Bray (2000).

2. Agnew et al. (2009).

3. FAO (2016).

4. Kara (2009), chapter 6.

5. Brooten (2015).
6. Morgan and Staples (2006); Sylwester (2014).
7. Data are from FAO (2016) and FAO country profile for Thailand available at http://www.fao.org/fishery/facp/THA/en.
8. Pitcher and Cheung (2013).
9. Sorajjakool (2013).
10. FAO (2016).
11. Early Mortality Syndrome (EMS) is a new disease that was first detected in China in 2010 and has since spread throughout Asian shrimp farms. The disease results in up to 100 percent mortality rates of shrimp within 20 to 30 days on farms stocked with infected *nauplii*.
12. FAO (2016).
13. Chantavanich et al. (2016).
14. FAO (2016).
15. See "American Seafood Consumption Up in 2015, Landing Volumes Even," available at https://www.seafoodsource.com/news/supply-trade/american-seafood-consumption-up-in-2015-landing-volumes-even, retrieved November 1, 2016.
16. NOAA (2016).
17. Data are from a search conducted on the NOAA website on October 4, 2016, available at http://www.st.nmfs.noaa.gov/commercial-fisheries/foreign-trade/applications/trade-by-country
18. FAO (2016).
19. New (2015) provides an insightful discussion on how current corporate social responsibility practices are inadequate to address slavery in global supply chains, and states that more robust inspection and auditing efforts will be required to do so.
20. Kara (2012), chapter 4.
21. Daily wage is calculated on an average of 29 days worked per month; hourly wage is calculated on an average of 15 hours worked per day in the cases documented.
22. Daily wage is calculated on an average of 27 days worked per month; hourly wage is calculated on an average of 13.5 hours worked per day in the cases documented.

8. A FRAMEWORK TO ERADICATE SLAVERY

1. Kara (2012), chapter 1.
2. Bhabha (2014).
3. For guidance on this point, see the United Nations Convention on the Rights of the Child (1989) and UNICEF Guidelines on the Protection of Child Victims of Trafficking (2006).
4. Kara (2011).
5. In criminal law, the principle of proportionality suggests that the punishment of an offender should be proportionate to the nature of the crime.

6. A few simplifying assumptions must be made. First, in the formula for the real economic penalty, I have treated the prosecution and conviction probabilities as independent, although several real-world conditions might render them dependent. In either case, the results of the calculations are not materially different. Second, calculating the probability of being prosecuted can be simplified such that each slave in a country represents one criminal act of slavery each year. This will understate the number of criminal acts, but it allows for a more meaningful analysis.

7. Calculated using data from the Ministry of Justice, Court of Justice, and Ministry of Social Development and Human Security in Thailand.

8. Kara (2009), chapter 1.

APPENDIX A: GLOBAL SLAVERY METRICS

1. The global weighted average revenues and profits for each type of slavery were calculated as follows. First, allocations of slaves by type are based on my slavery estimation model. For debt bondage, I created unit economic models for the following industries: South Asia: brick making, tea harvesting, agriculture (rice, wheat, maize, sugar, citrus, legumes, spices), carpet weaving, apparel, fireworks, shrimp and fish aquaculture, construction, gem cutting and polishing, stone breaking, bidi rolling, domestic work, mining (dimensional stones and minerals), leather processing, glass work, commercial sex; East Asia and the Pacific: tea harvesting, construction, domestic work, shrimp and fish aquaculture and processing, commercial sex; Middle East: construction, domestic work, commercial sex; Africa: construction, coffee harvesting, agriculture (potato, wheat, citrus, legumes, spices), conveyance, domestic work, commercial sex; Latin America and the Caribbean: dairy farm, coffee, agriculture (sugar, wheat, citrus, legumes), coal, construction, commercial sex; North America: construction, domestic work, commercial sex. For sex trafficking, the numbers are updated from the unit economic models by country for various types of venue (brothel, massage parlor, street, etc.), a selection of which is included in appendix B of this book (more examples can be found in appendix B of *Sex Trafficking*). For labor trafficking, I created unit economic models in the following industries: South Asia: brick making, tea harvesting, agriculture (rice, wheat, maize, sugar, citrus, legumes, spices), carpet weaving, apparel, fireworks, shrimp and fish aquaculture, construction, stone breaking, domestic work, mining (dimensional stones and minerals), leather processing, glass work, commercial sex, begging, forced military service, forced marriage; East Asia and the Pacific: tea harvesting, agriculture (rice, sugar, citrus, legumes, spices, palm oil), apparel, construction, domestic work, shrimp and fish aquaculture and processing, begging, manufacturing, forced military service, forced marriage; Middle East: construction, manufacturing, domestic work, camel jockey; Africa: construction, coffee harvesting, agriculture (potato, wheat, citrus, spices), conveyance, begging, forced military service; Latin America and the Caribbean: dairy farm, coffee, agriculture (sugar, wheat, citrus, legumes), coal, construction; West

Europe: apparel, domestic work, manufacturing, begging, forced marriage; Central and East Europe: apparel, domestic work, manufacturing, begging, forced marriage; North America: agriculture (potato, wheat, citrus), apparel, domestic work, forced marriage. For other forced labor, the industries of exploitation are the same as labor trafficking, with the addition of allocations in each region for commercial sex, as well as bidi rolling, gem cutting and polishing, and additional categories of carpet weaving in South Asia.

2. One could allocate a portion of the costs of the upkeep of the female slave who gave birth to the new slave as the cost of acquisition, but this value would not be a significant number, especially after it is amortized across other revenues.

3. Two finance concepts must be considered when multiplying monthly recurring contribution by the average duration of enslavement: the time value of money and the risk of future cash flows. The time value of money accounts for the fact that a dollar today is worth more than a dollar a year from now, primarily because of inflation. The risk of future cash flows is the risk that the exploiter will not possess the slave for as long as expected. Theoretically, the global weighted average duration of exploitation encapsulates these risks, but to be conservative, the slave owner's likelihood of achieving the average duration of enslavement can still be discounted. This discount rate is applied when calculating the operating exploitation value to depreciate the value of future cash flows in relation to the time value of money and the risk of future cash flows. Most models used to calculate discount rates include applying a country's inflation rate to capture the time value of money as well as a risk premium on future cash flows. I have applied hefty discount rates of 25 percent to all countries covered in this book.

WORKS CITED

BOOKS, REPORTS, AND PAPERS

Abdul-Rashid, Abdul-Aziz. 2001. "Bangladeshi Migrant Workers in Malaysia's Construction Sector." *Asia Pacific Population Journal* 16 (1): 3–22.

Acemgolu, Daron, and Alexander Wolitzky. 2011. "The Economics of Labor Coercion." *Econometrica* 79 (2): 555–600.

Agbu, Osita. 2003. "Corruption and Human Trafficking: The Nigerian Case." *West Africa Review* 4 (1). http://www.africaknowledgeproject.org/index.php/war/article/view/320.

Agnew, David, John Pearce, Ganapathiraju Pramod, Tom Peatman, Reg Watson, John R. Beddington, and Tony J. Pitcher. 2009. "Estimating the Worldwide Extent of Illegal Fishing." *PLoS One* 4 (2): e4570. http://dx.doi.org/10.1371/journal.pone.0004570.

Ajayi, J. F., and Okun Uya, eds. 2010. *Slavery and Slave Trade in Nigeria: From Earliest Times to the Nineteenth Century.* Lancashire, UK: Safari.

Ajibade, George. 2013. "Same-Sex Relationships in Yoruba Culture and Orature." *Journal of Homosexuality* 60 (7): 965–983.

Alaba, Olugboyega. 2004. "Understanding Sexuality in the Yoruba Culture." Africa Regional Sexuality Resource Centre. http://www.arsrc.org/downloads/uhsss/alaba.pdf.

Athanassia, Sykiotou. 2007. "Trafficking in Human Beings: Internet Recruitment." Council of Europe. https://rm.coe.int/CoERMPublicCommonSearchServices/DisplayDCTMContent?documentId=09000016806eeec0.

Awolalu, Omosade. 1968. "Ayelala: A Guardian of Social Morality." *Ibadan Journal of Religious Studies* 11 (2).

——. 1996. *Yoruba Beliefs and Sacrificial Rites.* Brooklyn, NY: Athelia Henrietta Press.

Bhabha, Jacqueline. 2014. *Child Migration and Human Rights in a Global Age*. Princeton, NJ: Princeton University Press.

Boer, Jan. 2003. *Nigeria's Decades of Blood 1980–2002: Studies in Christian-Muslim Relations*. Belleville, Ontario: Essence.

Bray, Kevin. ed. 2000. *A Global Review of Illegal, Unreported and Unregulated Fishing (IUU)*. Food and Agriculture Organization of the United Nations. http://www.fao.org/docrep/005/Y3274E/y3274e08.htm.

Bromfield, Nicole. 2016. "Sex Slavery and Sex Trafficking of Women in the United States Historical and Contemporary Parallels, Policies, and Perspectives in Social Work." *Affilia* 31 (1): 129–139.

Brooten, Lisa. 2015. "Blind Spots in Human Rights Coverage: Framing Violence Against the Rohingya in Myanmar/Burma." *Popular Communication: The International Journal of Media and Culture* 13 (2): 132–144.

Buckley, Michelle. 2012. "From Kerala to Dubai and Back Again: Construction Migrants and the Global Economic Crisis." *Geoforum* 43: 250–259.

Cadet, Jean-Robert. 1998. *Restavec: From Haitian Slave Child to Middle-Class American*. Austin: University of Texas Press.

Calavita, Kitty. 2010. *Inside the State: The Bracero Program, Immigration, and the I.N.S.* New Orleans: Quid Pro, LLC.

California Department of Food and Agriculture. 2016. "California Agricultural Statistics Review: 2014–2015." https://www.cdfa.ca.gov/statistics/PDFs/2015Report.pdf.

Campbell, John. 2013. *Nigeria: Dancing on the Brink*. Lanham, MD: Rowman & Littlefield.

Chantavanich, Supang, et al. 2016. "Under the Shadow: Forced Labour among Sea Fishers in Thailand." *Marine Policy* 68: 1–7.

Chawki, Mohamed and Mohamed Wahab. 2005. "Technology Is a Double-Edged Sword: Illegal Human Trafficking in the Information Age." Computer Crime Research Center. http://www.droit-tic.com/pdf/chawki-wahab3.pdf.

Cherney, Hollis, and T. N. Srinivasan. eds. 1988. *Handbook of Development Economics*. Vol. 1. Amsterdam: Elsevier.

Chuang, Janie. 2010. "Achieving Accountability for Migrant Domestic Worker Abuse." *North Carolina Law Review* 88: 1628–1656.

Clawson, Heather, et al. 2006. *Law Enforcement Response to Human Trafficking and the Implications for Victims: Current Practices and Lessons Learned*. Rockville, MD: National Institute of Justice.

Construction Intelligence Center. 2016. *Global Construction Outlook 2020*. New York: CIC.

Daniel, Cletus. 1982. *Bitter Harvest: A History of California Farmworkers, 1870–1941*. Berkeley: University of California Press.

Deshpande, Neha, and Nawal Nour. 2013. "Sex Trafficking of Women and Girls." *Reviews in Obstetrics and Gynecology* 6 (1): 22–27.

Dixon, Herbet. 2013. "Human Trafficking and the Internet." *Judges Journal, American Bar Association* 52 (1): 36–39.

Equaino, Olaudah. 1789. *The Interesting Narrative of the Life of Olaudah Equaino, 1789*. London: Author.

Estes, Richard, and Neil Weiner. 2001. *The Commercial Sexual Exploitation of Children in the U.S., Canada, and Mexico*. Philadelphia: School of Social Work, University of Pennsylvania.

Falola, Toyin. 1998. *Violence in Nigeria: Crisis of Religious Politics and Secular Ideologies*. Rochester, NY: University of Rochester Press.

Fogel, William. 1989. *Without Consent or Contract: The Rise and Fall of American Slavery*. Rochester, NY: Norton.

Frieden, Jeffrey A. 2006. *Global Capitalism: Its Fall and Rise in the Twentieth Century*. Rochester, NY: Norton.

Food and Agriculture Organization of the United Nations. 2016. *The State of World Fisheries and Aquaculture*. Rome.

Genicot, Garance. 2002. "Bonded Labour and Serfdom: A Paradox of Voluntary Choice." *Journal of Development Economics* 67 (1): 101–127.

Gortmaker, S. L., et al. 1998. "Improving the Request Process to Increase Family Consent for Organ Donation." *Journal of Transplant Coordination* 8 (4): 210–217.

Goyal, M., et. al. 2002. "Economic and Health Consequences of Selling a Kidney in India." *Journal of the American Medical Association* 288 (13): 1589–1593.

Green, Toby. 2014. *The Rise of the Trans-Atlantic Slave Trade in Western Africa, 1300–1589*. Cambridge, UK: Cambridge University Press.

Griego, Garcia. 1981. "Importation of Mexican Contract Laborers to the United States, 1942–1964: Antecedents, Operation and Legacy." Working Paper Series, Program in United States-Mexican Studies. San Diego: University of California.

Habib, Irfan. 1963. *The Agrarian System of Mughal India, 1562–1707*. Bombay: Oxford University Press.

Heinzelman, Jessica. 2013. "Crowdsourcing for Human Rights Monitoring: Challenges for Information Collection and Verification." In *Human Rights and Information Communication Technologies: Trends and Consequences of Use*, ed. John Lannon and Edward Halpin. Hershey, PA: Information Science Reference.

Hochschild, Adam. 2005. *Bury the Chains: Prophets and Rebels in the Fight to Free and Empire's Slaves*. New York: Houghton Mifflin.

Humanity United. 2013. "Exploitative Labor Practices in the Global Palm Industry." http://humanityunited.org/pdfs/Modern_Slavery_in_the_Palm_Oil_Industry.pdf.

International Labour Organization. 2005. *ILO Minimum Estimate of Forced Labour in the World*. Geneva: International Labour Office.

——. 2007. *Construction: Employment and Output Dimensions*. Geneva: International Labour Office.

——. 2009. *Indicators of Forced Labor*. Geneva: International Labour Office.

——. 2012. *ILO Global Estimate of Forced Labor*. Geneva: International Labour Office.

——. 2013. *Domestic Workers Across the World: Global and Regional Statistics and the Extent of Legal Protection*. Geneva: International Labour Office.

International Labour Organization International Programme on the Elimination of Child Labor (IPEC). 2010. "Child Trafficking—Essentials." http://www.ilo.org/ipec /Informationresources/WCMS_IPEC_PUB_14616/lang--en/index.htm.

Kara, Siddharth. 2009. *Sex Trafficking: Inside the Business of Modern Slavery.* New York: Columbia University Press.

——. 2011. "Designing More Effective Laws Against Human Trafficking." *Northwestern Journal of International Human Rights* 9 (2): 123–147.

——. 2012. *Bonded Labor: Tackling the System of Slavery in South Asia.* New York: Columbia University Press.

——. 2014. *Tainted Carpets: Slavery and Child Labor in India's Hand-Made Carpet Sector.* Boston: Harvard School of Public Health.

Khan, Raza Ali. 2014. "Malaysian Construction Sector and Malaysia Vision 2020: Developed Nation Status." *Procedia—Social and Behavioral Sciences* 109: 507–513.

Klein, Martin. 1993. *Breaking the Chains: Slavery, Bondage, and Emancipation in Modern Africa and Asia.* Madison: University of Wisconsin Press.

Kotrla, Kimberly. 2010. "Domestic Minor Sex Trafficking in the United States." *Social Work* 55 (2): 181–187.

Kumar, D. 1965. *Land and Caste in South India.* Cambridge, UK: Cambridge University Press.

Latonero, Mark. 2011. *Human Trafficking Online: The Role of Social Networking Sites and Online Classifieds.* Los Angeles: Annenberg School for Communications, University of Southern California.

——. 2012. *The Rise of Mobile and the Diffusion of Technology-Facilitated Trafficking.* Los Angeles: Annenberg School for Communications, University of Southern California.

Lewis, Bernard. 1992. *Race and Slavery in the Middle East: An Historical Enquiry.* Oxford: Oxford University Press.

Lutz, Helma, ed. 2008. *Migration and Domestic Work: A European Perspective on a Global Theme.* New York: Routledge.

Malaquais, Dominique. 1998. *Kingdom of Benin.* First Books—African Civilizations. London: Franklin Watts.

Malaysia Ministry of Human Resources. 2017. "Employment and Labour Statistics." http://www.mohr.gov.my/index.php/en/component/content/article?id=136.

McWilliams, Carey. 2000. *Factories in the Field: The Story of Migratory Farm Labor in California.* Berkeley: University of California Press.

Meltzer, Milton. 1993. *Slavery: A World History.* Boston: De Capo Press.

Mironov, Valdimir, et. al. 2003. "Organ Printing: Computer-Sided Jet-Based 3D Tissue Engineering." *Trends in Biotechnology* 21 (4): 157–161.

Morgan, Gary, and Derek Staples. 2006. *The History of Industrial Marine Fisheries in Southeast Asia.* Bangkok: Food and Agriculture Organization of the United Nations.

Murphy, Sean, and Anthony Atala. 2014. "3D Bioprinting of Tissues and Organs." *Nature Biotechnology* 32: 773–785.

Narayanan, Suresh, and Yew-Wah Lai. 2005. "The Causes and Consequences of Immigrant Labour in the Construction Sector in Malaysia." *Immigration Migration* 45 (5): 31–57.

Nathan, Howard, et al. 2003. "Organ Transplantation in the United States." *American Journal of Transplantation* 3 (Suppl. 4): 29–40.

National Oceanic and Atmospheric Administration. 2016. "Imports and exports of fishery products annual summary, 2015." http://www.st.nmfs.noaa.gov/Assets /commercial/trade/Trade2015.pdf.

New, Stephen. 2015. "Modern Slavery and the Supply Chain: The Limits of Corporate Social Responsibility?" *Supply Chain Management: An International Journal* 20 (6): 697–707.

Nnadi, Ine. 2013. "Sex Trafficking and Women—The Nigerian Experience." *Journal of Politics and Law* 6 (3): 179–188.

Okonofua, Friday. 2004. "Knowledge, Attitudes and Experiences of Sex Trafficking by Young Women in Benin City, South-South Nigeria." *Social Science & Medicine* 59 (6): 1315–1327.

O'Neill, Richard. 2000. "International Trafficking in Women to the United States: A Contemporary Manifestation of Slavery and Organized Crime," Washington, DC: Center for the Study of Intelligence, Central Intelligence Agency.

Patterson, Orlando. 1982. *Slavery and Social Death*. Cambridge, MA: Harvard University Press.

Pete, Daniel R. 1990. *The Shadow of Slavery, Peonage in the South, 1901–1969*. Champaign: University of Illinois Press.

Pitcher, Tony, and Willam Cheung. 2013. "Fisheries: Hope or Despair?" *Marine Pollution Bulletin* 74 (2): 506–516.

Radcliffe-Richards, J., et. al. 1998. "The Case for Allowing Kidney Sales." *Lancet* 351 (9120): 1950–1952.

Raymond, Janice, and Donna Hughes. 2001. "Sex Trafficking of Women in the United States." Coalition Against Trafficking in Women. https://www.ncjrs.gov/pdffiles1/nij /grants/187774.pdf.

Sayres, Nicole. 2007. "An Analysis of the Situation of Filipino Domestic Workers." Manila: International Labour Organization.

Scheper-Hughes, Nancy. 2003. "Keeping an Eye on the Global Traffic in Human Organs." *Lancet* 361 (9369): 1645–1648.

Schultz, Theodore W. 1964. *Transforming Traditional Agriculture*. New Haven, CN: Yale University Press.

Siminoff, L. A., et. al. 1995. "Public Policy Governing Organ and Tissue Procurement in the United States: Results from the National Organ and Tissue Procurement Study." *Annals of Internal Medicine* 123 (1): 10–17.

Smith, Thomas C. 1959. *The Agrarian Origins of Modern Japan*. Palo Alto, CA: Stanford University Press.

Sorajjakool, Siroj. 2013. *Human Trafficking in Thailand: Current Issues, Trends and the Role of the Thai Government*. Chiang Mai, Thailand: Silkworm Books.

Sowunmi, Zents. 2015. *The Political History of Nigeria since 1945: The Vultures and the Vulnerable*. Brooklyn, NY: Korloki.

Stephenson, Carl. 1952. *Mediaeval Feudalism*. Ithaca, NY: Cornell University Press.

Stiglitz, Joseph. 1989. "Rational Peasants, Efficient Institutions, and a Theory of Rural Organization: Methodological Remarks for Development Economics." In *The Economic Theory of Agrarian Institutions*, ed. P. Bardham. Oxford: Oxford University Press.

——. 2003. *Globalization and Its Discontents*. New York: Norton.

Sylwester, Joanna. 2014. "Fishers of Men: The Neglected Effects of Environmental Depletion on Labor Trafficking in the Thai Fishing Industry." *Pacific Rim Law & Policy Journal* 23 (2): 423–459.

Thomas, Hugh. 1999. *The Slave Trade: The Story of the Atlantic Slave Trade: 1440–1870*. New York: Simon & Schuster.

United Nations Department of Economic and Social Affairs. 2015. "International Migration Report 2015." New York: United Nations.

Vanderschaaf, Victoria. 2013. "Spotlight On: How the Internet Facilitates Underage Victimization in Human Trafficking." *Children's Legal Rights Journal* 34 (1): 135–138.

Vaught, David. 2002. *Cultivating California: Growers, Specialty Crops, and Labor, 1875–1920*. Baltimore: Johns Hopkins University Press.

Verité. 2010. *Help Wanted: Hiring, Human Trafficking and Modern-Day Slavery in the Global Economy*. Amherst, MA: Verité.

Walts, Katherine, ed. 2011. *Human Trafficking and Exploitation of Children and Youth in the United States*. Chicago: Center for the Human Rights of Children, Loyola University.

Wells, Jill. 2007. "Informality in the Construction Sector in Developing Countries." *Construction Management and Economics* 25 (1): 87–93.

Zargooshi, J. 2001a. "Iranian Kidney Donors: Motivations and Relations with Recipients." *Journal of Urology* 165 (2): 386–392.

——. 2001b. "Quality of Life of Iranian Kidney 'Donors.'" *Journal of Urology* 166 (5): 1790–1799.

LAWS AND CONVENTIONS

Declaration of Istanbul on Organ Trafficking and Transplant Tourism, 2009

European Convention on Human Rights and Biomedicine, 2002

Food and Agriculture Organization of the United Nations Code of Conduct for Responsible Fishers, 1995

India Bonded Labour System (Abolition) Act, 1976

International Labour Organization Abolition of Forced Labour Convention (No. 105), 1957

International Labour Organization Discrimination (Employment and Occupation) Convention (No. 111), 1958

International Labour Organization Domestic Workers Convention (No. 189), 2011

International Labour Organization Equal Remuneration Convention (No. 100), 1951

International Labour Organization Forced Labour Convention (No. 29), 1930

International Labour Organization Freedom of Association and Protection of the Right to Organise Convention (No. 87), 1948

International Labour Organization Minimum Wage Convention (No. 138), 1973

International Labour Organization Protocol to the Forced Labour Convention, 1930 (No. P029), 2014

International Labour Organization Recommendation Concerning Work in the Fishing Sector (No. 199), 2007

International Labour Organization Right to Organise and Collective Bargaining Convention (No. 98), 1949

International Labour Organization Worst Forms of Child Labor Conventions (No. 182), 1999

International Labour Organization Work in Fishing Convention, 2007 (No. 188)

League of Nations Slavery Convention, 1926

Malaysia Anti-Trafficking in Persons Act, 2007

Paris Principles on the Involvement of Children in Armed Conflict, 2007

Thailand Act Governing the Right to Fish in Thai Waters, B.E. 2482 (1939)

Thailand Anti-Trafficking in Persons Act, B.E. 2551 (2008)

Thailand Fisheries Act, B.E. 2490 (1947)

Thailand Narcotic Act, B.E. 2522 (1979)

Thailand Vessel Act, B.E. 2481 (1938)

UNICEF Guidelines on the Protection of Child Victims of Trafficking, 2006

United Kingdom Modern Slavery Act, 2015

United Kingdom Slave Trade Abolition Act, 1807

United Kingdom Slavery Abolition Act, 1833

United Nations Convention on Consent to Marriage, Minimum Age for Marriage and Registration of Marriages, 1964

United Nations Convention on the Elimination of All Forms of Discrimination Against Women (CEDAW), 1979

United Nations Convention on the Rights of the Child, 1989

United Nations Optional Protocol on the Sale of Children, Child Prostitution and Child Pornography, 2000

United Nations Protocol Against the Smuggling of Migrants by Land, Sea and Air, 2000

United Nations Protocol to Prevent, Suppress and Punish Trafficking in Persons Especially Women and Children, supplementing the United Nations Convention Against Transnational Organized Crime, 2000

United Nations Supplementary Convention on the Abolition of Slavery, the Slave Trade, and Institutions and Practices Similar to Slavery, 1956

United Nations Universal Declaration of Human Rights, 1948

United States Communications Decency Act, 1996

United States Fair Labor Standards Act, 1933

United States Lacey Act, 1900

United States Migrant and Seasonal Agricultural Worker Protection Act, 1983

United States Occupational Safety and Health Act, 1970

United States Portal-to-Portal Pay Act, 1947

United States Smoot-Hawley Tariff Act, 1930

United States Stop Advertising Victims of Exploitation (SAVE) Act, 2015

United States Trade Facilitation and Enforcement Act, 2015

United States Trafficking Victims Protection Act, 2000

United States Revised Uniform Anatomical Gift Act, 2006

World Health Organization Guiding Principles on Human Cell, Tissue and Organ Transplantation, 1991

INDEX

Page numbers in italics refer to figures or tables

Rafiq (migrant laborer), 199
Rama (fisherman), 252–53
refugee camps, 30, 233
remittance income: for domestic work, 182, 182–83; labor migration and, 262
Republic of Biafra, 72
researcher safety: Mexico drug cartels and, 132–33; organ recruiters and, 117–19; Thai fishing sector and, 237
research questionnaire: background and nature of work in, 300–301; categorization for, 305–6; child labor and, 299, 304–5, 306; consent and assent in, 300; debt bondage in, 303–4, 305–6; forced labor under ILO Convention No. 29 in, 301–3, 305; human trafficking and, 304, 306
return on investment (ROI), 24–25, 279, 280, 282, 283; defining, 310n41
revictimization, 207; law enforcement and, 38–39; policy reforms and, 271
Revised Uniform Anatomical Gift Act, U.S. (2006), 128
Rohingya, 224, 232; cargo holds for, 238; citizenship of, 237, 239; economic conditions of Thai seafood industry and, 237–39; human trafficking of, 237–39, 247, 260; international response to, 239; laws and conventions for, 250; mass graves of, 239; violence against (2012), 237
ROI. See return on investment
Russia: American romanticism and, 216; debt bondage and commercial sex from, 215–16

Samut Sakhon, Thailand, 225–32, 247
Sandra (sex trafficking survivor), 68–69
self-determination, 111

sex trafficking, ix, 12; baby factories and, 69–70; Bedia and, 1–2, 4; of children, 2–3, 4, 146, 151, 158; debt bondage and, 218–19, 220; demand-side policies and, 34–35; Dipali as survivor of, 156; economics of, 267, 279, 280, 281, 290; EU and, 51, 154–55; EV of, 35–36; false marriage offers and, 155–56; foster care system and, 213, 214, 216–18; India brothel economics, 288; Joyce and, 184–85; Katya (Moldova) and, 154–55; Lisu and, 232–33; madams for, 2–3, 52, 55, 66–70; Maria and U.S., 213–14, 215; Melanie and, 153–54; Nigerian street prostitution economics and, 291; organized crime groups and, 214; organ sale and, 111; profits of, 20–21, 21; in Singapore, 196; Sita and, 1–3; spirituality and, 49, 51; Stephanie and, 217–18; Sunee and, 219–20; in Thailand, 224, 231–32, 289; trolleys and, 53; U.S. economics and, 267, 290. See also brothel; child sex trafficking; Nigeria
sex trafficking and technology: Backpage.com and, 145–47, 146, 152–53, 173; Communications Decency Act and, 152–53; Craigslist and, 151–52; female degradation and, 147, 150; John's Chat Rooms and, 149–50; Lou and, 173–76; online advertisements for, 149; social media and, 153–56; in South Asia, 155–56; sporting events and, 150–51. See also technology, as prevention and intervention
Shell-BP, 71, 72
Sinaloa cartel, 215
Singapore: Alam in, 198; automobile tax in, 195–96; construction sector, ix; deportation in, 200–201; housing for construction workers in, 199;

CPSIA information can be obtained
at www.ICGtesting.com
Printed in the USA
LVHW092041020321
680404LV00003B/6/J

9 780231 158466